S0-BUG-035

# Popular Efficacy in the Democratic Era

———————————

# Popular Efficacy in the Democratic Era

## A Reexamination of Electoral Accountability in the United States, 1828–2000

*Peter F. Nardulli*

JK
524
·N 37
2005
West

PRINCETON UNIVERSITY PRESS

PRINCETON AND OXFORD

Copyright © 2005 by Princeton University Press
Published by Princeton University Press, 41 William Street,
Princeton, New Jersey 08540
In the United Kingdom: Princeton University Press,
3 Market Place, Woodstock, Oxfordshire OX20 1SY

All Rights Reserved

*Library of Congress Cataloging-in-Publication Data*

Nardulli, Peter F.
Popular efficacy in the democratic era : a reexamination of electoral
accountability in the United States, 1828–2000 / Peter F. Nardulli.
p.   cm.
Includes bibliographical references and index.
ISBN-13: 978-0-691-12285-4 (cl : alk. paper)
ISBN-10: 0-691-12285-7 (cl : alk. paper)
1. Presidents—United States—Election—History. 2. Voting—United States—
History. 3. Political participation—United States. 4. Social classes—
United States. 5. Democracy—United States. I. Title.
JK524.N37 2005
24.973—dc23      2005048696

British Library Cataloging-in-Publication Data is available

This book has been composed in Sabon

Printed on acid-free paper. ∞

pup.princeton.edu

Printed in the United States of America

1   3   5   7   9   10   8   6   4   2

*To Ann, for thirty-five years of patience
and endurance*

———————————————

# CONTENTS

# PREFACE

THIS BOOK is about ordinary citizens and their ability to play an efficacious role in their own governance. Its objective is to provide fresh and durable empirical insights into a fundamental tenet of democratic theory, popular efficacy. By popular efficacy I mean the capacity of citizens to drive, guide, and constrain the behavior of political elites. Popular efficacy is what makes democracy more responsive to broad societal interests than other forms of governance. The stronger the force of popular influences within a democracy, the greater its responsiveness to broader societal interests. Within representative democracies, popular efficacy derives principally, but not exclusively, from mechanisms that provide for electoral accountability. Despite the centrality of popular efficacy to democratic theory, the behavioral assumptions upon which it is based have been subjected to unrelenting criticism throughout the twentieth century.

In addressing matters such as popular efficacy, electoral accountability and democratic responsiveness, this work continues a long line of scholarly work on mass- elite linkages. This work differs from previous studies by positing and empirically examining a different political dynamic within the electoral arena. This dynamic involves the interactions among: (1) *exogenous events*, which are largely outside the control of political elites; (2) *citizens' core political desires*, which are largely invariant across individuals; and (3) *the core political interests of political elites*: their desire for electoral success. Within this dynamic, the radiated effects of exogenous events are posited to initiate intense episodes of information processing that lead citizens to update their political cognitions. These updates may generate deviations from their habitual voting behavior, thereby impinging on the core political interests of elites.

I use this political dynamic as the basis for conducting an unconventional reassessment of the image of voters as "manageable fools." V. O. Key offered this characterization of citizens as a summary of decades of empirical research on mass political behavior. I was motivated to scrutinize this durable image of voters by two considerations. The first is the disjuncture between the image of voters that has emerged from survey-based research and the behavior of political stewards. I term this disjuncture the *paradox of elected officials*. The paradox is as follows: Why do elected officials seem so preoccupied with the concerns of the public if citizens are "manageable fools"? Despite this dismissive conception of voters, elected officials frequently act as though citizens are concerned about political stewardship and have the capacity to act in a retributive

fashion. Providing a theoretically based and empirically supportable solution to this paradox would enhance our understanding of popular efficacy
immensely.

The second consideration that motivated this research is my belief that
scholarly efforts to generate inferences about citizen competence have
been hampered by conceptual and methodological limitations. These self-
imposed limitations have had profound consequences for our understanding of the role of citizens in democratic governance. Consequently, I use
the political dynamic sketched above to construct a theoretical framework that provides a relatively unique and potentially fruitful conception
of mass-elite linkages. I use this framework to conduct a macro-level analysis of presidential voting from the onset of Jacksonian democracy to the
present. These analyses gauge the capacity of voters to react electorally to
exogenous events whose radiated effects impinge upon their core political
desires; they also consider the impact of these electoral reactions on the
core interests of political elites. These analyses provide the basis for generating original and important empirical insights into popular efficacy and
democratic responsiveness.

At the core of the theoretical framework used to conduct this reexamination is a conceptual synthesis that addresses two questions that are
fundamental to the study of popular efficacy: (1) what we expect of democratic citizens (i.e., what does it mean to be efficacious?); (2) how we can
conceive of ordinary citizens as fulfilling those expectations? In answering
these questions, I integrate an evaluative (Schumpeterian) conception of
democratic citizenship with a conception of human decision making that
draws from advances in the cognitive sciences. The resulting model acknowledges that citizens "peripherally process" most political information most of the time. It also accepts as a given that voters adopt normal
voting routines and that the influence of inertial and centripetal forces on
electoral behavior is strong. At the same time, however, the model asserts
that uncontrollable and politically salient exogenous events can stimulate
interludes of intensive information processing that can generate departures from normal voting routines. The aggregate effect of these disrup-
tions can generate electoral jolts that impinge upon the core political interests of political elites.

In addition to offering a conceptual synthesis that explains why salient
exogenous events can generate modifications in political cognitions and
behavior, I provide an individual-level model of how exogenous events
are transformed into changes in voting behavior. The transformation of
exogenous events into evaluations of stewardship and vote choices involves the complex workings of several sets of factors that unfold over
time. Among the most important factors in this transformational process
are the activities of political stewards. Indeed, some of these activities

constitute what can be characterized as endogenous influences on electoral behavior. Endogenous influences are efforts by political elites to shape, direct, and control the political behavior of citizens. These influences are primal forces in democratic political orders. Currently, political parties are the most important source of endogenous influences within the electoral arena. Their influence can be seen in the prevalence of normal electoral behavior, habitual patterns of voting generated by deeply engrained partisan attachments.

Efforts by elites to spin and control the radiated effects of exogenous events interfere with citizens' objective evaluation of political stewardship. These elite efforts constitute the primary threat to popular efficacy within the conceptualization of mass-elite linkages offered here. If elite efforts to insulate themselves from performance-based evaluations of stewardship are successful, the concepts of electoral accountability and democratic responsiveness are little more than constructed myths used to mask and justify elite dominance. This means that the role of endogenous influences must be addressed in any assessment of mass-elite linkages in democratic orders. Thus, a primary focus of the empirical analyses presented here is on electoral independence. Electoral independence refers to the ability of citizens to overcome the inertial effects of habitual behavior and the centripetal pulls of partisan attachments; it is manifested in departures from normal voting behavior. Electoral independence is central to the study of popular efficacy because it speaks to the capacity of citizens to manifest evaluations of political stewardship in their voting behavior.

The focus on electoral independence within the conceptual framework developed here leads naturally to an analysis of electoral outcomes and settings. The impact of electoral independence upon outcomes and settings is important because it speaks directly to the effect of these electoral jolts on the core interests of political elites, their desire for electoral success. Thus, another important component of the empirical analyses presented here involves estimating the incidence of disequilibrating electoral outcomes (realigning, deviating, and endorsement elections) and competitive electoral settings. If disequilibrating elections and competitive electoral settings are rare occurrences, then it would reinforce the conventional wisdom concerning popular efficacy. If these electoral phenomena occur regularly, then it would suggest that elected officials have been taught that voters are discriminating consumers of public goods who can fitfully intervene within the electoral arena. Such findings would provide an explanation for the paradox of elected officials and undermine the prevailing conventional wisdom about popular efficacy.

To gauge electoral independence and its impact on electoral outcomes and setting, I develop a macro-level extension of the Michigan model of voting behavior; it provides the conceptual base for the disentangling of endogenous and exogenous influences on electoral behavior. I operationalize this model using a longitudinal, subnational design. The analytic focus of the operationalization is on the normal voting patterns of local electorates in presidential elections between 1828 and 2000. This provides the empirical base for generating inferences about popular efficacy. The temporal and spatial reach of the empirical analyses, in conjunction with a careful and conservative operationalization of key concepts, contributes to the goal of generating fresh and durable empirical insights about popular efficacy.

This unconventional approach to studying popular efficacy provides a set of empirical results that challenge the conventional wisdom about mass-elite linkages. The electoral independence analyses demonstrate that these departures from normal voting behavior are consistent with the political dynamic posited here. Estimates of the incidence of competitive electoral settings and disequilibrating electoral outcomes provide additional insights into popular efficacy. The distribution of these election types demonstrates that centrality of the electorate was underscored either going into a presidential campaign or in the outcome of the election, in two-thirds of all elections since the emergence of a two-party system. These results suggest that, over the course of the past two centuries, strategic political elites have learned that the electorate is a potent political force in democratic politics, a force with which to be reckoned. When joined with the findings of the electoral independence analyses, these results provide a solution to the paradox of elected officials. Moreover, they provide an image of voters as being neither foolish nor manageable.

# ACKNOWLEDGMENTS

I FIRST BEGAN work on this project in the summer of 1986. Since then I have accumulated an untold number of debts. Most of the work for this book was done while I served as the head of the Department of Political Science at the University of Illinois at Urbana-Champaign. This would not have been possible without the indulgence, as well as the financial and moral support, of Larry R. Faulkner and Jesse G. Delia. I could not imagine working for two finer individuals

My greatest intellectual debt is to my old friend and colleague, James H. Kuklinski. As I bored him with the details of this study for almost two decades, he patiently challenged and prodded me to do better. This effort is not as good as he would have liked, but it is a far better work than it would have been without the number of hours he spent reviewing parts of the work and discussing various problems. I am also enormously indebted to Paul J. Quirk, who also spent a great deal of time with me at the crucial early stages of this effort. Jeff Stonecash and Bryan Jones, two of my oldest and dearest friends in the profession, took the time to read the entire first draft of the manuscript. Many of the improvements in the final draft were due to their unselfish efforts and keen insights. James Gimpel also provided me with an insightful set of comments on a later version of the entire manuscript.

Brian Gaines also spent an inordinate amount of time reading various chapters as well as helping me address methodological issues. Wendy Tam Cho often joined our methodological discussions, contributed mightily to them, and provided me with key sets of advice at crucial junctures. During the formative stages of this work Gerry Munck, Melissa Orlie, and Richard Snyder provided me with a great deal of assistance in placing my work within the current debate over democratic governance. Their contributions provided for a much more broadly gauged effort, and for that I am greatly indebted to them. Other colleagues at Illinois who helped me at different points in this effort are Brian Sala, Scott Althaus, Thomas Rudolph, Paul Diehl, and Zachary Elkins. I also benefited greatly from intermittent conversations with Paul Sniderman and Chris Achen, both of whom provided me with much encouragement. Scott Gartner also was of great help in providing me with some key data. In this regard I should also mention the extraordinary contributions of Ted Bos and his "Economagic" data archive.

In a larger sense I have benefited greatly from the stimulating and supportive intellectual atmosphere that pervades the department at Illinois.

I received a great deal of feedback from several talks I gave at our informal seminar series, not to mention the patience of the faculty while I was distracted from my departmental responsibilities.

I have had invaluable help from several generations of talented graduate students at Illinois, beginning with Ellen Riggle and Michael Frank. Jon Dalager, Norman Hurley, Jeff Jenkins, and Colin McCoy ably succeeded them. The next generation of graduate students to contribute included Donald Greco and David Darmofal. The final wrap-up work fell to Phil Habel.

This book benefited enormously from several days I spent at Michigan State University presenting an early version of the manuscript. I am grateful to David Rohde for inviting me, for arranging the workshop at which I spoke, and for his insightful comments. Tom Hammond, Jeff Jenkins, Jamie Carson, and Charles J. Finocchiaro also provided me with excellent comments and feedback. I also benefited from the insights provided by Sam Kernell and Mat McCubbins and other faculty at the University of California-San Diego on an early version of chapter 8.

I am also sincerely grateful to Chuck Myers at Princeton University Press for his support and confidence in this project. His determination through a multiyear review process and three major revisions of the original text have provided for a vastly improved final product. I could not imagine working with a better editor. Enormously helpful were the reviews he solicited, which prompted me to make a number of changes in the presentation of the theoretical and empirical analyses. Thus, I am also indebted to the anonymous reviewers.

As all of the writing and analysis for this book was done while I was burdened with heavy administrative responsibilities, I must acknowledge the exceptional administrative support I received from Jean Paley and Margarita Ham, whose competence and hard work made it possible to steal away part of my day to complete this book. Even more directly supportive were Brenda Stamm and Delinda Swanson, who aided me in completing various book-related tasks on an untold number of occasions. Even though these tasks went well beyond their job requirements, they performed them superbly and graciously.

Throughout the process of completing this book I have benefited enormously from extended conversations with Sam Gove, Sam Buford, and Dick Cline. While only Sam Gove is a trained political scientist, the wisdom and insights I received from all three have made this a better product. My deepest debt, of course, is to my immediate family, Ann, Marc, and Beth. I began this project when Ann was just beginning her academic career as a post doc and Marc and Beth were in grade school. Far too many of my energies were drained by this project to have done all I should have as a husband and father. But Ann is now a senior professor at Illinois and Marc and Beth have gone on to successful careers and wonderful marriages, making it possible for me to bore their spouses, Joe and Jessica, with details of "the book" and its progress. Fortunately, I was able to finish "the book" before the arrival of the first product of these unions, Peter V. Nardulli.

Despite all the assistance I have received from a remarkable set of people, in the end they could not (entirely) save me from myself. Thus, I remain solely accountable for all of the error of fact, judgment, and execution that remain.

# Popular Efficacy in the Democratic Era

# CHAPTER ONE

# Democracy, Popular Efficacy, and the Electoral Arena

As mankind approaches the end of the millennium, the
twin crises of authoritarianism and socialist central planning have left only one competitor standing in the ring
as an ideology of potential universal validity: liberal democracy, the doctrine of individual freedom and popular
sovereignty. Two hundred years after they first animated
the French and American revolutions, the principles of
liberty and equality have proven not just durable, but
resurgent.

    —FRANCIS FUKUYAMA, *The End of History
    and the Last Man*

The founders of representative government expected
that the formal arrangements they advocated would
somehow induce government to act in the interest of the
people, but they did not know precisely why it would be
so. Neither do we, after two hundred years.

    —ADAM PRZEWORSKI, SUSAN C. STOKES, AND
    BERNARD MANIN, *Democracy, Accountability,
    and Representation*

THE WORLD experienced an extraordinary amount of societal change in
the latter third of the twentieth century. Colonial empires all but disap-
peared, and transnational organizations emerged for the purpose of ensur-
ing world order and furthering social welfare. Unprecedented levels of
international cooperation occurred across a number of areas (arms control, trade, health, environmental protection, etc.) and international conflicts were largely restricted to proxy wars and regional conflicts. In many
nations expectations for human rights were heightened and gender roles
transformed. The electronics revolution and fundamental changes in
modes of communication and transportation contributed to the globalization of economic activity, which generated dramatic increases in afflu-
ence—as well as increased disparities in wealth across and within nations.
Also significant was the widespread diffusion of liberal democratic governments and free enterprise economies.

Many have considered the emergence of liberal democracies and free market economies so significant that they attributed the increased pace of societal change and social progress to them. Indeed, Fukuyama (1992: 48) argues that the allure of these systems is so great, and the forces behind the liberal revolution so fundamental, that a "common evolutionary pattern" is emerging, one that will result in the widespread diffusion of liberal orders (representative democracy and free enterprise economics). Many proponents of the liberal revolution do not agree with Fukuyama's analysis. Most, however, would agree that liberal orders are uniquely capable of providing for the structure, stability, and dynamism needed to harness human, societal, and natural resources for the realization of broad societal interests. In contrast to its "competitors," the processes used by liberal orders to produce goods and services are tied much more closely to the preferences of individuals. On a *theoretical* level, they provide unparalleled opportunities for (1) individuals to develop, express, and enforce their preferences on matters affecting their welfare and (2) entrepreneurs to engage in activities aimed at satisfying the demands that flow from those individual preferences.

The appeal of liberal orders rests on a foundation of both value judgments and empirical assumptions. These value judgments took centuries to develop; they gained widespread acceptance in Western societies only after substantial changes were made in the initial formulations of both democracy and capitalism (direct democracy and laissez-faire capitalism). In contrast to the broad consensus that these value judgments currently enjoy, there is a good deal of skepticism about the empirics: Do they work the way they are supposed to work? Do they achieve what they are intended to achieve? This is especially true in the case of representative democracy.

The contemporary allure of representative democracy is based on its potential to make government responsive to the needs, interests, and desires of ordinary citizens, as opposed to those of political and social elites or specialized interest groups. Governmental responsiveness to broad societal interests has been a timeless concern, which is why democracy's "third wave" has achieved such acclaim. At a theoretical level, democracy appears more responsive than its competitors or its predecessors. But the uncertainties expressed in the epigraph to this chapter underscore the widespread concerns over how, or if, democratic political orders "induce government to act in the interest of the people." Uncertainties about *democratic responsiveness* such as those expressed by Przeworski and his collaborators feed the concerns of democratic skeptics.

These skeptics do not deny the dramatic increases in the standard of living experienced in Western democracies over the past century. Nor do they deny the ability of democracies to live in harmony with themselves and other democratic nations. Or their relative stability. Instead, they attribute these accomplishments to cultural and/or geophysical factors rather than political ones. Democratic skeptics are driven to seek alternative explanations because they doubt that the distinguishing features of democratic political orders can account for their accomplishments. That is, they are skeptical about the force of popular influences within representative democracies, what I term popular efficacy.

Popular efficacy can be understood as the capacity of citizens to drive, guide, and constrain the behavior of political elites. Popular efficacy is what makes democratic governance more responsive to broad societal interests than other forms of governance. The stronger the force of popular influences within a democracy, the greater its responsiveness to broader societal interests. Within representative democracies, popular efficacy derives principally, but not exclusively, from mechanisms that provide for electoral accountability.

Skepticism about popular efficacy is rooted in (1) institutional complexities and interdependencies and (2) the demanding normative expectations it places on democratic citizens, processes, and structures. Representative democracies are complex systems involving many players, institutions, norms, and processes. In order for ordinary citizens to play an efficacious role, the various players (citizens, legislators, judges, bureaucrats, political parties, etc.) must have the capacity, and the commitment, to fulfill democratic role expectations. Moreover, political institutions and processes must be structured to reflect democratic norms and values. Finally, popular efficacy requires a set of systemic interdependencies; the various components of democracy must work in harmony in order to insure governmental responsiveness. Deficiencies in any aspect of the system—disinterested citizens, insulated legislators, autonomous bureaucrats, unfair elections, restrictions on civil and political liberties, and the like—can dilute the force of popular influences.

These interdependencies make "real" democracy (i.e., responsive democracy) a highly vulnerable, fragile form of government—some would say an unattainable form of government: little more than a myth constructed by political elites to justify their control over the levers of societal power.

The skepticism about popular efficacy rooted in institutional and normative concerns has been reinforced by the work of empiricists who have studied the political behavior of ordinary citizens. Empirical democratic theorists have expressed concerns about citizens' cognitive limitations, the ability of political elites to mold and manipulate their political views, and the difficulties diffuse publics have penetrating and mobilizing complex institutional networks. In *The Responsible Electorate*, V. O. Key articulated the prevailing conventional wisdom concerning democratic citizens: the image of voters as *"manageable fools."* Key observed, in his imitable way, that

> By and large, the picture of the voter that emerges from a combination of the folklore of practical politics and the findings of the new electoral studies is not a pretty one. It is not a portrait of citizens moving to a considered decision as they play their solemn role of making and unmaking governments. The older tradition from practical politics may regard the voter as an erratic and irrational fellow susceptible to manipulation by skilled humbugs. One need not live through many campaigns to observe politicians, even successful politicians, who act as though they regarded the people as manageable fools. Nor does a heroic conception of the voter emerge from the new analyses of electoral behavior. They can be added up to a conception of voting not as a civic decision but as an almost purely deterministic act. Given knowledge of certain characteristics of a voter—his occupation, his residence, his national origin, and perhaps certain of his attitudes—one can predict with a high probability the direction of his vote. The actions of persons are made to appear to be only predictable and automatic responses to campaign stimuli. (1966: 5)

This image is rooted in empirical observations derived from a century's worth of experience with mass suffrage in industrial democracies.[1] Since Key wrote, a half-century of research conducted within the individual-level survey research paradigm has documented the durability of the image of voters as "manageable fools," as chapter 2 will document. This image is quite different from that embedded in most treatises on democratic theory, particularly utilitarian conceptions that underlie representative democracies. The problematic theoretical implications of the "manageable fools" caricature reinforce the normative and institutional concerns expressed above.

The problematic implications of institutional factors for popular efficacy are particularly true in the United States, which is the empirical focus of this study. The circumstances that led many of the original colonists to settle in America bred a disdain for unchecked concentrations of governmental power. That disdain was reinforced by the colonial experience, manifested itself in the complex constitutional design of governments in the United States, and has been an integral part of American political

---

[1] Political scholars have been studying citizens and making empirically based inferences about popular efficacy in large-scale industrial democracies since the latter part of the nineteenth century. The earliest assessments emerged from the insightful, but fairly unstructured, observations of scholars such as Mosca, Michels, Pareto, Bryce, Ostrogorski, Weber, and Schumpeter. This early body of work was followed by the early- and mid-twentieth-century work of empirical democratic theorists, most of whom used data derived from survey research.

culture for over two centuries. The institutional legacy of this disdain for unchecked power is the existence of diverse channels of influence and many veto points in American government. The implications of this institutional legacy for democracy have been compounded by the course of American political development. The pluralistic nature of American society, combined with its liberal underpinnings, has led to the emergence of a multitude of diverse, highly organized interest groups.

The confluence of these developments has led many to conclude that these groups have overwhelmed the role and concerns of ordinary citizens in American governance. Thus, American politics has been characterized as being dominated by cumbersome institutional structures and policy processes that serve and protect the interests of well-organized, upper-class groups. It is viewed as being capable of generating only incremental change and being largely unresponsive to the vaguely articulated needs of ordinary citizens. As such, it hardly seems capable of harnessing human, societal, and natural resources in a way that maximizes the welfare of ordinary citizens.

If institutional factors blunt, negate, or dilute the force of vaguely articulated sentiments emanating from a malleable and inattentive public, utilitarian accounts of democratic responsiveness are implausible. This dilemma has led various scholars to offer reconceptualizations of what democracy is and how it works. Some of the theoretical efforts to reconceive representative democracy have led to formulations (the elitist model, pluralism) in which the role of the *demos* is considerably less central than in nineteenth-century utilitarianism. These empirically based reformulations of mass-elite linkages within democracy have loosened the conceptual ties between the preferences of individuals and governmental outputs. At a theoretical level these revisions have made democracy less distinctively responsive to broad societal interests than its competitors, a development that has profound implications for how we understand, and normatively evaluate, democratic governance.

## POPULAR EFFICACY, ELECTORAL ACCOUNTABILITY, AND DEMOCRATIC RESPONSIVENESS

Despite the durability of the "manageable fools" image, the late-twentieth-century wave of democratization makes conducting research bearing on democratic responsiveness more important today than when Key wrote. Thus, this work joins the long tradition of research on mass-elite linkages in democratic regimes. Its principal objective is to determine whether there is a theoretically viable and empirically supportable basis for "bringing the people back in" to our understanding of how representative democracy works. This work builds on the retrospective voting tradition pioneered by Key and Fiorina. But it differs from earlier approaches to understanding mass elite-linkages by examining a different set of political dynamics to generate fresh empirical insights into democratic responsiveness.

Traditional studies of mass-elite linkages have been characterized by a primary focus on the actions of political elites (party platforms, legislative enactments, policy positions, administrative actions) and how they correspond to the ideological leanings and policy preferences of their constituents. These studies draw inferences about popular efficacy by examining the capacity of citizens to maintain and act upon stable, cohesive ideologies, which are held to vary across individuals. From this perspective, stable and cohesive ideologies, joined with information on the actions and views of elected officials, are what make representative democracies uniquely responsive. The inability of most voters to sustain cohesive ideologies, or to relate information on elite actions to their own preferences and manifest them in their votes, led to dismal conclusions about popular efficacy. More recent research on mass-elite linkages identifies elites as sources of political information. This has led many to draw the causal arrows *from elites to masses*, further undermining utilitarian conceptions of democratic responsiveness.

In contrast, the approach offered here focuses on (1) exogenous events, which are largely outside the control of political elites, (2) citizens' core political desires, which are largely invariant across individuals, and (3) political elites' core political interests, their desire for electoral success. It draws inferences about popular efficacy by examining the capacity of voters to react electorally to exogenous events whose radiated effects impinge upon their core political desires. The radiated effects of these exogenous events can initiate intense episodes of information processing that lead citizens to update their political cognitions and deviate from their normal voting behavior, thereby impinging on the core political interests of elites.

McCubbins and Schwartz's "1984" distinction between how police and fire departments function can provide some insights into the conception of mass-elite linkages offered here. Citizens do not constantly monitor political matters to determine whether political stewards are acting in ways that comport with citizens' preconceived and ideologically constrained conceptions. Rather, citizens' attention to political matters is activated by fire alarms—politically salient exogenous events. These fire alarms can cause individuals to deviate from their normal voting behavior. If widespread enough, these deviations will generate electoral jolts that will affect political elites' prospects for electoral success.

If voters (i.e., principals) regularly demonstrate their capacity to produce disequilibrating electoral jolts, political elites (i.e., agents) will be taught that it is in their interests to be attentive to the core political desires of citizens. Within this conception of mass-elite linkages, the capacity of voters to discipline elites electorally, joined with elites' rational anticipation of electoral rebukes, provides a political dynamic that makes representative democracy uniquely responsive to broad societal interests.

This posited dynamic, if empirically supportable, has the potential to provide unique and valuable insights into popular efficacy and democratic governance. The thrust of most extant research on mass-elite linkages notwithstanding, examining this dynamic empirically is not a fool's errand. My efforts in developing and empirically examining these theoretical dynamics are motivated by two considerations. One is the disjuncture between the image of voters that has emerged from academic research and the behavior of political stewards—what I term the "paradox of elected officials." The second is my belief that most scholarly efforts to understand popular efficacy have been handicapped by self-imposed conceptual and methodological limitations.

The next section introduces the paradox of elected officials and offers a metaphor to convey the approach to the study of popular efficacy driving this research. Then I develop the implications of this metaphor for the study of popular efficacy and the structure of the empirical analyses. Finally, I outline the methodological approach I use to conduct the empirical analyses.

## The Paradox of Elected Officials

The paradox of elected officials can be stated simply: Why do elected officials seem so preoccupied with popular concerns if citizens are "manageable fools"? Despite the findings of most empirical research on political behavior, elected officials make frequent trips home to measure the pulse of their constituents. They hire pollsters to gauge public opinion. They conduct strategy sessions to develop information campaigns to shape public perceptions. They worry about the timing of economic cycles, the impact of scandals, the effect of policies on their constituencies, and so forth and so on. In short, these officials act as though what the electorate thinks, and how it may act, affects their reelection prospects. This suggests that they may be laboring under an image of the electorate that is not informed by, or consistent with, the gist of the scholarly literature on political behavior.

A theoretically grounded and empirically supported conception of mass-elite linkages that could explain the paradox of elected officials would provide the basis for recentering citizens in our conceptions of democratic governance. To illustrate how such a conception is possible in light of the conventional wisdom generated by decades of research on political behavior, consider a simple culinary metaphor.

Restaurants, like governments, must satisfy the basic needs and desires of their patrons. However, while customers know what tastes good to them (and what does not), most want little more than palatable food at a fair price. The vast majority of customers know little about the intricacies of food preparation in a commercial setting and do not want to spend much time thinking about it. Consequently, they develop habitual patronage patterns that are influenced by those of their family and friends, as well as by their personal experiences with the restaurant. Out-of-towners and children coming of age are influenced by the patterns of those with whom they identify and interact.

Though much depends upon their profit margins and cash reserves, the strength of habitual patronage patterns provide restaurateurs with a good deal of latitude in structuring their day-to-day operations. Consequently, many decisions they make are highly susceptible to influence by those with more immediate interests in the operation of the restaurant (suppliers, cooks, wait staff, etc.) than by their clientele. Despite this there are limits to the autonomy of restaurateurs: being unresponsive to customers' desires entails a certain level of risk for the restaurateur. Moreover, important sources of threats to the restaurateur's grip on his customer base are out of his control.

Consider, for example, meat infected with mad cow disease that was unwittingly used in the preparation of entrees, generating a flurry of illnesses that lead to a major disruption in patronage patterns. This disruption could be exacerbated by revelations about (1) the restaurateur's unconventional choice of suppliers, (2) kickbacks to the restaurant by disreputable wholesalers, and (3) widespread disregard of industry standards in conducting health checks. The developments could lead their regular customers to eat fewer meals at restaurants altogether or to reevaluate their patronage, which could lead to the creation of new patronage patterns. If a sufficiently large number of regular customers departed from their patronage patterns, the restaurateur could experience financial setbacks, if not financial ruin.

In this metaphor, restaurateurs are assumed to be strategic actors motivated by their desire to maximize profits. Their behavior is determined by (1) the extent to which their customers are discriminating consumers and (2) their competitive environment. If the patronage patterns of the restaurant's clientele do not show them to be discriminating consumers, then the costs of the restaurant's indifference to their core desires are minimal. Thus, if the restaurant's customer base does not make large and enduring changes in their patronage patterns after an incident such as the mad cow infestation, over time restaurateurs will learn that they do not have to weigh customer concerns very heavily in determining what goes on in the kitchen. While the preferences of ordinary customers can seldom be wholly ignored, it may be possible to appease them with a few standby palliatives and an occasional advertising blitz. This is particularly true if consumers have few viable alternatives and the restaurant enjoys healthy profit margins.

A wholly different situation obtains, however, if the restaurant's customers are discriminating consumers. If events such as the mad cow incident result in enduring declines in patronage, then restaurateurs will learn to take seriously customer concerns and desires. They will have a powerful incentive to (1) learn from incidents that generate departures from habitual patronage patterns, (2) translate those lessons into changes in the structure and operation of the restaurant, and (3) anticipate potential problems and engage in preemptive actions designed to forestall future financial setbacks. Because the restaurateur's children aspire to inherit and run the restaurant he will also be motivated to transmit to them what he learned about the importance of being attentive to the core desires of customers. The restaurateur's incentives to act on the basis of market lessons increase when his profit margins are slim and the competition for customers is great.

### The Electoral Arena and Democratic Responsiveness

The political implications of this culinary metaphor are straightforward. If citizens are discriminating consumers of public goods, they can be efficacious political actors. The most important resource ordinary citizens have within representative democracies is the vote; their vote is their currency. Thus, democratic responsiveness hinges on the capacity of citizens to manifest discriminating behavior within the electoral arena. Moreover, because the din in "policy kitchens" is great, citizens must demonstrate the capacity to wield a big electoral stick. Popular sentiments and concerns will influence the decisional calculus of strategic political elites only if those elites view the electorate as a force that can impinge on their desire for elective office. This will happen only if voters demonstrate the capacity to depart from their normal voting behavior, regularly administering sharp, disequilibrating electoral jolts.

Electoral pressures are usually not as targeted or unambiguous as other forms of influence upon government (sophisticated information campaigns by interest groups, strategically placed campaign contributions, targeted lobbying efforts, etc.). But ordinary citizens have few other feasible alternatives. They do not have the resources or expertise to compete successfully with the powerful special interests huddled around the various "cooking stations" that generate public policy. Other forms of more focused popular expression (demonstrations, riots, protests) are much more difficult to organize and sustain. While electoral influences are often blunt and ambiguous, they can impact profoundly upon the core interests of political elites: their desire for electoral success. Thus, to generate fresh empirical insights into popular efficacy, the empirical analyses presented here focus on two phenomena that are crucial to electoral accountability: electoral independence and the competitiveness of electoral settings.

*Electoral independence* refers to the capacity of citizens to overcome the inertial tendencies in, and centripetal partisan pulls on, their electoral behavior. The dominance of these forces within the electoral arena is an important component of the "manageable fools" caricature of voters. If ordinary citizens do not evidence the capacity to overcome these forces on a regular basis, then it will be difficult to argue that they are efficacious political actors. Their capacity to compete with organized interests and to penetrate, mobilize, and integrate cumbersome policy-making networks would be suspect. The dominance of inertial and partisan forces in the determination of electoral outcomes would suggest that ordinary citizens are little more than "silent partners" in democratic governance.

On the other hand, if citizens demonstrate that they are discriminating consumers of public goods, it will be possible to conceive of them as efficacious political actors. By regularly demonstrating their capacity to administer disequilibrating electoral jolts, citizens can teach political elites that it is in their interest to be attentive to popular concerns, even to the point of anticipating threats to core political desires and acting preemptively. These "electoral lessons" become an important part of the political lore handed down from one generation of political elites to the next. Through this education in democratic politics elites would learn that elections are not ceremonial rites arranged to provide citizens with the opportunity to reaffirm partisan loyalties. Rather, they would be taught that elections are opportunities for citizens to scrutinize political stewardship. Thus, if citizens "fitfully intervene" with the electoral arena on a regular basis, political elites will internalize an image of the electorate that is akin to the fickle and discriminating clientele of a restaurant. And they will act according.

*Competitive electoral settings* facilitate electoral independence. They make it easier to translate evaluations of stewardship into electoral jolts; more competitive settings reduce the number of politically discerning voters needed to generate a disequilibrating electoral outcome. But electoral competitiveness also has an independent effect on popular efficacy. It plays an important role in the education of political elites by teaching elites about the importance of popular concerns in democratic politics. When electoral settings are competitive, party elites cannot be content to rely on time-tested techniques designed to mobilize party loyalists. Rather, they must think strategically and creatively about both retaining their electoral base and attracting inactive, unaligned, or marginally aligned voters. Thus, the persistence of electoral competitiveness over time will (1) teach strategic political elites that it is in their interest to be attentive to public concerns and (2) provide them with the incentive to identify and address those concerns.

## Reexamining Electoral Accountability

Compelling empirical evidence on the electorate's capacity for electoral independence and the impact of electoral independence on electoral outcomes could provide the basis for important new inferences about the responsiveness of representative democracy. Providing this empirical evidence, however, requires working outside the individual-level survey research paradigm that has dominated research on mass-elite linkages for over half a century.[2] Thus, the empirical results reported here are derived from analyses of election returns from all counties and most major cities in the continental United States for all presidential elections from 1828 to 2000 (44 elections, 3,131 locales, over 110,000 observations). I focus

[2] Aggregate electoral analysis was the norm before the emergence of survey research but the tradition continued even after the individual-level survey research paradigm became established (see, for example, Burnham, W. D. 1970. *Critical Elections and the Mainsprings of American Politics.* New York, W. W. Norton; Kleppner, P. 1970. *The Cross of Culture: A Social Analysis of Midwestern Politics, 1850–1900.* New York, Free Press; Jensen, R. 1971. *The Winning of the Midwest: Social and Political Conflict, 1888–1896.* Chicago, University of Chicago Press; McSeveney, S. T. 1972. *The Politics of Depression: Voting Behavior in the Northeast, 1893–1896.* New York, Oxford University Press; Silbey, J. H., A. G. Bogue, et al., eds. 1978. *The History of American Electoral Behavior.* Princeton, Princeton University Press; Kleppner, P. 1979. *The Third Electoral System, 1853–1892: Parties, Voters, and Political Cultures.* Chapel Hill, University of North Carolina Press; Clubb, J. M., W. H. Flanigan, et al. 1980. *Partisan Realignment: Voters, Parties, and Government in American History.* Beverly Hills, CA, Sage Publications; Kleppner, P., W. D. Burnham, et al., eds. 1981. *The Evolution of American Electoral Systems.* Westport, CT, Greenwood Press; Bartels, L. M. 1998. "Electoral Continuity and Change, 1868–1996." *Electoral Studies* 17 (3): 301–26. A very comprehensive compilation of citations to aggregate works in the realignment tradition can be found in Bass, H. F. 1991. "Background to Debate: A Reader's Guide and Bibliography," in *The End of Realignment? Interpreting American Electoral Eras,* ed. B. E. Shafer. Madison, University of Wisconsin Press.

Moreover, there has been a recent spate of longitudinal work using aggregated survey data (see, for example: Wright, G. C., R. S. Erikson, et al. 1985. "Measuring State Partisanship and Ideology with Survey Data." *Journal of Politics* 47:469–89; Wright, G. C., R. S. Erikson, et al. 1987. "Public Opinion and Policy Liberalism in the American States." *American Journal of Political Science* 31:980–1001; MacKuen, M. B., R. S. Erikson, et al. 1989. "Macropartisanship." *American Political Science Review* 83: 1125–42; Stimson, J. A. 1991. *Public Opinion in America.* Boulder, CO, Westview Press; MacKuen, M. B., R. S. Erikson, et al. 1992. "Peasants or Bankers? The American Electorate and the U.S. Economy." *American Political Science Review* 86:597–611; Erikson, R. S., G. C. Wright, et al. (1993). *Statehouse Democracy: Public Opinion and Policy in the American States.* Cambridge, Cambridge University Press; Erikson, MacKuen, et al. 2002.

on presidential elections because empirical analyses of these contests have played a major role in shaping our understanding of popular efficacy. The 1828 to 2000 period is employed because it spans the entire democratic era in American politics.

The subnational, longitudinal approach adopted here is essential for empirically examining the conception of mass-elite linkages outlined above, which has straightforward implications that are observable in the voting patterns of local electorates. For example, if the radiated effects of exogenous events that impinge upon citizens' core desires overcome endogenous influences on their voting behavior, then their electoral impact will be manifested in departures from normal voting patterns. The political dynamics that give rise to these departures from normal voting patterns require a long time frame such as the one employed here. A long temporal reach is essential both to define normal voting patterns and to capture sufficient numbers of salient exogenous events. Also, using a research design with a subnational focus and a broad geographic reach provides for both a more comprehensive and precise specification of the electoral effects of exogenous events, which are expected to vary spatially.

While the empirical analysis conducted here is at the local level, its conceptual underpinnings are rooted in the individual-level survey research paradigm. That is, the empirical analyses are based on a macro-level extension of *the Michigan model of voting behavior.* The Michigan model was used to structure the macro-level analyses because it is theoretically well developed and empirically supportable at the individual level. At the core of the Michigan model is the concept of a normal vote. Normal voting behavior reflects the major role played by endogenous (partisan) influences on electoral behavior; normal party votes reflect the size of a party's electoral base. Within this framework electoral independence is gauged by *changes in* and *deviations from* normal voting patterns; electoral competitiveness is determined by the *relative size* of the parties' electoral bases.

This normal vote framework, in conjunction with the structure of the research design developed here, makes it possible to conduct analyses that are beyond the scope of the survey research paradigm. In particular, the approach offered here permits a focus on (1) the role of exogenous factors in generating *departures* from normal voting patterns and (2) the *impact* of those departures on electoral settings and outcomes. The factors that generate departures from normal voting patterns provide important insights into *whether citizens can be viewed as discriminating consumers of public goods.* Examining the impact of those departures on electoral settings and outcomes provides insights into *the lessons political elites have been taught about the role of the electorate in democratic politics.* Considered together, the empirical findings from this approach can provide unique insights into the responsiveness of American democracy.

## ORGANIZATION OF THIS BOOK

The following three chapters provide the individual-level theoretical foundations for the empirical analyses. A half-century of individual-level research has raised so many questions about the efficaciousness of citizens that macro-level empirical analyses bearing on popular efficacy require a sound individual-level foundation. Chapters 2 through 4 provide this theoretical foundation.

Chapter 2 reviews some of the earlier literature on mass-elite linkages and offers a theoretical synthesis that differentiates the approach offered here from earlier efforts. This synthesis addresses two foundational issues concerning democratic citizenship and popular efficacy. What does being an efficacious political actor entail? Can we conceive of citizens fulfilling those expectations? It argues that an *evaluative conception of democratic citizenship*, in conjunction with the *emerging work in cognitive science*, provides the theoretical basis for believing that citizens may be capable of efficacious political behavior.

This conceptualization acknowledges the peripheral processing of most political information as well as the dominant role of endogenously tainted political heuristics. It also assigns a central role to exogenous events that impinge upon core political desires and lead citizens to initiate episodes of intensive processing of political information and induce political learning. These intensive interludes can generate experientially based cognitive reconfigurations of political matters that, in turn, can influence evaluations of stewardship and vote choice.

While the theoretical synthesis offered in chapter 2 demonstrates *why* exogenous events can be an important source of inferences about popular efficacy, chapter 3 demonstrates *how* exogenous events are manifested in macro-level electoral change. The transformation of exogenous events into evaluations of stewardship and vote choices involves the complex workings of several sets of factors that unfold over time. Chapter 3 presents an individual-level model of this transformational process. It shows how the interactions among these various factors can lead citizens to deviate from their normal voting behavior; the aggregate effects of these deviations produce macro-level electoral changes of varying magnitude, duration, and geographic scope.

The activities of political stewards play an important role in the transformational model presented in chapter 3. Indeed, some of these activities constitute what can be characterized as endogenous influences on electoral behavior. Endogenous influences are efforts by political elites to shape, direct, and control the political behavior of citizens. Efforts by elites to control the electoral effects of politically salient exogenous events undermine objective evaluation of political stewardship; these endogenous influences constitute the primary threat to popular efficacy within the conceptualization of mass-elite linkages offered in chapter 2.

Because endogenous influences represent individual-level factors that may negate the political dynamics described in chapter 2 and chapter 3, chapter 4 provides a broad introduction to the role of endogenous influences in democratic governance. Chapter 4 demonstrates that endogenous influences are primal forces in democratic political orders and argues that the political party is currently the dominant vehicle for the transmission of endogenous influences. It concludes by addressing the role of endogenous influences on voting. This analysis provides the theoretical basis for the derivation of normal voting patterns for local electorates, which are used in specifying departures from normal voting patterns.

Chapter 5 presents the subnational, longitudinal design used to structure the empirical analyses. It introduces the concept of a local electorate and details the historical data archive used to obtain profiles of them. It then presents an overview of the approach used to derive the normal voting patterns of local electorates, which are defined as the manifestation of endogenous (partisan) influences on individual voting behavior—aggregated to the local level. Some examples of normal voting patterns are presented and used to provide concrete insights into the concepts of electoral independence and competitiveness. Finally, the normal voting data are used to underscore the centrality of endogenous influences on the voting patterns of local electorates.

Because local normal voting patterns are defined as the manifestation of endogenous influences, only departures from those patterns are used to generate inferences about popular efficacy. Chapter 6 underscores the conservative nature of this approach by challenging the interpretation of normal voting patterns as the manifestation of endogenous influences on voting behavior. Defining normal voting patterns as the manifestation of endogenous influences rests on an interpretation of political parties as endogenous institutions dominated by party elites. It follows from this rather constricted view that partisan influences on voting reflect little more than the interests of party elites. The challenge posed in chapter 6 rests on a pluralistic view of parties that views partisan influences on voting as a reflection of the interests of the party's core constituencies. The analyses reported in chapter 6 suggest that partisan influences on voting cannot be viewed as wholly, or even largely, endogenous. These analyses provide empirical support for the assumptions underlying the transformational model presented in chapter 3, in addition to important insights into mass-elite linkages in American democracy.

Chapter 7 presents the first component of the electoral independence analysis. Its focus is on enduring electoral change (critical and secular), and it examines the incidence, geographic scope, and magnitude of these data. The data on enduring electoral change are distributed in a manner that comports with the transformational model presented in chapter 3. The temporal and spatial structure of these data is consistent with the assertion that they were generated by a series of reinforcing exogenous events rooted in transformative societal developments. It also demonstrates that the magnitude of these enduring changes is large enough to capture the attention of political elites and play a role in their political education.

Chapter 8 presents the second component of the electoral independence analysis. It uses data on electoral perturbations to generate inferences about popular efficacy. This analysis integrates two sets of independent variables with the normal vote data. The first is a set of performance indicators that captures variations in the realization of core political desires within three domains: prosperity, war and peace, and personal security. The second set includes data on partisan resources and actions designed to manage and control electoral behavior. The results demonstrate that while the effect of the performance indicators on electoral perturbations is substantial, the effects of partisan activities are weak and mixed. Indeed, some of the partisan factors have unanticipated effects rooted in the long-standing American fear of concentrated power. While these analyses cast doubt on the capacity of political elites to manage and shape electoral perturbations, they provide strong support for the notion that voters are discriminating consumers of public goods.

Chapter 9 speaks to the role of electoral independence in the education of political elites by examining its impact on electoral settings and electoral outcomes. Its focus is on the incidence of competitive electoral settings and disequilibrating electoral outcomes (realigning elections, deviating elections, endorsement elections). The distribution of these election types demonstrates that centrality of the electorate to the core interests of political elites was underscored either going into a presidential campaign or in the outcome of the election in two-thirds of all elections since the emergence of a two-party system. The results suggest that, over the course of the past two centuries, political elites are likely to have learned that the electorate is a potent political force in democratic politics.

When joined with the findings of the electoral independence analyses, these results shed a good deal of light on the paradox of elected officials. They suggest that strategic political elites are likely to have internalized an image of the electorate that is very different from that found in most academic research. Indeed, the image of the electorate that emerges here suggests that it is rational for political stewards to engage in anticipatory actions to guard against the consequences of electoral rebukes, as well as to reap the electoral benefits that accrue from wise stewardship. The empirical analyses presented here make it clear that strategic political elites driven by the desire for electoral success cannot afford to treat the electorate as a silent partner in democratic governance.

Chapter 10 summarizes the basic argument of this book. It also reviews the empirical evidence bearing on the debate over popular efficacy. Finally, it develops the broader implications of these findings for democratic theory, American politics, and future research.

## References

Bartels, L. M. 1998. "Electoral Continuity and Change, 1868–1996." *Electoral Studies* 17 (3): 301–26.

Bass, H. F. 1991. "Background to Debate: A Reader's Guide and Bibliography." In *The End of Realignment? Interpreting American Electoral Eras*, edited by B. E. Shafer. Madison, University of Wisconsin Press.

Burnham, W. D. 1970. *Critical Elections and the Mainsprings of American Politics*. New York, W. W. Norton.

Clubb, J. M., W. H. Flanigan, et al. 1980. *Partisan Realignment: Voters, Parties, and Government in American History*. Beverly Hills, CA, Sage Publications.

Erikson, R. S., G. C. Wright, et al. 1993. *Statehouse Democracy: Public Opinion and Policy in the American States*. Cambridge, Cambridge University Press.

Fiorina, M. P. 1981. *Retrospective Voting in American National Elections*. New Haven, Yale University Press.

Fukuyama, F. 1992. *The End of HIstory and the Last Man*. New York, Avon Books.

Jensen, R. 1971. *The Winning of the Midwest: Social and Political Conflict, 1888–1896*. Chicago, University of Chicago Press.

Key, V. O. 1966. *The Responsible Electorate: Rationality in Presidential Voting, 1936–1960*. Cambridge, Harvard University Press.

Kleppner, P. 1970. *The Cross of Culture: A Social Analysis of Midwestern Politics, 1850–1900*. New York, Free Press.

————1979. *The Third Electoral System, 1853–1892: Parties, Voters, and Political Cultures*. Chapel Hill, University of North Carolina Press.

Kleppner, P., W. D. Burnham, et al., eds. 1981. *The Evolution of American Electoral Systems*. Westport, CT, Greenwood Press.

MacKuen, M. B., R. S. Erikson, et al. 1989. "Macropartisanship." *American Political Science Review* 83: 1125–42.

MacKuen, M. B., R. S. Erikson, et al. 1992. "Peasants or Bankers? The American Electorate and the U.S. Economy." *American Political Science Review* 86: 597–611.

McCubbins, M., and T. Schwartz. 1984. "Congressional Oversight Overlooked: Police Patrols versus Fire Alarms." *American Journal of Political Science* 28:165–79.

McSeveney, S. T. 1972. *The Politics of Depression: Voting Behavior in the Northeast, 1893–1896*. New York, Oxford University Press.

Silbey, J. H., A. G. Bogue, et al., eds. 1978. *The History of American Electoral Behavior*. Princeton, Princeton University Press.

Stimson, J. A. 1991. *Public Opinion in America*. Boulder, CO, Westview Press.

Wright, G. C., R. S. Erikson, et al. 1985. "Measuring State Partisanship and Ideology with Survey Data." *Journal of Politics* 47:469–89.

Wright, G. C., R. S. Erikson, et al. 1987. "Public Opinion and Policy Liberalism in the American States." *American Journal of Political Science* 31:980–1001.

# CHAPTER TWO

# Democratic Citizenship, Democratic Citizens, and Mass-Elite Linkages

> From the perspective of twenty-five hundred years of Western political thinking, almost no one, until recently, thought democracy to be a very good way of structuring political life. This opinion was not always due to inattention. Thucydides, Plato, and Aristotle gave very close and critical attention to democracy within Periclean Athens, and to that city's later more radical experiences with democracy in the aftermath of the Peloponnesian War. They found Athenian democracy, both in theory and practice, to be vengeful, impolitic in war and peace, unstable and mean-spirited in its internal affairs. . . . [T]he great preponderance of political thinkers . . . have insisted on the perversity of democratic constitutions, the disorderliness of democratic politics, and the moral depravity of the democratic character.
> —PAUL E. CORCORAN,
> "The Limits of Democratic Theory"

> The sober second thought of the people is never wrong, and always efficient.
> —MARTIN VAN BUREN, 1829[1]

THIS CHAPTER addresses two foundational questions in the study of popular efficacy: What does it mean to say that democratic citizens are efficacious political actors? In light of what we know about political behavior, is it possible to conceive of ordinary citizens as being efficacious? In providing answers to these questions chapter 2 further illuminates the conceptualization of mass-elite linkages introduced in chapter 1. These answers also explain why this conceptualization has the potential to yield fresh insights into popular efficacy, insights that have important implications for our understanding of democracy as a uniquely responsive form of government.

---

[1] This quote is from Arthur M. Schlesinger, Jr. 1946. Boston, Little, Brown. *The Age of Jackson.*

The first section of this chapter reviews selected works in democratic theory and political psychology pertaining to democratic citizenship. A careful examination of the literature on democratic theory reveals different conceptions of citizenship embedded in different models of democracy. Each defines popular efficacy differently. I examine these different conceptions of citizenship in light of the literature on political behavior and argue that only one justifies continued empirical investigation: the evaluative conception of citizenship. When joined with some insights derived from research in political psychology, this conception of citizenship provides the basis for thinking that citizens *may* be capable of being discriminating consumers of public goods.

A central assertion in political psychology, which draws from research in the cognitive sciences, is that citizens use heuristic devices to aid them in making political judgments. This assertion has the potential to undermine the most damning inferences drawn from the seminal works in empirical democratic theory. However, research in political psychology has generated two normative concerns that undermine the notion that citizens are efficacious political actors. The first is that many cognitive psychologists view heuristic reasoning as a suboptimal form of decision making. The second is that many political information flows and heuristics are tainted by endogenous influences that erode the evaluative capacities of citizens. These two concerns are developed in the second section of this chapter; the third section offers a normatively appealing conception of mass-elite linkages that addresses them. The distinguishing features of this conceptualization are the significance it attributes to (1) core political desires and their effect on information processing and (2) exogenous events that are capable of generating intermittent episodes of intensive information processing.

## Democratic Citizenship and Democratic Citizens

How political thinkers have conceived democracy has changed considerably over time. Democratic theory has been affected by divergent intellectual traditions rooted in different historical epochs (Greek classical democracy, Roman republicanism, and Western European liberalism), as well as by institutional innovations in government, shifts in the scale and organization of society, and historical experiences with democratic forms of government. As a result, there is currently little consensus on the *specifics* of what constitutes a democracy. On an empirical level, there is a great deal of institutional variety in governments commonly considered democracies (Schmitter 1991). On a theoretical level there are several "models" of democracy (Macpherson 1977; Held 1987). Embedded in various models of democracy are different conceptions of the role of citizens: the participatory, the utilitarian, and the evaluative. These different conceptions can be, and have been, used to assess the viability, health, and functioning of democratic government. They provide different perspectives on popular efficacy.

In the participatory conception, citizens exert direct influences on democratic governance by performing the full range of governmental functions.[2] Within the culinary metaphor this is analogous to citizens drafting the menus, staffing the cook stations, and preparing the food, as well as serving it. In the utilitarian conception, citizens play an indirect role by being informed and active political actors who maintain informed preferences on public matters, communicate those preferences to their elected representatives, and monitor the performance of their representatives.[3] Metaphorically, this conception is analogous to patrons having views as to what should be on the restaurant's menu, providing detailed information on their preparation preferences, and gauging their patronage to the proprietor's responsiveness to their preferences.

In the evaluative conception citizens exert an even more indirect effect on governance matters. They do this by acting as monitors of political elites.[4] Within this conception democratic citizens do not have to maintain informed and stable preferences about the *specifics of public policy*. However, they must have: (1) stable core political desires; (2) the cognitive capacity to evaluate political stewardship in light of those core desires; and (3) the ability to register those evaluations within the electoral arena. Put metaphorically, the restaurant's patrons must be discriminating consumers of public goods. They must be able to determine whether what they are being served is palatable, and whether it is priced fairly.

Because the United States is a representative democracy the most relevant conceptions of citizenship are the utilitarian and the evaluative. Of the two, the utilitarian conception has played a far more prominent role in the development and assessment of American democracy. Utilitarian-based arguments, combined with an emerging commitment to egalitarianism, provided the basis for the expanded political role of citizens in early-nineteenth-century America. Moreover, the rhetoric of many scholars,

---

[2] The participatory conception of democratic citizenship has its roots in the experiences of Athenian democracy; its classic statement can be found in Pericles' Funeral Oration.

[3] The utilitarian conception of democratic citizenship emerges from a nineteenth-century model of representative democracy with its roots in the work of Jeremy Bentham and James Mill; the most succinct contemporary statement of the utilitarian conception is in Berelson, Lazarsfeld, and McPhee's *Voting* (Berelson, Lazarsfeld et al. 1954: 306–9).

[4] The evaluative conception of democratic citizenship emerges from the twentieth-century work of Joseph Schumpeter (1942) and "process models" of representative democracy (Held 1987).

pundits, and public officials suggests that the expectations embodied in the utilitarian conception define the criteria that *should* be used to evaluate the efficaciousness of citizens.

The problem with the utilitarian conception of citizenship is that it is unsustainable on empirical grounds. If this were the standard for assessing popular efficacy, there would be little justification for continued empirical research.

The ability of most citizens to meet utilitarian ideals has been questioned ever since empiricists began to study democracies (Ostrogorski 1902; Wallas 1909; Mosca 1939; Michels [1915] 1962). Early suspicions that citizens were "manageable fools" were confirmed in a series of surveys on political knowledge administered to U.S. citizens during the middle of the twentieth century (Niemi and Weisberg 1993a). The results of these surveys were dismal and cumulative. They led Smith to note that, by the late 1960s, "The public's lack of information was so well established that scholars lost interest in studying the subject (Smith 1989: 159)." These findings have important implications for utilitarian conceptions of citizenship. Without adequate information citizens would not have the capacity to make meaningful electoral choices. These conclusions were compounded by Converse's findings that mass belief systems were unstructured (Converse 1964). Metaphorically, it is difficult for ordinary citizens to plan a menu or stipulate preparations if they know little about restaurant management and vacillate in their food preferences.

In reviewing the research on empirical democratic theory Niemi and Weisberg (1993a) acknowledge that political sophistication varies considerably across individuals, political systems, and time. Their review suggests that voters are neither supersophisticated nor abysmally ignorant. In the end, however, they conclude that

> empirical research has forever ruined our picture of mass electorates as comprised of idealized good citizens. Along with that fictional person's high levels of political interest, knowledge, and participation, we must discard an all-encompassing ideological view of politics and a clear understanding of political coinage such as liberal/conservative. Too many results . . . have found voters . . . whose understanding and use of ideological thinking are minimal at best. Too many attempts have been made to lower the standards required to declare voters ideological—only to find that many voters still could not qualify. (50)

Lupia and McCubbins second this view in a recent assessment:

> Cicero's observation that "in the common people there is no wisdom, no penetration, no power of judgment" is an apt summary of modern voting studies. . . . Many scholars argue that voters, because of their obstinance or

their inability to educate themselves, become unwitting puppets of campaign and media puppet-masters. . . . Iyengar (1987: 816) summarizes the literature on voting and elections: "the low level of political knowledge and the absence of ideological reasoning has lent credence to the charges that popular control of government is illusory." These studies suggest that voters who lack information cannot use elections to control their governors. (1998)

In assessing the implications of these studies for popular efficacy Lupia and McCubbins concede that "people lack information" (1998:1). They do not, however, concede that this makes democratic citizens unable to "control their governors." This is because of the import of scholarly advances in the cognitive sciences, particularly cognitive psychology (Tversky and Kahneman 1974). Political psychologists have extended these advances to the study of political behavior. This research has built upon and enriched earlier observations that limited information does not prevent citizens from making informed judgments.

> In the 1950s . . . Berelson, Lazarsfeld, and McPhee (1954) and Downs (1957) argued that voters rely on opinion leaders and political parties to overcome their information shortfalls. More recently, a generation of scholars led by Fiorina (1981), Kuklinski, Metlay, and May (1982), Calvert (1985), Grofman and Norrander (1990), the contributors to Ferejohn and Kuklinski (1990), Popkin (1991), Sniderman, Brody, and Tetlock (1991), and the contributors to Lodge and McGraw (1995) has furthered countered the view that the "democratic citizen is expected to be well informed about political affairs (Berelson, Lazarsfeld, McPhee, 1954: 308)." Collectively, these scholars have demonstrated that voters can use a wide range of simple cues as substitutes for complex information. (Lupia and McCubbins 1998: 5)

On a metaphorical level, the research to which Lupia and McCubbins refer suggests the following: Ordinary customers can make judgments on continued patronage without knowing much about meal planning, cooking, or the restaurant business. They also do not need to know what is going on at every cooking station; nor do they need to have tried everything on the menu. Sampling from the menu, absorbing information cues, and using judgmental heuristics (simplified rules to integrate information cues) may be enough to make reasoned judgments about what is going on in the kitchen—and whether it is sufficient to sustain their patronage.

Cognitive models of decision making provide the basis for believing that ordinary citizens may be able to make reasoned political judgments despite manifest informational deficiencies. But they are antithetical to the rational deductivism embodied in utilitarian thought. These models do not support the notion that citizens have the ability or inclination to (1) maintain comprehensive, well-structured preferences concerning complex public policies, (2) collect and absorb large amounts of relevant political information through the vigilant surveillance of political elites, or (3) do the cognitive work needed to integrate the collected political information with their policy preferences. This means that the potential utility of cognitively based models for enhancing our understanding of mass-elite linkages can best be realized by adopting an evaluative conception of democratic citizens, a conception that emerges from process models of democracy. This potential is rooted in the role of ordinary citizens within process models of democracy.

Process models define democracy as a *method* of selecting political leaders. Democracy derives its effectiveness as a governing mechanism from the *processes* by which it generates collective decisions. Democratic processes involve the interaction of political elites within a prescribed institutional setting composed of both public and private entities and procedural checks and guarantees. The capacity of ordinary citizens to formulate, and act upon, detailed policy preferences is less central to policymaking within process models of democracy than to utilitarian models. Within process models, the primary responsibility of citizens is to (1) evaluate the stewardship and/or vision of competing elites and (2) act on those evaluations at election time. *The fear of electoral retribution is what leads strategic, self-interested political elites to be attentive to popular concerns and adopt inclusive conceptions of social welfare.*

Cognitive models of human decision making suggest that citizens may be capable of making the type of discriminating evaluations expected of them within process models of democracy. Combined with the evaluative conception of citizenship, cognitive models provide the basis for conceiving citizens as efficacious political actors. This conceptual synthesis provides the justification for continued empirical research into popular efficacy. However, the results of cognitive research have produced too many normative concerns to conclude, a priori, that this conceptual synthesis is capable of undermining the characterization of citizens as "manageable fools." The next section reviews these normative concerns and the following section presents a conceptualization of mass-elite linkages that addresses them.

### COGNITIVE SCIENCE AND DEMOCRATIC THEORY: NORMATIVE IMPLICATIONS AND CONCERNS

A key goal of the cognitive sciences is to develop models of individual decision making that comport with the cognitive abilities that human beings are thought to possess. Extensions of cognitive research into the political arena are based on the premise that political behavior is structured similarly to behavior in other spheres of life. McGraw and Lodge note that the most important contribution of cognitive research to political science is the development of information-processing models of behavior.

> The notion that information about the world is represented in memory in an organized way and that how this knowledge is "bundled together" affects the way we comprehend and respond to the world is not new, dating back to Aristotle (Bartlett 1932). What is new is the treatment of thinking as "information processing." The information-processing approach to thinking is concerned with identifying the processes by which people acquire, store, retrieve, transform, and use information to perform some intelligent, goal-based activity. This approach sees the individual as a purposive actor whose behavior, while routinely deviating from rational expectations, nevertheless can be viewed as a reasonable response to an experience-based representation of the world. (1995: 1)

Most of the political research drawing from information-processing models of decision making has been concerned with improving our understanding of political behavior. Political psychologists have generated some of the most important contributions to our understanding of political behavior since the seminal work in the field.[5] Despite the thrust of most cognitively based research, its utility for political science is not limited to behavioral applications: It can make important normative contributions by providing insights into our understanding of democratic processes. Its formidable potential notwithstanding, political psychology has made only limited contributions to democratic theory. Indeed, its principal contribution here has been to demonstrate that the dismal inferences that have been drawn about popular efficacy are due more to the inadequacies of the utilitarian paradigm than those of ordinary citizens. While the value of undermining these rather dismal inferences should not be minimized, political psychology has the potential to make more positive contributions.

A cognitively based understanding of mass-elite linkages would be invaluable because it would be derived from broadly based and empirically informed conceptualizations of human behavior. Such a model could contribute to our understanding of what democratic governance means by providing insights into what it *can* mean—or at least what it is likely to mean. Herein lies the potential utility of cognitive psychology in help-

---

[5] This research has dealt with, among other things, the makeup and use of judgmental heuristics, the role of on-line processing of information as opposed to memory-based processing, and the analysis of differences in cognitive processes (see Ferejohn and Kuklinski 1990; Sniderman, Brody, et al. 1991; and Lodge and McGraw 1995 for examples of, and citations to, this field of work).

ing us understand the role of the *demos* in democratic governance. This notwithstanding, it cannot be assumed that cognitively based research will necessarily provide a scientific basis for "bringing the people back in" to democratic theory. Its potential contributions are clouded by two factors: the prevalence of peripheral processing of political information and the tainting of information flows and judgmental heuristics by endogenous influences.

### Peripheral Processing and Democratic Decision Making

It is not at all clear from a review of research in political psychology that information-processing models yield a normatively satisfying picture of democratic decision making. For example, cognitively based research has established that individuals absorb only a small proportion of the information to which they are exposed, that biases exist in the information flows to which different groups of individuals are exposed, and that individuals vary in their predisposition to seek or avoid exposure to diverse sources of information. Is it also clear that the use of stereotyping and projection is widespread and that emotional considerations play a role in how some information is evaluated. Finally, individuals with high levels of preexisting information on a topic are most likely to reject new information. This, of course, minimizes the impact of new information on the judgments of political elites.

Given some of the preliminary findings in political psychology, research in this tradition may ultimately reinforce the image of citizens as "manageable fools." This, of course, would undermine the idea of electoral accountability and democratic responsiveness. The likelihood of this possibility is clear in a recent work by Kuklinski and Quirk (2000). It is one of the few analyses that deals explicitly with the implications of cognitive research for democratic theory. They note that the picture of political decision making that has been generated in political psychology has ominous normative implications.

Crucial to Kuklinski and Quirk's analysis is the distinction that cognitive psychologists draw between central and peripheral processing of information. Central processing makes greater use of human mental capacities. But most political evaluations are the result of peripheral processing and make extensive use of simple heuristics and stereotypic inferences. The implications of this for democratic governance are fairly dismal. Peripheral processing is not necessarily an effective means of dealing with information. Information shortcuts, like many others, often have costs. They are often unreliable and do not necessarily translate into reasonable judgments.

Ironically, political scientists have borrowed the concept of heuristics from psychology while overlooking its main significance in that literature. Viewing heuristics as rational strategies for dealing with ignorance, political scientists have stressed how they enhance competence. . . . For the most part, cognitive psychologists look at heuristics differently. They see the use of heuristics as automatic, unconscious, and frequently dysfunctional (see, for example, Kahneman, Slovic, and Tversky 1982; Nisbett and Ross 1980). Research has shown that people use arbitrary starting points to anchor estimates, use accessibility in memory to estimate frequency; use a source's attractiveness to judge her credibility; and draw inferences from predetermined scripts and stereotypes. In cases that do not fit their implicit assumptions, heuristic judgments produce serious departures from rationality. (2000: 166).

The most basic conclusion Kuklinski and Quirk draw from these observations is that the cognitive capacities of humans may not be well suited for the responsibilities of democratic citizenship. Humans have the ability to make effective decisions. But, due to the nature and origins of human cognitive capacities, people will use available information effectively only under certain conditions. Unfortunately, the context within which most electoral decisions are made undermines the effective use of information.

### Endogenous Influences upon Information Flows and Judgmental Heuristics

Within information-processing models of political decision making, citizens rely heavily upon heuristic devices to assimilate political information that is largely mediated. This is troubling from the perspective of democratic theory because political elites are the dominant source of both information flows and heuristic devices. Thus, from the perspective of democratic theory, cognitively based conceptions of decision making may not merely be suboptimal and irrational; they may also be biased in a way that undermines the evaluative capacities of citizens. Zaller, for example, highlights the role of elites in how citizens process political information and contends that it is unavoidable.

The argument of this book is, on first inspection, scarcely encouraging with respect to domination of mass opinions by elites. . . . If many citizens are largely uncritical in their response to political communications as carried in the mass media, and if most of the rest respond mechanically on the basis of partisan cues, how can one deny the existence of a substantial degree of elite domination of public opinion?

It all depends on how one defines elite domination. If one takes it to mean any situation in which the public changes its opinion in the direction of the "information" and leadership cues supplied to it by elites, indeed, there is not much to argue about. Not only the present study but several others provide abundant evidence of this sort of elite domination (Iyengar and Kinder 1987; Page, Shapiro, and Dempsey 1987; Fan 1988).

. . . [So] of course the public responds to elite-supplied information and leadership cues. How could it be otherwise in a world in which events are ambiguous and in which the public must regularly have opinions about matters that are, to use Lippman's phrase again, "out of reach, out of sight, out of mind" (1922, 1946: 21)? (1992: 311)

Delli Carpini and Keeter develop the normative implications of elite domination:

In [these] approaches . . . "the voice of the people is but an echo" of the elites who dominate the information environment at any given time (Key 1966: 2). The opinions and behaviors of most citizens are treated as either uninterpretable background noise or the mere reflections of a more informed minority. All three models assume the "unavoidable dependency of [the mass public] on elite discourse." . . . [This is a problem because] one of the main justifications for citizen participation in liberal democracies is to serve as a check on the tendency of those in power to use their position for their own gain. Herein lies the catch-22 of any model of democracy solely dependent on information filtered through political elites—even through competing elites. (1989: 46)

What Delli Carpini and Keeter find crippling from the perspective of democratic theory is not problematic from Zaller's perspective. These scholars arrive at radically different conclusions because they fail to distinguish endogenous sources of political information and heuristics from other sources. This distinction has profound normative implications. Consider, for example, Kuklinski and Quirk's list of political heuristics:

In elections, the classic voting cue is of course the political party (Campbell, Converse, Miller, and Stokes 1960). By merely attending to party labels, voters can compensate for a lack of reliable information on the candidates' policy positions. Popkin (1991) identifies a multitude of other voting strategies on which people can draw. These include attributing issue positions on the basis of a candidate's demographics or those of his supporters; using evidence about personal character to make inferences about political character; assuming that the president controls the economy; and using returns in early primaries as evidence of the candidates' merit.

In judging either candidates or policies, people can use public statements by elected officials, interest-group leaders, or others as cues. Citizens who know very little about a pending bill, for example, can look to the statements of particular officeholders they have come to trust (Carmines and Kuklinski 1990; Mondak 1994). Alternatively, they can consider the positions of interest groups whose policy preferences they are generally inclined to support or oppose (Lupia 1994). Such cues arguably eliminate the need for substantive information about an issue. . . . Brody and Sniderman (1985) argue that people can use the likability of certain political groups—blacks and whites, liberals and conservatives—to make reasonable judgments of where they stand on policy. (2000: 155)

Reasonable minds can differ over whether these heuristics provide a sound basis for making political evaluations. But it is clear that their *origins* differ in ways that have significant normative implications. While some derive from affectations toward social groups, immutable demographic traits, and exogenous factors, others are traceable to *political stewards*. This is especially true of the political party as a heuristic device and any information that flows from party elites. The unique relationship of political parties to the policy-making process, and to their loyalists, makes their influence on the evaluative processes of citizens suspect on normative grounds.

Party elites either are, or aspire to be, the public's political stewards. The pursuit of elective office is the political party's *raison d'etre*. It is the driving force behind most party actions and it affects what information political parties present as well as the "spin" they put on it. This is of consequence for democratic governance because political parties have a strong grip on their adherents' beliefs and behavior. Zaller is simply summarizing decades of research when he contends that the party's core constituencies "respond mechanically on the basis of partisan cues." These mechanical responses dull the evaluative capacities of citizens in a context in which peripheral processing dominates decision making.

## CORE POLITICAL DESIRES, EXOGENOUS EVENTS, AND MASS-ELITE LINKAGES

These normative concerns cloud the utility of the conceptual synthesis offered earlier in constructing a view of mass-elite linkages that is consistent with the notion of an efficacious citizenry. To overcome these normative concerns, several salient individual-level findings must be addressed. Some of these findings are rooted in the seminal literature on empirical democratic theory, others in the more recent literature in political psychology. Two are particularly important: (1) Converse's finding that mass political belief systems are unstable and (2) research in political psychology documenting that the peripheral processing of mediated political information dominates democratic decision making.

Converse's work on mass belief systems (1964) is problematic because implicit in the concept of electoral accountability is the idea that individuals have a set of political preferences, views, and attitudes that are deeply rooted in their psyches and, hence, meaningful, important, and stable. Without such preferences the question of whether the governed can control their governors becomes irrelevant because, as Achen notes, "Democratic theory loses its starting point" (1975: 1218). The gist of the political psychology research on decision making is problematic because recent normative critiques of this research stress the suboptimal nature of peripheral processing and the potential for bias in mediated information flows and political heuristics, as just noted.

These bodies of empirical work pose formidable, but not insurmountable, problems. Any normatively appealing conception of mass-elite linkages must be premised on the assertion that democratic governance has a "starting point." The fact that many political beliefs and preferences are unstable does not mean that citizens do not have any durable basis for evaluating political stewardship. Political belief systems are complex cognitive configurations. Some components are more important and durable than others; they provide a starting point for democratic governance.

Any conception of mass-elite linkages based on the synthesis offered earlier must be based on the assertion that the peripheral processing of mediated political information dominates democratic decision making. But the fact that most citizens routinely rely on suboptimal and biased modes of information processing that are frequently tainted by endogenous influences does not mean that their evaluative capacities are always compromised. Exogenous events can affect the manner in which at least some citizens process political information some of the time by generating intense episodes of information processing, which can lead to cognitive and behavioral changes.

The next section discusses mass belief systems in light of an information processing perspective on political decision making. The second section discusses the impact that exogenous factors can have on the processing of political information.

## Political Belief Systems and Core Political Desires

In one of the seminal contributions to political psychology, Sniderman, Brody, and Tetlock challenge the implications that have been drawn from Converse's highly influential work on mass belief systems. In discussing what they term as Converse's "minimalist" model they note

The root question to ask of the minimalist model is this: What things, according to the model, are there in a belief system? Chiefly, according to Converse, issue preferences—opinions, for example, about government responsibility for housing, American policy overseas, urban renewal, and the like. Given the indefinitely large number of issues of consequence in politics, the ontological commitments of minimalism would seem numerous indeed.

But also remarkably meager: In practice the minimalist model proceeds as though a belief system contains opinions on specific issues, and not much else. Values of many sizes and shapes are thus excluded—the importance people attach to achievement and hard work, to protecting liberty and equality, to preserving tradition, to assuring diversity and change. (Sniderman, Brody, et al. 1991: 17–18)

Sniderman and his colleagues stress the need to "outline a different perspective on belief systems, not because we doubt that there are issues about which the public has only the most superficial opinions, but because we believe that there are issues about which it possesses strong convictions (1991: 18)." They offer a more refined and inclusive conception than Converse's elite-oriented conception. I strongly endorse the view that citizens have strong convictions on some political matters. At the same time, I offer a somewhat different conception of a political belief system than Sniderman and his coauthors. I conceptualize a political belief system in terms of citizens' views toward core political desires, regime traits (symbols, norms, institutions, etc.), and political instruments (issues and policies). This conceptualization is outlined in table 2–1.

This characterization flows from what I term a "mass perspective" on politics. That is, it organizes political phenomena in light of how ordinary citizens, as opposed to political sophisticates, are likely to view and deal with the political system. Moreover, it is based on the premise that in politics, like every aspect of life (child rearing, finance, work, marriage, etc.), some concerns are more important than others. Consequently, information that bears on more important political concerns is handled differently from information that does not. Furthermore, information that bears on more important political concerns also has more consequential behavioral effects.

To illustrate these points, consider an example derived from family life. It is extremely important to most parents that their child develops as a healthy, happy, and socially responsible person. Different parents may prioritize these desires differently. But the high value they place on them is not likely to fluctuate much over time. Also, because these fundamental aspirations are primal desires that are deeply engrained in the psyche of most parents, they are not highly susceptible to manipulation by others. Moreover, all but the most dysfunctional of parents are likely to (1) notice important signs that suggest their child may not be developing properly (illness, enduring malaise, delinquency) and (2) invest a good deal of cog-

TABLE 2.1
Structure of U.S. Political Belief System

| Core Political Desires | | Regime Traits | | | Political Instruments | |
| --- | --- | --- | --- | --- | --- | --- |
| Basic | Derivative | Symbols and Norms | Institutions and Groups | Political Figures | Policies and Issues with Broadly Based Effects | Policies and Issues with Narrowly Based Effects |
| Life | Personal Security | U.S. Constitution | Presidency | Political Candidates | Tax | Telecommunications |
| Happiness | Peace | Bill of Rights | Congress | Government Leaders | Social Security | Anti-trust |
| Liberty | Prosperity | Declaration of Independence | Supreme Court | Party Leaders | Health Care | Securities Regulation |
| Equality | Positive Liberties | | Democratic Party | Religious Leaders | Monetary | Sea Rights |
| | Negative Liberties | | Republican Party | Business Leaders | Environmental | International Trade |
| | Democracy | Majority Rule | Media | Education Leaders | | |
| | | Minority Rights | African-Americans | | | |
| | | Political Tolerance | Homosexuals | | | |
| | | | Labor Unions | | | |
| | | | Multi-nationals | | | |

nitive energy in thinking about these signs. Finally, even if parents do not understand the causes behind the developments that threaten their primal desires, most are likely to take some action.

The same cannot be said about other parental desires. In addition to the above-mentioned aspirations, parents may want their children to be cheerleaders, on the wrestling team, members of the French club, or to attend a particular college. These are clearly secondary concerns, perhaps important to parents only because they have a dim perception that these goals may contribute to their more fundamental desires. Moreover, rather than being deeply engrained in their psyche, these secondary desires may have their origins in transient social norms. If they moved to another neighborhood, these secondary desires might change substantially. Thus, because of differences in neighbors, a higher priority may be given to their child belonging to the computer club, being on the basketball team, or going to a trade school. In addition to being less stable, these secondary preferences are probably less consequential for parental behavior. If a daughter does not get the leading part in the school play, most parents would not call the principal. If their child dropped out of the French club, they may not even notice. The same is not true for most parents if their child was arrested or was diagnosed with a serious illness.

It is important to recognize distinctions among the political phenomena embodied in table 2–1 for the same reason it is important to recognize distinctions among objects of parental concern. These distinctions affect how individuals process political information. Moreover, information on different types of political phenomena has different behavioral consequences. Table 2–2 outlines some of the key differences across the categories depicted in table 2–1 in light of an information-processing perspective on political behavior. They are (1) the role these phenomena play in the political realm, (2) their relationship to an individual's life, (3) the stability of their cognitive representations, (4) the sources of new information flows relevant to them, (5) the amount of cognitive energy ordinary citizens are likely to expend in dealing with new information pertinent to them, and (6) the likelihood that relevant new information will have a behavioral impact.

When considered collectively these differences have important implications for a normatively appealing conceptualization of mass-elite linkages. Reflecting on these matters suggests that peripheral processing of political information does not dominate all political cognitions. The notion that more cognitive energy is expended on some political information is noteworthy. It suggests that discriminating judgments and thoughtful actions based on durable and deeply embedded political desires—and not subject to elite manipulation—are possible.

TABLE 2–2
Differences in Components of Political Belief Systems

| Component Characteristic | Core Political Desires | Regime Traits | Political Instruments |
|---|---|---|---|
| Role in political realm of life | The most fundamental desires, wants, and needs that fall within the purview of the political system | Help individuals make sense of processes that affect fundamental desires and contribute to the legitimacy of these processes | Provide the means by which the political system addresses issues that affect fundamenat political desires |
| Importantance to individual's life | They have great instrumental and symbolic importance | Some are likely to be of great symbolic importance; others will be of instrumental importance only to the extent that they impact on basic political values | Some are likely to be of great symbolic importance; others will be of instrumental importance only to the extent that they impact on basic political values |
| Stability of cognitive representations | Highly stable | Views and beliefs toward basic symbols and political institutions are highly stable; those toward groups and individuals are less stable | Attitudes toward some issues (longstanding, "easy" issues) are stable; most others are likely to be very unstable |
| Sources of new information | Some information can be directly received (i.e., experientially based) | Secondary information sources only (i.e., elite mediated) | Secondary information sources only (i.e., elite mediated) |
| Cognitive effort likely to be expended on new information | A relatively great amount; new information likely to be received; role of judgmental heuristics less dominant | Minimal; much information will not be received; role of judgmental heuristics expected to be dominant | Minimal; much information will not be received; role of judgmental heuristics expected to be dominant |
| Behavioral consequences of new information | New information evaluated as having great import for preferences likely to generate widespread and enduring behavioral consequences | New information evaluated as having great symbolic import may generate some behavioral consequences for some individuals | New information evaluated as having great symbolic import may generate some behavioral consequences for some individuals |

ROLE AND IMPORTANCE

Core political desires in a Western society such as the United States include such basic yearnings as life, liberty, happiness, democracy, and equality—as well as a larger set of derivative preferences (personal security, prosperity, a sense of control over one's destiny, equal treatment under the laws, etc.). These are important components of any political belief system; they relate to the most basic human desires that fall within the purview of a political system. While hierarchies of core political desires may vary across individuals and over time, as a whole they are far more important to the welfare of citizens than are other political referents. Consequently, the ability of a political system to satisfy these basic desires will have both real and symbolic effects on the lives of its citizens. The enduring prominence of themes such as prosperity, peace, liberty, equality, and the like in political rhetoric is a testament to the importance of these values to citizens.

The regime traits category in table 2–1 includes a diverse set of political phenomena: symbols, norms, institutions, groups, and leaders. These phenomena differ considerably in both their political role and their impact on the lives of citizens. Some of these traits (symbols, norms, and institutions) are the very embodiment of the process by which collective actions are taken to satisfy basic political desires. Citizens' cognitive representations of these phenomena define the broad contours of the political system as well as its operating rules. The role of other political objects (groups and leaders) is quite different. They are an integral part of the system of heuristics that aid citizens in making political judgments. Cues from these groups and leaders help ill-informed and inattentive citizens deal with processes that provide for their most basic political desires. Without these heuristics it would be very difficult for citizens to make sense of a wide array of political matters.

The final category in table 2–1, political instruments, includes a broad range of more mundane and transient objects: the issues and policies that constitute the "stuff" of day-to-day political debate, discussion, and maneuverings. These political instruments are the means by which political actors are able to formulate collective actions on behalf of the body politic. The importance of these political instruments for the lives of citizens varies enormously. Some (tax matters, social security) have direct, instrumental, and broadly experienced effects; others have symbolic and broadly experienced effects (abortion, the ERA). There are other issues that have indirect and instrumental, but widely experienced, effects (monetary policy). Still others have very narrow effects that are usually direct and instrumental (trade policy, telecommunications policy).

#### STABILITY OF COGNITIVE REPRESENTATIONS

The cognitive stability of the wide range of the phenomena included in table 2–1 varies considerably, both within and across categories. Cognitive representations of core political desires are the most stable because these values are the most deeply embedded in the human psyche. Some of these political desires and their derivatives (life, personal security, peace, prosperity, etc.) parallel those basic human concerns that anthropologists date to the Stone Age (Kuklinski and Quirk 2000). Those core political desires of more recent standing (liberty, democracy, equality, etc.) are derived from the views and pursuits of political and social elites of an earlier era. However, they have been embodied in, or can be derived from, fundamental political documents. These include the American Declaration of Independence and the Preamble to the United States Constitution. The centrality of these values is continually reinforced in political rhetoric. Consequently, these core political desires are stable cognitions that are deeply embedded in the psyche of citizens. They anchor the political preferences of ordinary citizens and provide the "starting point" for any analysis of electoral accountability.

The cognitive stability of regime traits varies considerably, largely because this category includes such a wide range of phenomena. Some of the symbols, norms, and institutions included in this category are enduring components of the American political system. As a result, most citizens have well-grounded, stable representations of them. But they are far from immutable. Views toward such basic institutions as the Supreme Court, Congress, and the presidency have fluctuated considerably just in the last half of the twentieth century. Moreover, support for norms such as political tolerance ebbs and flows with internal crises and external threats; it also varies across referent groups (terrorists, immigrants, atheists, etc.). Cognitive representations of groups and political leaders are even more unstable. All political leaders and many groups are transient parts of the political scene, and citizens are constantly developing and updating their evaluations of them.

Cognitive representations of political instruments are the least stable component of political belief systems. However, even within this category the stability of cognitive representations varies considerably. Views toward issues and policies that are long-standing and of widespread concern (social security) are likely to be fairly well embedded in the psyche of citizens, and more stable. Views on issues that are narrowly focused and/or highly technical are likely to be highly unstable and subject to manipulation.

### SOURCES OF NEW INFORMATION

Not all components of an individual's political belief system are "out of reach, out of sight, out of mind" in Walter Lippmann's oft-quoted phrase. Some information relevant to basic political desires is experientially based. The existence of an experiential base is crucial here. It makes ordinary citizens less dependent on elite mediation of political information. This is important because while the availability of an experiential base does not eliminate elite influence over mass cognitions, it does limit it. The existence of this experiential base is undoubtedly what led Lincoln to assert that while all of the people could be fooled some of the time, and some of the people could be fooled all of the time, all of the people could not be fooled all of the time. However, Lincoln's maxim is not equally applicable across political referents. It is most relevant to core political desires. Indeed, some of these core political desires are so important that it is impossible for at least some citizens *not* to receive directly at least some pertinent information.

Citizens *experience* reductions in take-home pay or its purchasing power, as well as unemployment. They also notice increased purchasing power, "wealth effects" from a mushrooming stock market, and the availability of high-paying jobs, not to mention local siblings who are sent to fight wars in foreign lands, as well as those who do not return. Citizens who drive from their unkempt, pothole-ridden neighborhoods through well-kept neighborhoods with well-maintained roads and attractive parks can *sense* inequitable treatment. A new senior citizens center, a branch library, or park renovations in their neighborhood will provide people with the sense that they are getting treated equitably. Citizens who have been victims of violent crimes or who know their neighbors have been victimized will *feel* that their personal security is jeopardized. Falling crime levels and a visibly more active nightlife (neighborhood strolls, street corner chats) will reassure them about their safety.

Ordinary citizens are apt to take note of important changes in regime traits, but they rarely *experience* them. Rather, they are dependent on mediated information. Some information on regime traits is more likely to be absorbed by them than other information. Information about fundamental symbols of American democracy (the Constitution, the flag, minority rights, etc.) is likely to be noticed. On the other hand, important institutional and processual changes frequently occur without the public noticing. For example, major changes took place in both the executive office of the president and the organization of Congress over the past quarter century. Most citizens took little note of these changes because they did not perceive them as consequential for their lives. Even if such changes impacted upon their lives, the vast majority of citizens would be unable to trace the linkages, for reasons noted by Kuklinski and Quirk (2000).

Much the same can be said for the ability of citizens to *experience* events and developments concerning political instruments. Most people care deeply about the *consequences* of policies for their core political desires. But there are many issues and policies swirling about the political arena at any given time. Their effect on matters citizens care about is indirect and diffuse. It would be virtually impossible for citizens to determine, a priori, the impact of these matters on their well-being, even if they chose to invest the cognitive energies it would require. As a result they are highly dependent on elite cues concerning likely impacts as well as elite interpretations of causal linkages.

### COGNITIVE EFFORT INVESTED IN EVALUATING NEW INFORMATION

Also important for a normatively appealing conception of mass-elite linkages is the amount of cognitive energy that citizens are willing to expend on political matters. Berent and Krosnick (1995: 92) note that not all attitudes are created equally. Some are more important than others, and these differences have important implications for information processing. While they deal only with policy-specific attitudes, their findings have direct implications for the structure of political beliefs outlined in table 2–1. Core political values are the most fundamental component of political belief systems. Thus, more cognitive energy is likely to be expended in processing of information relevant to them than on other political referents. Moreover, the information absorbed concerning political values is likely to the most accessible and organized the most effectively. The cognitive investment in regime traits and political instruments is likely to be much less and more diverse.

### BEHAVIORAL CONSEQUENCES OF EVALUATED INFORMATION

Berent and Krosnick's work also has implications for the last dimension in table 2–2: the behavioral consequences of evaluated information. They assert that behavioral consequences are most likely to flow from evaluated information pertaining to the most important attitude referents. This assertion provides additional support for the organization of political phenomena embodied in table 2–1. The centrality of core political desires stands out on this dimension as it does on the others, further underscoring their importance in understanding democratic governance. Throughout history it has been dissatisfaction with these core values that have led people to risk life itself in order to transform political orders. Threats to these values have led to wars of liberation, incited slave revolts and riots, given rise to freedom marches, hunger strikes, and the like. These core political desires may not be as fundamental as the most basic human drives. But within the political realm, they constitute the very definition of well-being.

This is less true for the other political phenomena incorporated in table 2–1. Matters that impact upon important political symbols and institutions may be noticed by, and provoke strong reactions on the part of, ordinary citizens. On the other hand, institutional change is frequently welcomed. However, even when it is not welcomed, it seldom precipitates spontaneous political action. Changes in political leadership, being an integral part of the political process, are of much less consequence. The likelihood that evaluated information concerning political instruments would generate behavioral consequences is even less. As noted earlier, citizens do not ordinarily invest large amounts of cognitive energy on most policy matters. Experience has taught them that most political leaders are simply speculating about their impact. As a result, most changes in most policies take place without citizens knowing or caring about them. Most citizens take a "wait and see" attitude, acting only if core political desires are threatened.

### Exogenous Events and Cognitive Reconfigurations
### of Political Phenomena

Much of the work in political psychology has been focused on the identifying the processes individuals use to handle information, defining the limits to their information-processing abilities, outlining the tools they have developed to deal with those limitations, and delineating how those tools are used. And understandably so. These are extremely complex phenomena whose interactions have profound behavioral implications that require a good deal of scholarly attention. However, in focusing on these matters most political scientists, Popkin (1991), Marcus and MacKuen (1993), and Jones (1994) being important exceptions, have neglected the impact of exogenous events on decision al processes. This is lamentable because the impact of these phenomena on information processing has important implications for democratic governance.

Exogenous events are "happenings" that are the manifestation of ongoing human intercourse and unfolding societal developments. A wide range of interactions and developments can generate politically salient exogenous events. The most important are fundamental societal transformations such as the emergence of a new religious order; the creation, formation and/or reconfiguration of a nation-state; the forging of a commercial, industrial, postindustrial or global economy, and so forth. Also relevant are less fundamental but profoundly unsettling developments. These include economic crises (the depressions of the 1830s, the 1870s, the 1890s; the stock market crash of 1929; the stagflation of the 1970s, etc.), civil unrest (the urban riots of the 1910s and 1960s), wars (the Civil War, World War One, World War Two, etc.); major population changes (frontier settlement, immigration, urbanization, suburbanization); and important social movements (abolitionism, temperance, populism, the labor movement, women's rights, the environmental movement, civil rights, the campaign for family values, etc.).

The interactions and developments noted above are rooted in primal forces such as scientific and technological innovations, ecological dictates and limits, extranational developments, fundamental psychological drives, and deeply embedded cultural values. Because these are such primal forces a change in one often affects others. Their interplay at a given point in time can initiate an isolated event or a chain of related events.

Sometimes the radiated effects of these events impact upon the core political desires of citizens. When this happens it will cause politically discerning citizens to refocus their attention and cognitive energies on political matters, generating periods of intense processing of political information. This episodic scrutiny can affect citizens' evaluations of political stewardship by leading citizens to reevaluate the past, rethink the present, and reassess their prospects for the future.

### EXOGENOUS EVENTS AND INFORMATION PROCESSING

The importance of exogenous events for political behavior is underscored in Jones's emphasis on attention shifts (1994). His Herculean effort to integrate economic, psychological, and biological perspectives on decision making is motivated by a desire to account for nonincremental policy shifts in American politics (Baumgartner and Jones 1993). Jones argues that these can be accounted for only by shifts in attention because shifts in political preferences are difficult to generate and, hence, more infrequent. His analysis is relevant here because exogenous events are an important source of attention shifts.

Exogenous events can put electoral pressure on political elites to engage in nonincremental policy shifts because they provide the stimulus for relatively intensive reflections on, and reevaluations of, political stewardship. Evidence for this proposition can be found in the groundbreaking work of Marcus and MacKuen (1993). They are concerned with the role of emotions in presidential voting, which they view as a catalyst for political learning. Their findings with respect to anxiety are of most relevance here. They argue that "emotion is a catalyst for political learning. . . . Generally inattentive to politics, citizens may require sharp notice before they become motivated to learn anything. . . . [Thus,] anxiety works co-operatively with learning to shift attention to political matters and to diminish reliance on habit in voting decisions" (673).

Anxiety is important to information processing because it provides citizens with the incentive to gather strategic information. Marcus and MacKuen go on to note that "[E]xperiments in cognitive psychology demonstrate that negative events increase attention and that emotional reactions are crucial to the stimulation of attention (Derryberry 1991; Pratto and John 1991). Thus, current work in psychology and neuropsychology supports a theoretical view about how people come to learn about politics: they abandon complacency and start to pay attention when the world signals that something is not right" (673). Thus, to the extent that exogenous events trigger feelings of anxiety on the part of voters, they can play an important role in enhancing the scrutiny of political stewardship.

What makes exogenous events particularly important to our understanding of popular efficacy is the primal nature of the forces that generate them. In a political realm dominated by powerful endogenous influences and the peripheral processing of political information, exogenous events can generate a cleansing revitalization of evaluative processes. It is extremely difficult for political stewards to control exogenous events or their radiated effects on citizen evaluations of their stewardship. Rather than being controlled, manipulated, and used by political elites to further their own interests, the emotions generated by these exogenous events are likely to disrupt citizens' political inertia. As Marcus and MacKuen note, this can generate political learning that can lead citizens to realize that their political heuristics require reevaluation and, perhaps, replacement. This, of course, creates problems for political elites desiring to influence citizens' perceptions of political matters. It makes it difficult for party elites to trade on enduring partisan attachments or to put a partisan "spin" on unfolding events.

### EXOGENOUS EVENTS AND THE POLITICS OF UPHEAVAL

The political significance of exogenous factors can be illustrated by contrasting the politics of normalcy with the politics of upheaval.[6] During periods of normalcy the electoral constituencies of the major parties are relatively well defined and stable. The core issues that divide them are fairly clear. Electoral strategies during these periods involve shoring up the party's electoral base, attracting swing voters, and mobilizing inactive voters. To implement their electoral strategies parties rely on venerable and revered leaders as well as enduring party themes, issues, and symbols. Another defining trait of the politics of normalcy is that the major parties exercise a good deal of control over the issue agendas of the day. Party agendas are determined by largely internal interactions; party leaders have a good sense of who they must please and what it will take to please them. Moreover, as the most pressing political issues tend to be distributional, parties can depend on battle-tested strategies to further their agendas and satisfy their constituents: pork barrel politics, logrolling, and symbolic political acts.

During periods of uncertainty and upheaval party elites face a very different situation. Their electoral strategies must be forged with the recognition that the erosive effects of exogenous events may have weakened the loyalties of groups that make up their electoral base. Traditional party issues, themes, and symbols may no longer resonate with their loyalists. Further constraining their electoral strategies is the possibility that the unsettling effects of exogenous events may have discredited longtime party leaders. Parties may also face additional electoral challenges in the

---

[6] Jones (1994) provides a nice analogue to this contrast within policy-making arenas when he discusses the shift from parallel processing to serial processing (1994: 164–204).

form of new leaders, movements, and parties. Moreover, party leaders have much less control over the political agenda. Exogenous events can force party elites to deal with issues that will potentially disrupt an already tenuous and weakened electoral coalition. Finally, pork barrel politics, logrolling, and symbolic political acts may no longer be sufficient to satisfy important electoral constituencies. The times may call for bold political initiatives. Party leaders may be incapable of conceiving such initiatives, or citizens may simply be skeptical of their commitment to them.

In sum, exogenous events can make citizens (1) refocus their attention on politics, (2) initiate intensive episodes of information processing, and (3) generate cognitive reconfigurations of political phenomena. When citizens are stimulated to reevaluate and redefine their political heuristics, politics shifts from a predictable, comfortable, normal state to a state of upheaval. The uncertainties inherent in states of upheaval can lead voters to deviate from their normal voting behavior, which could have profound implications for the core interests of incumbent and aspiring stewards. This makes the processes that generate these cognitive reconfigurations vital to our understanding of mass-elite linkages in democratic regimes.

## SUMMARY

This chapter argues for the utility of integrating an evaluative conception of democratic citizenship with insights derived from work in the cognitive sciences. This theoretical synthesis negates the rather dismal inferences that have been drawn from the seminal work on empirical democratic theory. Those inferences were drawn using a utilitarian conception of citizenship, and they reinforced the image of voters as "manageable fools." The distinctiveness of the synthesis offered here is the importance it places on core political desires and exogenous events whose radiated effects impinge on those desires. Core political desires are rooted in fundamental human yearnings; politically salient exogenous events are rooted in human intercourse and societal developments often orchestrated by primal forces. Because of their roots, neither core political desires nor exogenous events are susceptible to elite manipulation, at least in the short run. These assertions, when combined with episodes of relatively intense information processing generated by politically salient exogenous events, provide the theoretical basis for a normatively appealing conception of mass-elite linkages.

The conception of mass-elite linkages produced by the theoretical synthesis proposed in this chapter holds great theoretical promise. However, it simply addresses *why* exogenous events impinging upon core political desires have potentially important implications for our understanding of democratic processes. Chapter 3 addresses *how* salient exogenous events are transformed into evaluations of stewardship that can lead citizens to deviate from their normal voting behavior. A detailed examination of this transformational process is essential to understanding how exogenous events can affect electoral accountability and democratic responsiveness. A refined understanding of this process can yield insights into incentives that stewards have to engage in preemptive actions to protect and provide for core political desires, as well as the role that political elites can play in influencing stewardship evaluations. Thus, chapter 3 is a crucial part of this effort to understand the force of popular influences in democratic governance.

<h2 style="text-align:center">REFERENCES</h2>

Achen, C. H. 1975. "Mass Political Attitudes and the Survey Response." *American Political Science Review* 69: 1218–31.

Baumgartner, F. R., and B. D. Jones. 1993. *Agendas and Instability in American Politics*. Chicago, University of Chicago Press.

Berelson, B. R., P. F. Lazarsfeld, and W. N. McPhee. 1954. *Voting: A Study of Opinion Formation in a Presidential Campaign*. Chicago: University of Chicago Press.

Berent, M. K., and J. K. Krosnick. 1995. "The Relationship between Political Attitude Importance and Knowledge Structure." In *Political Judgment: Structure and Process*, edited by M. Lodge and K. M. McGraw. Ann Arbor, University of Michigan Press.

Converse, P. E. 1964. "The Nature of Belief Systems in Mass Publics." In *Ideology and Discontent*, edited by D. E. Apter. New York, Free Press.

Delli Carpini, M. X., and S. Keeter. 1989. *What Americans Know about Politics and Why It Matters*. New Haven, Yale University Press.

Held, D. 1987. *Models of Democracy*. Stanford, CA, Stanford University Press.

Jones, B. D. 1994. *Reconceiving Decision Making in Democratic Politics*. Chicago, University of Chicago Press.

Kuklinski, J. H., and P. J. Quirk. 1999. "Reconsidering the Rational Public: Cognition, Heuristics, and Mass Opinion." In *Elements of Reason: Cognition, Choice, and the Bounds of Rationality*, edited by A. Lupia, M. McCubbins, and S. Popkin. New York, Cambridge University Press.

Lupia, A., and M. D. McCubbins. 1998. *The Democratic Dilemma: Can Citizens Learn What They Need to Know?* Cambridge, Cambridge University Press.

Macpherson, C. B. 1977. *The Life and Times of Liberal Democracy*. Oxford, Oxford University Press.

Marcus, G. E., and M. B. MacKuen. 1993. "Anxiety, Enthusiasm, and the Vote: The Emotional Underpinnings of Learning and Involvement during Presidential Campaigns." *American Political Science Review* 87 (3): 672–85.

McGraw, K. M., and M. Lodge. 1995. Introduction. In *Political Judgment*, edited by K. M. McGraw and M. Lodge. Ann Arbor, University of Michigan Press.

Michels, R. [1915] 1962. *Political Parties: A Sociological Study of the Oligarchical Tendencies of Modern Democracy.* New York, Free Press.

Mosca, G. 1939. *The Ruling Class.* New York, McGraw-Hill.

Niemi, R. G., and H. Weisberg, eds. 1993a. *Classics in Voting Behavior.* Washington, DC, Congressional Quarterly Press.

Ostrogorski, M. (1902). *Democracy and the Organization of Political Parties.* New York Haskell House Publishers.

Popkin, S. L. (1991). *The Reasoning Voter.* Chicago, University of Chicago Press.

Schlesinger, A. M. (1946). *The Age of Jackson.* Boston, Little, Brown.

Schmitter, P. (1991). "What Democracy Is . . . and Is Not." *Journal of Democracy* 2 (3): 75–88.

Schumpeter, J. A. (1942). *Capitalism, Socialism, and Democracy.* New York, Harper and Row.

Smith, E.R.A.N. (1989). *The Unchanging American Voter.* Berkeley and Los Angeles, University of California Press.

Sniderman, P. M., R. A. Brody, et al. (1991). *Reasoning and Choice: Explorations in Political Psychology.* Cambridge, Cambridge University Press.

Tversky, A., and D. Kahneman. 1974. "Judgment under Uncertainty: Heuristics and Biases." *Science* 185: 1124–31.

Wallas, G. (1909). *Human Nature in Politics.* London, Archibald Constable.

Zaller, J. R. 1992. *The Nature and Origins of Mass Opinion.* New York: Cambridge University Press.

# CHAPTER THREE

# Exogenous Events, Evaluations of Stewardship, and Citizens' Normal Voting Behavior

Gentlemen, the select classes of mankind are no longer the governors of mankind. The fortunes of mankind are now in the hands of the plain people of the whole world. Satisfy them, and you have not only justified their confidence, but established peace. Fail to satisfy them, and no arrangement that you can make will either set up or steady the peace of the world.
—WOODROW WILSON, in a speech given to the League of Nations, January 25, 1919

To an extent that few like but none can avoid, citizens in large societies are dependent on unseen and usually unknown others for most of their information about the larger world in which they live. . . . The "others" on whom we depend, directly or indirectly, for information about the world are, for the most part, persons who devote themselves full time to some aspect of politics or public affairs—which is to say, political elites.
—JOHN ZALLER, *The Nature and Origins of Mass Opinion*

THE CONTRASTING implications of the two perspectives articulated in the epigraphs to this chapter nicely frame the debate over representative democracy as a distinctively responsive form of government. While Wilson stresses the importance of "the select classes" satisfying "the plain people," Zaller emphasizes the centrality of political elites as information sources. To the extent that political elites (1) control and filter the information that is vital to evaluations of stewardship and (2) serve as opinion leaders who provide signals to responsive masses, the principal-agent relationship embodied in democratic theory is compromised.

The approach to mass-elite linkages offered here offers new insights into the responsiveness of democratic governance. This conceptualization draws inferences about mass-elite linkages from a set of political dynamics that focuses on exogenous events whose radiated effects impinge upon citizens' core political desires. These events can foster episodes of intensive information processing, causing reevaluations of political stewardship that could lead voters to depart from their normal voting routines. The aggregated effect, over time, of these departures generates macro-level electoral changes that vary in their *magnitude, duration,* and *geographic scope.* These departures are the principal means by which citizens express their evaluation of political stewardship. The aggregate effects of these departures are of paramount importance to political elites because these departures impinge upon elites' core political interests.

This chapter provides a model of the process by which exogenous events are transformed into vote choices. As aggregations of these vote choices produce the voting patterns that are the key focuses of the empirical chapters, this transformational model provides the individual-level foundations for these macro-level analyses. The next section introduces the model and a metaphor that is useful in illustrating it. The following three sections present propositions drawn from the model that specify how macro-level electoral changes are generated by the model's dynamics. Examples from the metaphor are used to illustrate key propositions.

## EXOGENOUS EVENTS AND VOTE CHOICE: A MODEL

Vote choices do not simply mirror exogenous events. Rather, exogenous events are transformed into evaluations of stewardship, and then vote choices, by the complex workings of several sets of factors that unfold over time. The cognized effects of exogenous events are not the only influences upon either stewardship evaluations or vote choices. However, under the proper conditions, they can be important in generating departures from normal voting behavior. The model of the transformational process presented below provides important insights into *how* these events can affect vote choice. I begin by introducing the model's axioms; then I outline its components. Finally, I introduce the Walled City metaphor.

### The Model's Axioms

The transformational model presented below is premised on assumptions involving the two principal human actors involved in the evaluations that influence vote choice: citizens and stewards. The conception of stewards used here is an institutional one; it includes stewards, members of their parties, and their administrations. Also, for ease of presentation, the term *steward* will include both incumbent stewards and aspiring stewards, unless otherwise specified. The basic assumptions underlying the model are:

- *Citizens are purposeful actors whose primary political motivation is the realization of a small set of core political desires (life, liberty, happiness, etc.).* (A1)
- *Stewards are strategic actors whose primary political motivation is the desire for electoral success.* (A2)

Positing that citizens are purposeful actors implies that while they are not fully rational actors, they structure their political behavior in ways that enhance the realization of their basic desires. The centrality of core political desires to political behavior does not mean that all citizens have identical hierarchies of core desires. Different citizens have different hierarchies, and a citizen's hierarchy of political desires can change over time. That having been said, at any given time, the realization of these core political desires is posited to be far more important to their political thoughts and actions than other considerations (ideological factors, policy preferences, group solidarity, etc).

Positing that stewards are strategic actors implies that their political actions are more considered than those of ordinary citizens. The priority stewards are posited to attach to electoral success does not mean that they do not also have policy goals, career ambitions, and ideological objectives that influence their behavior, or that different stewards do not prioritize these matters differently. It simply means that electoral success is usually essential to the achievement of these other goals. Thus, they will deploy whatever resources they control (individual, public, partisan) to maximize their chances for electoral success.

A handful of corollaries follow from these basic premises. Because citizens are purposeful actors whose political behavior is driven by their core political desires:

- *Citizens' existing political predispositions, including their normal voting behavior, are grounded in satisficing judgments that these predispositions are serving their core political desires.* (C1)
- *Citizens will depart from their existing political predispositions only if they conclude it will enhance their realization of core political desires.* (C2)
  - *Citizens will sustain departures from their existing political predispositions only if they conclude that adopting these changes will enhance their realization of core political desires.*

Because stewards are strategic actors whose political behavior is influenced heavily by their desire for electoral success, it follows that:

- *Stewards will structure their governmental actions, policies, and programs so as to maximize their electoral success.* (C3)
  - *Stewards' past priorities and effectiveness in providing various types of action, policies, and programs will provide them with policy reputations.* (C3.1)

- Stewards' policy reputations will provide them with loyal electoral bases. (C3.2)
- *Stewards' electoral bases will constrain their future actions, policies, and programs.* (C3.3)
- *Stewards will engage in preemptive actions, policies, and programs to protect and preserve citizens' core political desires if they believe preemptive measures are necessary to assure their electoral success.* (C3.4)
- *Stewards will deploy their partisan resources so as to maximize their electoral success.* (C3.4)
- *Stewards will deploy their individual resources so as to maximize their electoral success.* (C5)

## THE MODEL'S COMPONENTS

It follows from assumption A1 that an exogenous event's electoral relevance (i.e., its bearing on stewardship evaluations) is determined by two *necessary conditions*. The first derives from the centrality of core political desires to their political behavior. If an event's radiated effects do not impinge on core political desires, it is unlikely to (1) generate the emotional energy required to reassess a citizen's stewardship evaluations, (2) be viewed as relevant to stewardship evaluations, or (3) have the cognitive force required to generate a departure from normal voting behavior. Thus

- *An exogenous event's radiated effects must impinge upon a citizen's core political desires in order for it to affect vote choice.* (D1)

The second necessary condition derives from the fact that exogenous events are *happenings*. As happenings, they have a temporal component to them: they occur at a particular point in time. This is important because of assumption A1, as well as corollaries C1 and C2. It is posited that a citizen's normal voting behavior is grounded in satisficing judgments about the relative capacity of competing stewards to provide for their welfare. Thus, citizens will not depart from their "standing decision" without concluding that doing so will enhance their realization of core political desires. In order to determine an event's electoral relevance citizens must be able *to obtain and process information*. Doing so frequently takes time.

The amount of time required to gather and process relevant information will vary across events. In some cases, information on the electoral implications of an exogenous event is plentiful, straightforward, and immediately available. Thus, timing is irrelevant. Indeed, for this category of events, the closer to the election, the greater the event's electoral relevance. But other exogenous events are convoluted affairs that require time to collect and process relevant information, a task often complicated by

Does the Event Impinge on the Voter's Core Political Desires?

|  |  | No | Yes |
|---|---|---|---|
| Does the Citizen Have Sufficient Time to Process Information on the Event Before the Election? | No | Q1 (Irrelevant events) | Q2 (Ambiguous events) |
|  | Yes | Q3 (Inconsequential events) | Q4 (Critical events) |

Figure 3–1. Exogenous Events and Vote Choice: Necessary Conditions for Electoral Relevance

partisan efforts to confuse, mislead, or distract voters. The proximity of these events to Election Day can preclude the consideration of its electoral implications. If citizens do not have the ability to process relevant information, an exogenous event is likely to be little more than noise that is filtered out of stewardship evaluations. Thus, it follows that

- *Voters must be able to gather and process information on the political implications of an exogenous event before it will affect their vote choice.* (D2)

These two conditions can be used to construct a fourfold categorization of exogenous events that is depicted in figure 3–1. Within this categorization events are politically irrelevant (Q1), politically inconsequential (Q2), politically ambiguous (Q3), or politically critical (Q4). Only critical events will affect vote choice. But not all politically critical events will be electorally relevant. The conditions depicted in figure 3–1 are necessary but not sufficient conditions for electoral relevance. The electoral impact of seemingly identical critical events will differ because the process by which a critical event is transformed into electorally relevant considerations is influenced by factors quite independent of the event itself.

A model of the factors that affect this transformational process is depicted in figure 3–2. These factors include (1) the event's catalysis (catalyst, catalytic agent, reaction time), (2) key characteristics of the event (impact, timing, location), (3) voter attributes (proximity to the event's radiated effects, hierarchy of political desires, proximity to voters with similar profiles, political discernment, intensity of partisan attachments), (4) socio-political context (composition, density, and spatial distribution of accumulated societal residue), (5) subsequent events (impact, timing, location), and (6) the actions and resources of competing political stewards (levels of available resources, strategies used to deploy resources, effectiveness in implementing resources).

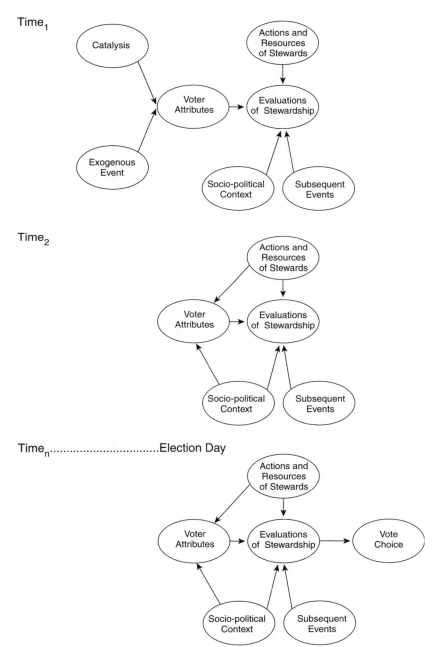

Figure 3–2. Exogenous Events and Vote Choice

The dependent variable in the model depicted in figure 3–2 is vote choice. Vote choice is defined in terms of a departure from a voter's normal voting behavior: it is either consistent with a citizen's normal voting routine (vote for party A's candidate, vote for party B's candidate, do not vote), or it is not. Thus, the electoral implications of a critical event will vary with a voter's existing predisposition; it will reinforce normal voting behavior for some and generate a departure for others. Therefore, in the sections that explicate the model, propositions will be specified in terms of *electoral relevance* rather than in terms of impact on either the incumbent or aspiring steward.

At the core of the model depicted in figure 3–2 is a citizen's evaluation of political stewardship. These evaluations can unfold over time—up to the point at which a vote choice must be made. As is evident in figure 3–2, factors that both *precede* and *follow* a critical event can affect its electoral relevance. For example, the circumstances that precipitated the critical event, its *catalysis*, are a key component of this model. A critical event's catalysis can affect whether a citizen holds the steward accountable for the event's impact on her realization of core political desires. The event's catalyst and catalytic agent can also affect voters' perceptions of the threat it poses.

Key characteristics of the *exogenous event* also affect its electoral relevance. While critical events impinge upon core political desires by definition, their impact can vary considerably. Likewise with an event's timing. Critical events vary considerably in their proximity to Election Day, and these temporal variations play an important mediating role in the model depicted in figure 3–2. That is, proximity to Election Day can affect the role other factors play in stewardship evaluations and vote choice. Finally, because exogenous events are *happenings*, they often have a spatial dimension to them. *Where* some critical events happen can affect the impact of their radiated effects on core political desires. Thus, depending upon when and where they occur, identical critical events can generate markedly different effects on vote choice.

*Voter attributes* also affect the transformation of critical events into vote choices. A voter's proximity to an event's radiated effects can affect how the event impinges on that voter's realization of core political desires. A voter's proximity to other voters with similar socio-political profiles is important because it can generate electorally relevant contextual effects. Differences in hierarchies of core political desires can also affect an event's impact on vote choice. Finally, differences in political discernment and the intensity of partisan attachments will affect how voters integrate the "felt effects" of critical events into their electoral evaluations. Political discernment refers to the capacity of citizens to recognize the link between critical events and political stewardship; it speaks to their ability to act as discriminating consumers of public goods. The intensity of partisan affiliations affects a voter's ability to manifest the implications of critical events in their vote choice; it speaks to a citizen's capacity for electoral independence.

Also important in the transformation of critical events into vote choices is the *socio-political context* upon which they unfold. Because exogenous events are happenings, it is useful to think of socio-political contexts as landscapes littered with piles of accumulated societal residue. Piles of societal residue accumulate as a result of the interaction among (1) ongoing human intercourse and unfolding societal developments, (2) a locale's unique historical setting, and (3) its civic norms, leadership, and associations (i.e., its stock of social capital). The interaction among these factors leads to piles of residue that vary in their composition, density, and spatial distribution.

Some of these accumulations of residue are composed of *combustible debris* (raw racial, ethnic, or religious tensions; deeply rooted, class-based animosities; festering political grievances; high levels of distrust, anxiety, or apathy); others are more akin to fertile *compost piles* (inclusive and broadly based civic associations; high levels of trust, mutual concern, and community mindedness; strong traditions of civic involvement and leadership). Still others are little more than heaps of spent materials, historical artifacts made harmless by the vicissitudes of time or the foresight/neglect of societal actors. At any given place and time, the mix of the piles will vary, along with their density and spatial distribution.

A society's socio-political context is extremely important to the transformational process depicted in figure 3–2: how a critical event affects electoral decisions can depend on interactions between the event and accumulations of societal residue. Under the proper conditions, an event's radiated effects can transform a critical event into a catalysis that ignites secondary reactions with electoral ramifications. The denser the distribution of piles, the more likely a critical event's radiated effects will be transformed into a catalysis that ignites secondary reactions. When the location and density of piles of debris vary geographically, so will the electoral effects generated by secondary reactions.

*Subsequent events* are also important to the transformational process depicted in figure 3–2. The impact, timing, and location of events that occur subsequent to a critical event can mediate the critical event's electoral impact. Some subsequent events can override a critical event's electoral impact; others can reinforce it. Also, crucial interactions can occur between subsequent events and efforts by stewards to influence a critical event's electoral impact.

The *actions and resources* of competing *political stewards* are also a central part of the process by which critical events are transformed into vote choices. Even though political stewards may be responsible for some aspects of an exogenous event's catalysis, these events are, by definition, beyond the control of political stewards. However, the fact that critical events can impinge upon their core political interests means that political stewards will use whatever resources they have to shape stewardship evaluations and vote choices in ways that will enhance their chances for electoral success.

Two categories of resources are important here: stewardship resources and partisan resources. Stewardship resources include both individual traits (wisdom, integrity, vision, credibility, policy innovativeness, administrative effectiveness, communication and bargaining skills, entrepreneurship, etc.) and the tools of public policy (tax revenues, social welfare policies, administrative actions, agenda control, etc.). Partisan resources include both the personal skills and styles of office seekers and holders (hortatory oratorical skills, political instincts, campaign skills, etc.) and party resources (patronage jobs, public contracts, campaign contributions, sizes and commitment of electoral base, precinct workers, media and public relations staff, pollsters, etc.). Stewards will deploy these resources using one of two general strategies: stewardship strategies and partisan strategies.

### The Walled City Metaphor

To assist in illuminating the dynamics of the model depicted in figure 3–2, I use a Walled City metaphor. The Walled City is a vibrant entity that has a diverse array of institutional structures that provide for the economic, social, and political needs of the city's inhabitants. While the Walled City's inhabitants share a small set of core political desires, their diversity leads certain citizens to value some more than others. As a result, while all of the city's structures are held in relatively high esteem, esteem varies across citizens. The vibrancy of the Walled City generates, over the normal course of development, accumulations of societal residue. These accumulated piles of residue are distributed throughout the city. But their composition and density vary across neighborhoods, which differ in their civic norms and stock of social capital.

To provide for its general well-being, the Walled City's populace selects stewards in regularly scheduled elections. There is one general steward and one responsible for each of the city's four sectors: the southeast, the northeast, the southwest, and the northwest. Being selected as one of the city's stewards brings many rewards to the victorious candidate and his/her supporters. Thus, two political organizations have emerged that routinely put forward nominees to compete in the Walled City's elections and work for their candidates' election. The city's vibrancy attracts a continual influx of immigrants who are wholly unsocialized into the city's political norms. Because of the city's generous voting laws, these immigrants, in conjunction with the city's youth, join to make the eligible electorate a fluid entity. This fluidity provides ongoing challenges for the political parties, which vary in their priorities, vision, and stewardship capacities.

The equanimity of the Walled City is affected, from time to time, by a variety of incendiary events. Examples of these incendiary events can illustrate the classification presented in figure 3–1. A match dropped by a child on a desolate street in the Walled City is an incendiary event. However, if the match simply falls to the ground and extinguishes, it is a *politically inconsequential event* (Q3); it would be a *politically irrelevant event* (Q1) if the match were dropped while citizens were voting. In either case, the event would be electorally irrelevant. In contrast, a major fire that destroys an entire neighborhood is an incendiary event with potentially relevant electoral effects. If the fire began at noon on Election Day it would be a *politically ambiguous event* (Q2) with little electoral relevance. If the fire occurred a month before Election Day it would be a *politically critical event* (Q4); its electoral relevance will be determined by the operation and interaction of the sets of factors outlined in figure 3–2.

## Critical Events and the Magnitude of Electoral Change

The magnitude of electoral change refers to *the proportion of the electorate deviating from normal voting behavior in a given election*; it is the most fundamental component of electoral change. The impact of a critical event on the magnitude of electoral change speaks directly to the event's effect on the core interests of political elites. Moreover, if a critical event impacts only a negligible proportion of the electorate, its geographic scope and duration are of little consequence. The proportion of the electorate whose vote choice is affected by critical events will depend upon each of the factors outlined in figure 3–2; the following sections explicate the role of each.

### Catalysis

A critical event's catalysis is electorally relevant because it speaks to an incumbent's responsibility for the event's radiated effects. Corollaries C1 and C2 assert that citizens' political predispositions are grounded in satisficing judgments about their utility; they will modify them only if they believe doing so will enhance their realization of core political desires. It follows from these corollaries that various aspects of a critical event's catalysis will affect its impact on vote choice. Consider first the event's *catalytic agent*. It is posited that:

- *The clearer the incumbent's responsibility for the catalytic agent, the greater a critical event's electoral relevance.*                    (P1)

The neighborhood fire introduced earlier to introduce the categorization depicted in figure 3–1 can be used to illustrate this proposition. If a bolt of lightning started the fire, it is not likely to have direct electoral repercussions. If a worn transmitter in a public utility operated by city employees started the neighborhood fire, however, then the steward's responsibility would be clear.

In situations where the incumbent steward had responsibility for the catalytic agent, assumption A1 and corollary C2, considered jointly, lead to several propositions about the effect of a critical event's *catalyst* and *reaction time* on its electoral relevance. With respect to the catalyst it is posited that

- *The greater the implications of the catalyst for a citizen's realization of core political desires, the greater a critical event's electoral relevance.*   (P2)

If the fire in the public utility were due to a technologically flawed transmitter that was used throughout the city, it would be of profound electoral significance to everyone living near a transmitter. If the fire were attributable to a drunken city employee who violated safety standards, the electoral effects would not be as widespread.

The reaction time of a critical event's catalysis affects its electoral relevance because it can lead to important inferences that affect evaluations of stewardship. The implications of reaction time for these evaluations will vary, however, depending upon whether the event's radiated effects had beneficial or undesirable effects. Where these effects are beneficial it is posited that:

- *The shorter the reaction time, the greater a critical event's electoral relevance.*                    (P3)

Where those consequences are undesirable it is posited that:

- *The longer the reaction time, the greater a critical event's electoral relevance.*                    (P4)

Consider flames emanating from the opening of a foundry made possible by the steward's creation of an industrial park in anticipation of innovative technological advances. The foundry's opening is a critical event with beneficial consequences because it provides hundreds of new jobs. The steward's farsightedness could produce electoral dividends. But long delays in bringing the plant on-line will reduce those electoral dividends as memories fade and his role in planning for the park becomes clouded and diffuse. Reaction time will have the opposite effect in situations where the critical event had undesirable effects. Consider a neighborhood fire caused by a worn transmitter that was a result of the city's long-term, and well publicized, neglect. Because the city knew about the problem and had time to address it, the incident generates more damning implications for stewardship evaluations than if the reaction time of the fire's catalysis was instantaneous.

## Event Characteristics

A critical event's impact on a citizen's vote choice will be affected by its (1) impact on core political desires, (2) timing, and (3) location. The magnitude of a critical events' impact on core political desires has an independent effect on vote choice, while the timing and location of these events have largely joint effects. These joint effects will be discussed in later sections. With respect to a critical event's impact on citizens' welfare, it follows from assumption A1 that

- *The greater a critical event's radiated effects on the realization of core political desires, the greater its electoral relevance.*                    (P5)

Consider the fire from the worn transmitter. If it affected only 10 percent of the city's inhabitants, the magnitude of its electoral impact would be less than if it affected 90 percent of the inhabitants. If the power outages lasted a day, the magnitude of the fire's electoral impact will be less than if it lasted a month.

## Voter Attributes

It follows from assumption A1 and the earlier discussion of voter attributes that these attributes will play an important role in the transformation of critical events into vote choices. Particularly important here are a citizen's (1) hierarchy of core political desires, (2) proximity to a critical event's radiated effects, (3) level of political discernment, and (4) intensity of partisan attachments.

Because hierarchies of core political desires vary across individuals, a given critical event can generate *varied reactions* from voters with *different hierarchies*. Thus,

- *The more a critical event's radiated effects impinge upon core political desires valued highly by a citizen, the greater its electoral relevance to that voter.*                                                      (P6)

Consider differences in the electoral implications of the new foundry for two citizens. Both are concerned with economic prosperity and good health. But one is a tenured professor in the Walled City's most prestigious university; the other is a blue-collar worker who was unemployed until he got a job in the foundry. The foundry's opening led the tenured professor to evaluate the incumbent's stewardship negatively because of her concern for the foundry's effect on pollution. While the blue-collar worker is also concerned with pollution, the foundry's opening generated positive evaluations of the incumbent's stewardship by the blue-collar worker. In that particular election, the blue-collar worker's electoral calculus gave more weight to the economic benefits of the foundry than to its environmental costs.

Because critical events are happenings, they often have a spatial dimension to them. Consequently, their radiated effects on core political desires can vary spatially. Sometimes there is an inverse spatial relationship; other times there is a positive one. Citizens' life activities also have a spatial dimension to them; they work, live, and play in different places. When an exogenous event's radiated effects vary spatially, it follows from assumption A1 that their electoral relevance will be affected by the proximity of voters to those radiated effects. This means that a critical event could have *different electoral effects* on voters with *identical hierarchies of core desires*. Thus,

- *When an exogenous event's radiated effects vary spatially, its electoral relevance will vary with the proximity of voters to those radiated effects.*   (P7)

Consider again the foundry's opening. It could generate different electoral reactions from two blue-collar workers who benefited economically from the foundry but lived in different neighborhoods. A worker whose neighborhood was directly affected by the foundry's stench and smoke is not likely to be as pleased with the incumbent's stewardship as one who was miles away from the steward's industrial park.

It follows from assumption A1 and corollary C2 that the level of a voter's political discernment and the intensity of their a priori commitment to a political party will also affect the electoral relevance of critical events. Voters who are politically more discerning are more likely to incorporate the implications of critical events into their stewardship evaluations than are less discerning voters. A critical event's radiated effects are less likely to affect a highly committed partisan's stewardship evaluations than the evaluations of one who lacks strong attachments. Even if committed partisans are dissatisfied with their steward's performance, they are likely to conclude that competing stewards would not have done any better. And, from their perspective, may not have done as well. Thus,

- *The greater the political discernment of the voter, the more likely that links between critical events and political stewardship will be made.* (P8)
- *The stronger the a priori commitment of a voter to a political party, the less likely that a critical event will affect their evaluations of political stewardship.* (P9)

The role of discernment and partisanship can be illustrated with respect to the fire caused by the worn transmitter. Politically discerning voters are more likely to see the link between stewardship and the maintenance of the transmitter than others. Also, less discerning voters are more likely to accept "explanations" that absolve the incumbent from responsibility for the fire, particularly if the incumbent is a skillful politician and speaker. Hard-core partisans of the incumbent's party will be even more willing to accept these self-absolutions, while committed partisans of the out-party are likely to dismiss the assertions and explanations of the incumbent.

The partisan affiliations of new entrants to the Walled City's electorate (first-time, youthful voters, and immigrants) are likely to be influenced by the preferences of those with whom they interact most frequently on political matters (family, friends, coworkers, etc.). The partisan attachments of new entrants are not likely to be strong initially. Thus, these attachments are susceptible to being molded by the interactions among critical events, stewardship, and the new entrants' realization of core political desires early in their political life. This is especially true for the more politically discerning new entrants.

It also follows from assumption A1 and the discussion of voter attributes that these attributes will interact with event catalyses to affect vote choice. Thus,

- *The greater the implications of the catalytic agent for a voter's realization of core political desires, the greater its electoral relevance.* (P10)
- *The greater the implications of an event's catalyst for a voter's realization of core political desires, the greater its electoral relevance.* (P11)

The importance of the voter/catalytic agent interaction can be illustrated by considering a fire set by a member of an alienated ethnic minority. To members of the majority population, the fact that the fire was set by a political dissident may take on added significance in terms of their personal safety, making them support get-tough tactics. The fire may be far less alarming to members of the minority sect, and get-tough tactics may be viewed as politically oppressive. The importance of the voter/catalyst interaction can be illustrated using the example of the opening of the new foundry. The foundry's opening may mean higher wages for the new employees and substantial returns for the foundry's operators and stockholder, thus generating electoral dividends for the incumbent. But the potential implications of this new technology are ominous for workers in the older foundry who have lost their jobs or who fear losing their jobs.

## Socio-Political Context

It follows from assumption A1 and corollary C2, as well as the discussions surrounding figure 3–2, that the socio-political context within which a critical event unfolds can affect vote choice. If the radiated effects of critical events reach accumulated piles of societal residue, they can act as catalyses that can ignite kinetic reactions. These secondary reactions can enhance the electoral relevance of the event. Indeed, contact with a pile of residue can turn a politically inconsequential event (Q3) into a politically critical event. The density of accumulated piles of residue is particularly important in affecting the magnitude of an event's electoral effect. Thus,

- *The existence of densely distributed accumulations of societal residue in-*
  *creases the likelihood that an inconsequential or critical event will affect*
  *a voter's evaluation of the incumbent's stewardship.*                    (P12)

To illustrate the detrimental effect of densely distributed piles of debris consider a modified version of the lighted match incident, which earlier was categorized as an inconsequential event. Rather than falling harmlessly, in this example it ignites a trail of fuel oil leaking from a highly combustible pile of debris. The pile's combustibility leads to a fire that rages out of control, igniting others piles of combustible debris densely distributed throughout the neighborhood and affecting stewardship evaluations.

A modified version of the foundry example will be useful in illustrating the beneficial effects of compost piles. Consider an entrepreneur who invited bids to develop the manufacturing capacity of a new incinerator. The Walled City was able to outbid its competitors because its association of civic, business, and labor leaders had laid the foundations for an industrial park and the steward acted on their vision. The park was very attractive to the discerning entrepreneur. Thus, the Walled City attracted the foundry, which created prosperity and enhanced the well-being of its residents.

## Subsequent Events

Events that are temporally subsequent to a critical event can have both independent and joint effects on its electoral relevance. The most important joint effects have to do with the impact subsequent events have on the effectiveness of stewards' strategies for controlling the electoral impact of critical events; they will be addressed in the next section. The independent effects of subsequent events are such that they can either *override* a critical event's electoral impact or *reinforce* it. Subsequent events can change the political agenda dramatically, overriding the electoral impact of a critical event. But they can also reinforce inferences concerning stewardship precipitated by an earlier critical event, thereby enhancing their electoral impact. Thus, it is posited that

- *Subsequent events will affect a critical event's electoral relevance.*   (P13)

To illustrate this proposition, consider a major arson committed during the first week of a steward's term. If it was an isolated event, it may well be forgotten by Election Day. If, however, a series of arsons occurred intermittently before Election Day, the impact of the initial arson could still play a role in the electoral calculus of many voters. This is particularly true if other events make the steward susceptible to the notion that she is "soft" on public safety issues. Consider also the new foundry for which the incumbent claimed credit. Subsequent leaks of poisonous pollutants into the Walled City's main water supply could eliminate whatever popularity boost the incumbent received from the opening. So would an influx of undesirable immigrants moving into the city to take advantage of employment opportunities. Each of these effects is also likely to interact with salient voter attributes in affecting stewardship evaluations and vote choice.

### The Actions and Resources of Competing Stewards

Exogenous events are, by definition, beyond the control of political stewards. However, because critical events can affect their prospects for electoral success, it follows from assumption A2 and corollaries C3 through C4 that stewards will try to mediate their electoral impact. To do this, stewards will use both performance-based strategies and partisan-based strategies, which are not mutually exclusive. Performance strategies are rooted in ideals epitomized by Progressive conceptions of politics; they deploy both political leadership and tools of public policy to protect and enhance citizens' realization of their core political desires. Partisan strategies are rooted in Machiavellian conceptions of politics; they deploy mostly political resources to obfuscate accountability and dull the evaluative capacities of citizens by distracting and misleading them, evoking partisan loyalties, using demagoguery and scare tactics, and so forth.

Enterprising stewards will devise performance strategies to capitalize on the opportunities that critical events generate, as well as ameliorate their undesirable effects. Wise stewards will use performance strategies to anticipate and plan for the unforeseeable effects of critical events by maintaining effective public safety agencies and viable social safety nets.

Because the adverse effects of some critical events are unavoidable, visionary and articulate stewards will use their leadership skills to help citizens understand the events. In addition to providing them with succinct explanations of exogenously induced societal changes, they can convey an understanding of how to address and/or capitalize upon them. Finally, stewards who successfully used performance strategies to deal with earlier problems can create a stock of credibility and trust that can be used to survive the deleterious effects of critical events. The skillful use of leadership, credibility, and trust are sources of stability for democratic governments.

Political stewards will also use partisan strategies to enhance their prospects for electoral success. These strategies can involve hindering, or at least delaying, the release of politically sensitive information. Partisan strategies also include the release of misleading information, denying responsibility for pivotal acts, and using their control of agendas and/or events to distract the electorate's attention. When stewards fail in escaping responsibility, they will attempt to prevent citizens from translating negative evaluations into vote choices by evoking political symbols. Finally, stewards will mobilize their loyalists to dilute the impact of negative electoral reactions by others.

The level of resources available to stewards will vary across stewards, as well as over time and space; so will their skill in devising and implementing strategies to deploy the resources they control. Stewards' efforts to mediate the electoral effects of critical events will be affected by other factors depicted in figure 3–2. Despite the potentially confounding effects of these uncontrollable factors, the importance of critical events to stewards' core interests insures that they will deploy whatever resources they control in mediating an event's electoral impact. Thus, it follows from corollary C3 that

- *Political stewards will use both performance and partisan strategies to influence a critical event's electoral relevance in ways that will enhance their chances for electoral success.*                                    (P14)
  - *The greater the relative level of resources, the greater the steward's ability to influence a critical event's electoral relevance.*          (P14.1)
  - *The more skillful the deployment of available resources, the greater the steward's ability to influence a critical event's electoral relevance.*   (P14.2)

To illustrate these propositions, consider a series of arsons in each of the Walled City's four sectors, which are governed by sector stewards with fundamentally different conceptions of politics. All four incumbents enjoy roughly equal levels of resources, but they are not endowed with identical resources. Moreover, they deploy their resources differently. In the southeast and northwest sectors the stewards are committed to Progressive conceptions of politics and performance strategies of dealing with critical events. In the northeast and southwest sectors the stewards are committed to Machiavellian conceptions of politics and partisan strategies of dealing with problems.

In responding to the arsons, all four stewards activate additional police patrols and put the fire department on high-alert status. However, in the northeast and southwest sectors, the police and firefighters are patronage employees who hold second jobs and frequently do not show up for work. Moreover, the fire equipment that is available to the firefighters was provided by political cronies and is substandard. In the southeast and northwest sectors the public employees are trained professionals outfitted with state-of- the-art equipment. Because the fires in all four sectors were unsettling but fairly limited, their effects in the southeast and northwest sectors were fairly well contained. Consequently, the arsons were only a minor issue in the next election. Because of performance deficiencies the fires in the northeast and southwest sectors did far more damage to homes and businesses, and the arsons were a hot campaign issue.

In the southeast and northwest sectors the incumbent stewards campaigned vigorously on their successful efforts to curb the impact of the fires, contrasting the impact of the fires in the northeast and southwest sectors. The incumbent steward in the northeast sector united his supporters by blaming the arsons on a culprit from the southeast sector who was preying on locals; the southwest sectors incumbent blamed the arsons on a member of a despised minority group. Both Machiavellian incumbents made a dramatic, but questionable, arrest the week before the election.

Despite the differences in resources and strategies deployed, all four incumbents were reelected in easy campaigns against weak opponents. It is, however, easy to see how differences in the level of resources stewards enjoyed, or their skill in deploying them, would lead to different electoral effects and outcomes. But it is less obvious how other factors embedded in figure 3–2 affect stewards' efforts to control these electoral effects. This notwithstanding, these other factors have important implications for the relative effectiveness of different strategies. Most important here are event catalyses, citizen attributes, socio-political context, and subsequent events.

When a critical event's catalysis clearly establishes accountability with the incumbent steward, a variety of options embedded in political strategies for mediating the events electoral effects are eliminated. Most affected are strategies that deny responsibility, delay the release of information, or present misleading information. Thus,

- *An event's catalysis can limit the effectiveness of partisan strategies in influencing a critical event's electoral relevance.* (P15)

To illustrate this proposition, consider a modified version of events in the southeast and northeast sector fires. Rather than being caused by an arsonist, the fires were caused by a defective transmitter in the sector's public utility plant. In the southeast sector a well-trained city employee activated the manual sprinkling system, confining the fire to the plant and causing power outages that lasted only two days. In the northeast sector the fire spread to the neighborhood because the responsible city employee was a patronage worker who was at his other job, which was reported by the local newspaper.

The event's catalysis so clearly established accountability in the northeast sector's steward that his options for devising a partisan strategy to control the electoral fallout from the fire are severely limited. The southeast sector's steward was as responsible for the defective transmitter as the northeast sector's steward. But her reliance on performance strategies were unaffected by the fact that the catalysis made her politically accountable. In this instance her strategies were effective in minimizing the impact of the fire on citizens' lives, thus curtailing its electoral impact.

Citizen attributes also affect the relative effectiveness of different strategies. The most relevant attributes here are the level of political discernment and the intensity of partisan attachments. Effectively implemented performance strategies are likely to be applauded by a steward's electoral base, persuasive to politically discerning voters, and ineffectual with her opponent's intense partisan loyalists. Effectively implemented partisan strategies are likely to be persuasive to a steward's electoral base, dismissed by politically discerning voters, and derided by her opponent's intense partisan loyalists. Moreover, the effectiveness of partisan strategies is also vulnerable to impact of skillfully implemented competing partisan strategies. In many cases partisan appeals will amount to little more than noise for unaligned voters, having little impact on their vote choice. In contrast, the electoral impact of performance strategies is likely to be determined largely by its success in protecting and enhancing citizens' core political desires. Thus,

- *The greater the level of a citizen's political discernment, the less effective partisan strategies will be in mediating a critical event's electoral relevance.*                                                                 (P16)
  - *The greater the level of a citizen's political discernment, the more effective performance strategies will be in mediating a critical event's electoral relevance.*                                                          (P16.1)
- *The greater the intensity of a citizen's partisan attachments to a steward's party, the more effective partisan strategies will be in mediating a critical event's electoral relevance.*                                     (P17)

- *Performance strategies will be more effective in mediating a critical
  event's electoral relevance for citizens without strong partisan
  attachments.*                                                    (P17.1)

To illustrate these propositions consider the public utility fire example
introduced above. While the Machiavellian steward's partisan options in
mediating the fire's electoral effects are limited, they are not eliminated.
But even skillful efforts to distract the electorate, evoke party symbols, or
to attack opponents are likely to be effective only with committed partisans. Political appeals to undiscerning voters without strong partisan loyalties are subject to counterappeals. The southeast sector's steward will
be able to contrast the sequence of events in her sector with those that
unfolded in the northeast sector. She may also be able to point to her
credible record in handling problems of this genre. If well documented,
these arguments will be compelling for politically discerning voters, effectively stemming the fire's electoral fallout.

The socio-political context upon which a critical event occurs can also
influence the relative effectiveness of elite strategies. Partisan strategies
are predicated on the belief that stewards can mediate the electoral effects
of critical events with post-hoc efforts designed to obfuscate accountability and dull citizens' evaluative capacities. To the extent that Machiavellians engage in preemptive strategies, they are designed to enlarge their
electoral base, intensify the loyalties of their supporters, and undermine
the electorate's general perceptions of the opposition. Performance strategies are predicated on the belief that stewards can mediate the electoral
effects of critical events by affecting their impact on citizens' realization
of their core political desires. Thus, performance strategies rely on the
effective post-hoc deployment of resources to ameliorate the deleterious
effects of critical events, as well as enterprising efforts to capitalize on
their potential. But preemptive efforts to fortify social safety nets, properly equip and train agents of public safety, and improve the socio-political context are also an integral part of performance strategies.

Improving a locale's socio-political context—removing combustible
piles of societal debris and facilitating the accumulation of compost
piles—is an important preemptive component of performance strategies.
These activities are essential to minimizing the chances that (1) a politically inconsequential event will be transformed into a critical event or (2)
a critical event with deleterious effects will ignite secondary reactions.
They are also essential to capitalizing on the potential societal benefits of
these events. Machiavellians who are indifferent to combustible piles of
debris may find that partisan strategies are ineffective in curtailing the
secondary effects of an otherwise manageable event. Also, while Machiavellians can attempt to claim credit for the beneficial aspects of critical

events, the failure to lay the groundwork needed to capitalize on them means that many potential benefits may not be realized. This will reduce the set of benefits available for credit claiming. Moreover, if the benefits of critical events are simply fortuitous, claims of credit will be tenuous and refutable. Thus,

- *The socio-political context upon which a critical event unfolds can limit the effectiveness of partisan strategies in influencing its electoral relevance.* (P18)

Subsequent events can also affect the relative effectiveness of elite mediating strategies. As noted earlier, subsequent events can either undermine or reinforce the electoral relevance of critical events. However, because partisan strategies are composed of efforts to obscure, delay, or "spin" facts relevant to political accountability, their effectiveness is uniquely vulnerable to subsequent events. These subsequent events can cause politically motivated accounts of an event to unravel, undermining "spins" and leading to embarrassments with electoral repercussions. Thus,

- *Partisan strategies to influence a critical event's electoral relevance will be most vulnerable to subsequent events.* (P19)

## CRITICAL EVENTS AND THE DURATION OF ELECTORAL CHANGE

The duration of electoral change generated by a critical event refers to the number of elections in which it generates departures from *ex post ante* normal voting behavior. The duration of a critical event's electoral effect determines whether it produces an election-specific perturbation or enduring electoral change. Enduring electoral change can be either secular or critical, depending upon the magnitude of the initial shift. Critical events that produce small, cumulative electoral effects generate secular change; those that produce sharp and large electoral effects generate critical realignments. The shape of critical realignments can vary over time, in conformance with one of three general models of temporal change. One is a step model, which involves a simple shift to a new steady-state equilibrium. A second form is an impulse-decline model; it involves a sharp initial shift that deteriorates over time. The third form of enduring temporal change is a dynamic growth model; it involves a sharp initial shift that grows over time.

The duration of an exogenous event's electoral effects is important because it speaks to the type of education political elites receive about democratic politics. In particular, the duration of electoral effects will teach political elites about the hierarchy of core political desires within the electorate, as well as the distribution of intensely held feelings about them. This, of course, is useful in educating elites about policy priorities, as well as the latitude they enjoy in policymaking.

I begin by discussing the factors that produce departures from normal voting behavior that last for multiple elections. Then I briefly note the implications of the transformational model depicted in figure 3–2 for the contours of critical realignments.

## The Duration of Electoral Effects

In chapter 2 it was noted that exogenous events are the manifestation of ongoing human intercourse and unfolding societal developments. These interactions and developments differ substantially across time and space, as do the exogenous events they generate. Most of these events have no electoral relevance, and most of those with electoral relevance are *isolated* events. Isolated critical events can lead a large proportion of the electorate to depart from their normal voting routines, generating a sizable electoral jolt. But because they are isolated events, they can be overridden by subsequent events, dealt with by effective stewardship, diffused by partisan appeals, or just fade from voters' consciousness over time. Thus, the electoral effects of these critical events are unlikely to endure, producing only an election-specific deviation.

In contrast, some societal developments are so transformative that they produce *a series of related critical events* that affect stewardship evaluations. If these initial evaluations are *reinforced* by later events in the series, their impact on vote choice will endure across a series of elections. One critical event may stand out as the *triggering event* (a stock market crash, a bloody conflict, a currency collapse, an emotion-laden act, etc.) and it may be of enormous symbolic importance. But it is the existence of a series of reinforcing critical events rooted in some common societal development that leads to enduring electoral effects. If the effect of these events endures long enough, it can define a new normal voting pattern. Given the cumulative impact of this series of critical events on citizens' core political desires, two propositions follow from assumption A1:

- *The greater the impact of a series of related, reinforcing critical events on a citizens' core political desires, the greater the likelihood that the events' electoral relevance will endure across a series of elections.* (P20)
- *The longer the series of related, reinforcing critical events, the greater the likelihood that the events' electoral relevance will endure across a series of elections.* (P21)

To illustrate this proposition consider the innovative technology that powered the southeast sector's new foundry. If it represents just a minor advance over earlier technologies, its economic and electoral effects may be isolated and short-lived. But if the technology is truly revolutionary, it could generate a series of related events, with the foundry opening merely being the triggering event. Extensions of the technology could lead to additional foundries and other uses in the southeast sector. These events feed both the economic boom in the southeast sector and the economic malaise in the northeast sector. Eventually, this malaise infects the north-west sector, whose economy is tightly integrated with that of the northeast sector. Excess productive capacity in the southeast sector also generates a flow of cheap exports that undermines the economic viability of sur-rounding cities. This leads to a large influx of jobless immigrants looking for work, most of whom locate within the low-income northeast sector. The influx of immigrants leads to ethnic conflicts that compound the lin-gering tensions generated by the economic malaise, generating a series of ethnic-based confrontations and some violent incidents.

The series of related events generated by the revolutionary new technol-ogy would almost certainly be reflected in stewardship evaluations. More-over, because the unfolding events span a decade and reinforce the initial impact of the triggering event, their electoral impact is felt across a series of elections. The series of events generated by the revolutionary technol-ogy, and the way they were handled, will create durable images of the competing stewards. These images are likely to last well after the event's impact on citizens' core political desires dissipates—especially if compet-ing parties are effective in reminding voters about how the economic crisis was handled.

Few isolated critical events can, by themselves, generate the force to maintain their electoral impact across a series of election, and not all criti-cal events that have the potential to be triggering events will realize that potential. Moreover, the durability of the electoral effects produced by a series of critical events will vary considerably. Durability will be affected by several factors depicted in figure 3–2: voter attributes, socio-political context, subsequent events, and the actions of competing stewards.

### VOTER ATTRIBUTES

It follows from assumption A1 that citizen attributes will affect the likeli-hood that the electoral effects of a series of related critical events will be enduring. The profound effects of societal developments capable of generating a series of related events means that attributes such as a citi-zen's political discernment, hierarchy of core political desires, and prox-imity to those with similar socio-political profiles are less important to durability. A citizen's proximity to these events' radiated effects, as well as the intensity of their partisan attachments will, however, have an im-portant effect on durability. Thus,

- *The greater the radiated effect of a series of related, reinforcing critical events on a citizen's core political desires, the greater the likelihood that the events' electoral relevance will endure across a series of elections.* (P22)
- *The more intense a citizens' partisan attachment, the less the likelihood that the electoral relevance of a series of related, reinforcing critical events will endure across a series of elections.* (P23)

Consider again the example of the revolutionary technology that led to the new foundry in the southeast sector. It is clear that the radiated effects of this technology would vary even across citizens who shared similar profiles and hierarchies of political desires. Consider the differential impact on blue-collar workers in different locales.

- Blue-collar workers in the *northeast sector* were the most directly and adversely affected by the innovative technology.
  - Those who were (1) members of the incumbent's party and (2) lost their jobs with the new foundry's opening are the most likely to make enduring changes in their normal voting behavior.
    - Contextual effects may lead other blue-collar supporters (i.e. those who did not lose their jobs) of the incumbent in the northeast sector to develop new voting norms.
    - The most diehard loyalists of the incumbent's party are less likely to adopt their initial departure as part of their ongoing political predispositions.
    - The aggregate effect of these changes in the behavior of citizens could lead to a critical realignment in the voting patterns of the northeast sector that favored the out-party.
- Blue-collar workers in the *southeast sector* were the most directly and positively affected by the innovative technology.
  - Those who were 1) members of the opposition party and (2) realized direct economic gains as a result of the foundry's opening are the most likely to adopt new voting norms.
    - Contextual effects may lead other blue-collar supporters (i.e. those who did not experience direct economic gain) of the out-party in the southeast sector to develop new voting norms.
    - The most diehard loyalists of the out-party are less likely to make enduring changes in the voting behavior.
    - The aggregate effects of these changes in the behavior of citizens could lead to a critical realignment in the voting patterns of the southeast sector that favored the incumbent party.
- Blue-collar workers in the *northwest sector* were only indirectly affected.
  - Those who were (1) members of the incumbent's party and (2) adversely affected by the new foundry's opening are the most likely to make enduring changes in their voting routines. Those who were (1)

members of the out-party and (2) positively affected by the new foundry's opening are equally likely to make enduring changes in their voting
routines.

- Contextual effects may lead other blue-collar citizens to develop new
  voting norms.
- The most diehard loyalists are less likely to make enduring changes
  in their voting behavior.
- The indirect and offsetting effects of the technology impact on the behavior of citizens could lead to secular changes in the voting patterns of the northwest sector, or to no change at all.

SOCIO-POLITICAL CONTEXT

The socio-political context within which a series of related and reinforcing critical events unfold will have an important effect upon the durability
of their electoral effects. The existence of densely distributed piles of combustible debris will enhance the chances that these events will ignite secondary reactions. These kinetic effects will compound the deleterious impact of these events and extend their electoral relevance over time. They
can transform what would be a critical event into a triggering event. The
existence of strategically conceived and distributed compost piles will
truncate the deleterious effects of a triggering event's wake, thereby limiting its electoral effects. They can also truncate the effects of a potential
triggering event, transforming it into an isolated critical event. In addition, compost piles will enhance the chances that the beneficial effects of
a series of critical events will be maximized, thus extending their electoral
effects. Therefore, it follows from assumption A1 and corollary C2.1 that:

- *The greater the density of piles of combustible debris, the greater the
  likelihood that the electoral relevance of a series of related and reinforcing critical events adversely affecting core political desires will endure
  across a series of elections.*                                      (P24)
- *The existence of strategically conceived and distributed compost piles
  will reduce the likelihood that the electoral relevance of a series of related and reinforcing critical events adversely affecting core political desires will endure across a series of elections.*                    (P25)
- *The existence of strategically conceived and distributed compost piles
  will reduce the likelihood that the electoral relevance of a series of related and reinforcing critical events positively affecting core political desires will endure across a series of elections.*                    (P26)

Consider again the example of the revolutionary technology. The electoral impact of the foundry closings in the northeast sector would have
been truncated if decades of ethnic, class-based conflicts had not pre-
vented the residents from mounting a unified effort to provide a social

safety net. Instead, the economic turmoil simply resuscitated lingering recriminations about how some residents were incapable of providing for their well-being. The beneficial impact of the technology would not have been as great in the southeast sector had it not been for farsighted civic, business, and labor groups who laid the groundwork for well-designed and environmentally sound industrial parks.

### SUBSEQUENT EVENTS

Overriding subsequent events can also have a profound impact on the duration of electoral effects. It follows from assumption A1 that

- *Overriding subsequent events will reduce the likelihood that the electoral relevance of a series of related, reinforcing critical events will endure across a series of elections.* (P27)

To illustrate this proposition, consider a twist on the innovative technology example. In this version, the Moated City launches a military attack the month after the first election in which the technology's electoral effects are manifested. The impact of the attack on the realization of citizens' core desires and stewardship evaluations is likely to override the effects generated by the innovative technology. Thus, the duration of the technology's electoral effects will be highly truncated for many voters.

### ACTIONS AND RESOURCES OF COMPETING STEWARDS

The actions and resources of competing stewards affect duration similarly to the way they affect magnitude. Because the workings and logic of these factors are so similar to the detailed discussion provided earlier, it will not be repeated here. Suffice it to say that effective performance strategies by the incumbent can truncate the duration of adverse electoral effects and can extend the duration of beneficial electoral effects. Partisan strategies are even less successful in dealing with a series of related and reinforcing critical events with deleterious effects. The extended unfolding of these events minimizes the effectiveness of partisan strategies and frays the loyalties of all but the most diehard partisans. It also increases the chances of igniting combustible debris.

## The Contours of Critical Realignments

A series of related and reinforcing events having a widespread and immediate effect on core political desires can generate a critical realignment. But the aggregate effects of new normal voting routines can generate temporal electoral patterns that vary across critical realignments. Three basic models of change were noted earlier: step models, impulse-decline models, and dynamic growth models. It would be both tedious and challenging to generate a comprehensive set of straightforward propositions concerning these temporal contours. This notwithstanding, that model does have one straightforward implication:

- *Critical realignments will seldom follow a step model of temporal change.* (P28)

This proposition may not appear to be profound. But it is at odds with much conventional thought about the shape of critical realignments and has important methodological implications (which will be addressed in chapter 5). While the traditional literature on critical realignments gave their temporal contours little thought, most scholars operated under the presumption that a step model of change was the norm. This was consistent with (1) the social-psychological model of voting and (2) cyclical theories of the timing of critical realignments. However, within the approach offered here, it would take an unlikely set of circumstances to produce critical realignments that simply moved from one steady-state equilibrium to another.

Absent other profound events affecting normal vote choices in the wake of a critical realignment, normal attrition rates would produce a deterioration of a normal vote trend line, leading to an impulse-decline model of change. Intergenerational socialization effects are not irrelevant within the conceptualization offered here. But they are not viewed to be as influential as they are in the traditional social-psychological model. Thus, the normal vote choices of new entrants after a critical election would be highly susceptible to the effects of isolated critical events, making the maintenance of a steady-state equilibrium highly unlikely. Also, subsequent events, in conjunction with efforts of competing stewards, would either reinforce or undermine existing normal vote choices. Partisan strategies, in conjunction with critical events with deleterious effects on recent converts, are likely to erode their partisan loyalties, leading to an impulse-decline pattern of change. Successful efforts to deal with the adverse consequences of subsequent or related events, or capitalize on their potential, would generate a dynamic growth pattern of change. So too would effective partisan strategies and contextual effects.

## CRITICAL EVENTS AND THE GEOGRAPHIC SCOPE OF ELECTORAL CHANGE

The geographic scope of a critical event's electoral impact refers to the spatial distribution, in a given election, of voters who depart from their normal voting routine because of the event's radiated effects. It is a key dimension to a critical event's electoral impact because it reveals a great deal about voters' political discernment. It also speaks to the impact of the electorate's discerning evaluations on the core interests of political elites. Geographic scope is influenced primarily by interactions between the critical event and voter attributes. Most important here are interactions among the event's location and impact on core political desires, on the one hand, and a voter's hierarchy of political desires and realization of core political desires, on the other. Also important, however, are sociopolitical contexts and competing stewards.

Because critical events are *happenings,* most *happen* in a particular place. In most cases an event's locus will affect the reach, impact, and salience of its radiated effects. As a result, few critical events have spatially uniform effects on voters. Thus,

- *The greater a critical event's radiated effects are spatially concentrated, the more likely its electoral relevance will be geographically variegated.* (P29)

To illustrate this proposition consider an effort by the Moated City to intimidate citizens in the Walled City by deploying a sophisticated missile. By design, the missile lands harmlessly in a deserted field, both as a warning and a demonstration of military might. The electoral effects of this event are likely to be evenly distributed across sectors of the Walled City. Its greatest electoral impact would be on voters with low tolerance for uncertainties over their security, who are randomly distributed throughout the city. In contrast, a spatially variegated electoral effect would be generated if the Moated City had very limited military capacities and launched a crude, but lethal, attack on the Walled City's southwest sector. The electoral effects of this attack are likely to be greatest within the southwest sector because the radiated effects of the attack are focused there.

The attack on the southwest sector is likely to elicit a very uniform response from residents of that sector because it represents a threat to the most basic of political desires: life. As a result, virtually all of the residents in the southwest sector will respond favorably to stewards they believe will protect them; they will respond negatively to those who they believe are unable to protect them or who are indifferent to their security concerns. But citizens in other sectors are beyond the reach of the Moated City's military capacity. Moreover, while some may be concerned with its military threat, many others' vote choices will be affected by more immediate concerns. This will result in aggregated vote choices that are very distinct from those in the southwest sector, making the missile attack's electoral effect spatially variegated.

Unlike the missile attack on the southwest sector, most critical events do not impinge upon such a basic core political desire. Thus, in most instances, the electoral relevance of a critical event with spatially concentrated effects will vary across voters with different hierarchies of core desires. This will dilute the geographic distinctiveness of the event's electoral effects. Therefore, it follows from assumption A1 that:

- *The greater the diversity in hierarchies of core political values among spatially concentrated voters, the less likely the electoral relevance of a critical event will be geographically variegated.* (P30)

Consider a transmitter fire that caused power outages in the northwest sector. Because citizens in its wealthier neighborhoods had worried about the reliability of the utility for years, they installed backup systems in their homes and businesses. They were unaffected by the fire, which, correspondingly, had little impact on their voting choices. Thus, while the electoral effects from the transmitter fire are spatially concentrated in the northwest sector, the geographic scope of the fire's effect will not be as sharply defined as those generated by the missile attack in the southwest sector.

Another factor affecting the geographic scope of a critical event's electoral impact is the extent to which subsets of voters with similar hierarchies of core political desires are spatially concentrated. In settings where these voters are concentrated, contextual factors may exacerbate the magnitude of a critical event's local electoral effects, generating more sharply defined geographic variations. Voters with similar reactions to the event will reinforce one another's interpretation of it. There will also be "snowball" effects as spiraling numbers of concerned voters articulate their grievances to friends and neighbors not directly affected. On the other hand, if a critical event's impact falls on voters who are geographically isolated from those with similar socio-political profiles, contextual effects can minimize the magnitude of its electoral effect. Individuals whose interpretation of an event is not reinforced by others may well be more inclined to dismiss the event's political implications, or at least not act on them. Thus, it follows from assumption A1 and corollary C2 that:

- *The greater the spatial concentration of voters with similar hierarchies of core political values, the more likely that a critical event's electoral relevance will be geographically variegated.* (P31)

This proposition can be illustrated by considering an incident involving young members of a group that was pointedly hostile to an oppressed racial minority. These teenagers set a fire that destroys the minority group's church and kills several children. The moral overtones of this fire may resonate in neighborhoods dominated by groups that are sympathetic to the minority group's plight. A relative handful of concerned citizens in these areas may be successful in underscoring the moral implications of the fire to others. A snowball effect may develop as aroused citizens articulate their feeling to others who, while sympathetic, may not have otherwise been motivated to act. The lack of a sympathetic population base in other neighborhoods may make the activities of concerned citizens ineffectual, and a snowball effect may never materialize. Neighborhoods in which voters were hostile to the minority group may be receptive to local leaders dismissing the event as nothing more than the act of misguided delinquents.

Socio-political context can also affect the geographic scope of electoral changes. Piles of combustible debris that are disproportionately concentrated in various locales can be ignited by exogenous events and generate electoral reactions that do not materialize elsewhere. Compost piles that have been carefully constructed by civic groups, or accumulate naturally within a locale, can lead to electorally relevant gains that do not appear elsewhere. Thus, it follows from assumption A1 and corollary C2 that:

- *The greater the spatial patterning of accumulated societal residue, the greater the likelihood that the electoral relevance of a critical event will be geographically variegated.* (P32)

To illustrate this proposition consider an arsonist who sets fires in three different sectors of the Walled City. In the southeast sector the fire is highly contained because the piles of debris are almost nonexistent due to civic actions and pressures. As a result, the fire destroys only one house, barely affecting the residents' stewardship evaluations. In the northeast sector the house fire went unnoticed by neighbors who, because of ethnic tensions, kept largely to themselves. As a result, the fire spread to a series of spatially patterned piles of debris that cut a swath through several ethnic areas, destroying many older homes. The series of fires leads to charges of neglect and discrimination. In the northwest sector the house fire ignites several piles of debris. But some neighbors observed the fire, rushed to the scene, removed a number of debris piles in the vicinity of the fire, and called the fire department. As a result, the fire did not spread beyond a few houses in the neighborhood, barely affecting stewardship evaluations.

One last important point to make about the geographic scope of electoral change is the impact that competing stewards can have.

- *Actions and resources of competing stewards will affect the likelihood that the electoral relevance of a critical event will be geographically variegated.* (P33)

The arson example just introduced can be used to illustrate the impact of different stewardship strategies. The reason that the fire in the northeast sector had a devastating effect is that untrained patronage workers working with antiquated equipment purchased from the steward's political cronies staffed the fire department. One of the reasons the fire in the northwest sector was contained is that the fire department was equipped with the latest technology and its firefighters were well trained.

## Summary

The transformational model discussed in this chapter, in conjunction with the theoretical synthesis presented in chapter 2, demonstrates how the conceptualization of mass-elite linkages offered here yields insights into democracy as a uniquely responsive form of government. It shows how exogenous events that impinge upon core political desires can lead voters to generate electoral jolts of varying magnitude, duration, and scope that impinge upon the core political interests of elites. The dynamics of this model address some of the theoretical ambiguities presented by the prevalence of peripheral processing of political information noted in chapter 2. These dynamics also underscore relative benefits of performance strategies, providing insights into the electoral incentives stewards have for engaging in preemptive actions designed to enhance the core political desires of citizens.

The discussion of exogenous influences presented thus far provides the theoretical basis for recentering citizens in our understanding of how democracy works to "induce government to act in the interest of the people." These individual-level theoretical analyses provide the underpinnings and justification for continued empirical analysis. But they do no more than that. Nothing in the analyses presented here addresses the ambiguities rooted in partisan strategies designed to dull and manipulate citizen evaluations of stewardship. Or to distract citizens by setting off false alarms. The transformational model depicted in figure 3–2 makes it clear that that political elites exercise some influence over the information democratic citizens receive, what they do with it, and its behavioral consequences. Thus, the impact of endogenous influences upon popular evaluations of political stewardship cannot be summarily dismissed.

The potential role of endogenous influences has troubling normative implications that require empirical analysis. Endogenous influences are the proverbial eight-hundred-pound gorillas that stalk an evaluation process dominated by the peripheral processing of most political information.

# CHAPTER FOUR

# Endogenous Influences and the Evaluative Capacities of Democratic Citizens

> By the time the Revolution had run its course in the early nineteenth century, American society had been radically and thoroughly transformed. . . . [Americans] had fundamentally altered their society and their social relationships. Far from remaining monarchical, hierarchy-ridden subjects on the margin of civilization, America had become, almost overnight, the most liberal, the most democratic, the most commercially minded, and the most modern people in the world. . . . [It] destroyed aristocracy as it had been understood in the Western world for at least two millennia.
> —GORDON WOOD, *The Radicalism of the American Revolution*

> Those who do not believe in the god of democracy contend . . . that the eternal struggles between aristocracy and democracy of which we read in history have never been anything more than the struggles between an old minority, defending its actual predominance, and a new and ambitious minority, intent upon the conquest of power, desiring either to fuse with the former or to dethrone and replace it. On this theory, these class struggles consist merely of struggles between successively dominant minorities. . . . Thus the majority of human beings, in a condition of eternal tutelage, are predestined by tragic necessity to submit to the dominion of a small minority, and must be content to constitute the pedestal of an oligarchy.
> —ROBERT MICHELS, *Political Parties*

ENDOGENOUS influences—efforts by elites to shape, direct, and control the political behavior of ordinary citizens—are primal factors that constitute an enduring component of all political systems. These influences were clear in the presentation of the transformational model presented in chapter 3, but the thrust of endogenous influences and the manner in which they are transmitted will vary across political systems and over time. Within the Anglo-American experience, the impact of endogenous influences upon electoral behavior has been evident since the incorporation of a popular component into the political order. Ordinary citizens were selectively and haltingly admitted into the political arena—and only then under the scrutiny and control of social elites. After the demise of traditional society and its deferential politics, a different set of elites emerged to lay claim to the mantle of the people. The emergence of a pluralistic democracy was accompanied by a set of professional political operatives who created, perfected, and institutionalized mass-based political parties.

The institutionalized efforts of political parties to shape, direct, and control the political involvement of ordinary citizens—like the earlier, more informal efforts of social elites—have never been wholly successful. However, in order to further our understanding of popular efficacy and democratic responsiveness, a much more precise sense of the relative importance of endogenous forces is required, one that resolves the unavoidable ambiguities that pervaded the discussions in chapter 3. This, of course, is the aim of the macro-level empirical analyses. In order to complete the individual-level underpinnings for these analyses, however, more needs to be said about the role of endogenous factors in affecting citizens' evaluative capacities and vote choices. These influences could well negate the impact of the political dynamics outlined in earlier chapters on the behavior of citizens.

Chapter 4 addresses, using broad strokes, the theoretical relationship between endogenous influences and vote choice. I begin by providing a very brief historical overview of endogenous influences in the Anglo-American democratic experience. This analysis demonstrates endogenous influences are deeply rooted in the modern democratic experience and must be an integral part of any empirical assessment of popular efficacy. I then provide a theoretical analysis of partisanship as the dominant source of endogenous influences since the Jacksonian period. This analysis provides the individual-level theoretical base for the derivation of macro-level normal vote estimates presented in chapter 5. Departures from these normal voting patterns will be used to generate assessments of electoral independence and generate inferences about mass-elite linkages.

## TRADITIONAL SOCIETY AND DEFERENTIAL POLITICS: COMMONERS AND THE GRAVITATIONAL PULL OF SOCIAL ELITES

Because of the views summarized by Corcoran in the epigraph to chapter 2, democratic political orders were virtually nonexistent in Western society for nearly two millennia. They began to reemerge in the latter part of the eighteenth century, albeit in modified form, due to a combination of major societal transformations, monumental shifts in intellectual thought, and opportunistic tactics by social elites. Among the most important societal changes were the demise of feudal society, the emergence of a commercial middle class, and the Protestant Reformation (Poggi 1978). The rise of humanism became reflected in the primacy attached to individual liberty and personal happiness. These values affected the manner in which various intellectuals viewed government and underscored the need for restraints on governmental power. Because of these societal transformations, the demarcation of the proper sphere of governmental authority could not be trusted to pope, king, or noble. This realization stimulated thinking about the origins and objectives of government, as well as the locus of ultimate sovereignty.

While the locus of political authority was found to reside in "the people," it did not follow that democratic political orders were the best way to organize political authority or to protect liberty. Indeed, as Charles Lindblom makes clear, democracy was a by-product of this intellectual revolution, but not a necessary or even desirable one.

> The history of democracy is largely an account of the pursuit of liberty. . . . In the early development of constitutional liberalism, from the Magna Carta through the Puritan and Glorious revolutions of the seventeenth century, the liberal constitutional movement was not associated with democracy. . . . It was a movement to enlarge and protect the liberties first of nobles and then of a merchant middle class, incorporating as a means of so doing constitutional restrictions on the prerogatives of government. As the movement came gradually to be associated with ideas of popular rule in the late eighteenth century, it maintained its preoccupation with liberty, to which popular rule was, however, never more than a means, and a disputed means at that. (1977:162–63)

The paradigmatic shifts in thinking about the objectives of government and the source of political authority were necessary, but not sufficient, conditions for the reemergence of democracy. The more immediate stimulus was a contracted battle among English elites in the middle part of the seventeenth century. The story is eloquently and skillfully told in Edmund S. Morgan's *Inventing the People* (1988). Morgan bases his analysis on the concept of a political fiction, which he uses to address Hume's puzzling about "the easiness with which the many are governed by the few."

In order to free themselves from papal dominance, the divine right of kings became a necessary political fiction for Protestant nations by the seventeenth century. By the early 1640s, however, long-simmering battles between the English king and Parliament over religion, money, and political power led to civil war. This rendered the doctrine of the divine right of

kings useless for Parliament; it could not provide the fictional basis necessary to justify parliamentary rule. What Parliament's supporters offered in
its place was the fiction of popular sovereignty. The intent of the elites who
espoused the fiction of popular sovereignty was not to vest the people with
real political authority. Nor was such an outcome likely to occur given the
makeup of English society at the time. As Ostrogorski notes,

> The state of political society in England on the eve of its transformation may
> be summed up in a single sentence: it was the absolute domination of an
> aristocratic class. The English aristocracy's . . . authority rested almost en-
> tirely on its property and its social influence. . . . Thanks to its wealth, the
> landed aristocracy monopolized all the approaches to public power. . . . The
> leading squires would simply select one of themselves for public office and
> use their influence to insure the choice of their nominee. Lessor electors
> would gravitate in the orbit of the great landlords. (1902: 6, 20)

This situation notwithstanding, a number of developments in the Inter-
regnum (the emergence of the Diggers and the Levelers, the movement to
institute the Agreement of the People) gave the gentry some cause for
concern. The gentry's fear and loathing of the "meaner sort" were calmed
by both suffrage norms and institutional factors, both of which reinforced
the dominant role of social elites. Suffrage norms provide important insights into the endogenous constraints on popular efficacy because they
reflect the same type of disingenuousness as the gentry's efforts on behalf
of popular sovereignty. These norms divided the commoners into two
groups: small rural landowners formed one; peasants and proletarians
formed the other. Peasants and proletarians could not be allowed to vote
because they were insufficiently independent, according to arguments put
forward by Montesquieu and echoed in Blackstone: "The 'true reason
requiring any qualification with regard to property in voters,' wrote
Blackstone, 'is to exclude such persons as are in so mean a situation as to
be esteemed to have no will of their own.' . . . [Blackstone] argued that a
large number of country folk were tenants who could easily be coerced
to vote as they were told. The same was true of urban working people.
. . . These working people were as vulnerable, if not more so, to the blan-
dishments and threats of their employers as were tenants to those of their
landlords" (Williamson 1960: 10–11).

In contrast to these vulnerable and dependent commoners was the pillar
of the English liberty, the small landowner who worked his own property
and lived off the fruit of his own labors. This stout soul was exalted in
what Morgan refers to as "the myth of the yeoman farmer," which is "the
notion that the ability of the people to exercise sovereignty and control
their government rested on the righteousness, independence, and military
might of the yeoman farmer, the man who owned his own land, made his

living from it, and stood ready to defend it and his country by force of arms" (1988: 153–54). However, despite the myth of the yeoman farmer, he was anything but independent. The myth was perpetuated for reasons that had nothing to do with independence and judgment. Rather, it existed because it created a palpable yet nonthreatening definition of the "people" thereby bolstering the legitimacy of popular sovereignty (i.e., making the fiction believable).

The yeoman's "ingrained deference to his big neighbors" (Morgan 1988: 173) was reinforced by the public nature of voting at the time; viva voce was the norm. Both Montesquieu and Blackstone's opposition to the secret ballot underscored the importance of public voting (Williamson 1960: 11). In their view, the cure (secret ballot) would be worse than the disease (threats to the independence of the yeomen). Public voting was important, according to Montesquieu because "the lower class ought to be directed by those of higher rank, and restrained by the gravity of eminent personages" (1949: 12). Thus,

> the glorification of the yeoman in the seventeenth and eighteenth centuries, which seemed to elevate the ordinary man, served paradoxically as the central ideological tenet of deferential politics. . . .
>
> [But] the paradox appears only from our modern perspective. We assume too easily that that popular sovereignty was the product of popular demand, a rising of the many against the few. It was not. It was a question of some of the few enlisting the many against the rest of the few. Yeoman did not declare their own independence. Their lordly neighbors declared it, in an appeal for support against those other few whom they feared and distrusted as enemies to liberty and to the security of property. (Morgan 1988: 169)

### Political Rhetoric, Societal Change, and the Demise of Traditional Society: From Deference to Partisanship

Momentous political changes occurred in England during the seventeenth century, and a radically different social setting existed in its American colonies. Yet life in the colonies during the middle of the eighteenth century "still bore traces of the medieval world of personal fealties and loyalties out of which it arose" (Wood 1991: 11). Gordon Wood's *Radicalism of the American Revolution* provides unusually rich insights into the social dependencies in early American life and the intricate web of patriarchal relations that integrated it. His work illustrates the factors that led ordinary folks to be "directed and restrained by the gravity of eminent personages." These observations underscore the extent to which endogenous influences on popular rule have been deeply embedded in the American political experience.

The deferential politics that characterized early American life were rooted in the traditional assumptions colonists held about the nature of society. They believed colonial life was shaped by a natural order derived from perceived social distinctions, an order that structured interpersonal relationships. Although there were important differences within social strata, the most basic social distinction in colonial society was between the gentry and commoners. Common folks walked differently, talked differently, dressed differently, ate differently, and thought differently from the gentry. From these perceived social distinctions flowed different societal roles, privileges, and obligations. The gentry were expected to live on the fruits of their accumulated wealth and to prepare themselves for the obligations of their rank. Their moral authority was derived from their training and education, their freedom from the demands of ordinary life, and their personal character (which was thought to be honorable and virtuous). Their upbringing and their independence put them in a unique position to *define* the common good; their noble character insured that they would *pursue* it. They were society's leaders and they expected deference from the masses.

The hierarchical structure of colonial society was maintained and perpetuated by an incredibly expansive and intricate web of personal relationships. Personal and familial ties reached across the local social milieu; intermarriage among the gentry was common. The web also extended vertically. The lack of paper currency and financial institutions made the gentry the primary source of capital for common folks. Moreover, the gentry dominated public offices. Indeed, it was not unusual for offices to be passed down across generations of the same family. Political factions were often organized around individuals and families, not broad sets of interests or ideologies. Thus, despite their professed independence, the colonists were "enmeshed in the diffuse and sometimes delicate webs of paternalistic obligation inherent in a hierarchical society. . . . It was taken for granted that 'Dependence and social Obligation take place at the first Dawn of Life, and as its Thread lengthens,' they would 'continually multiply and invigorate.' . . . 'Every service or help which one man affords another, requires its corresponding return.' These 'returns' were in fact 'the bands of society by which families, neighborhoods, and nations are knit together.' Society was held together by intricate networks of personal loyalties, obligations, and quasi-dependencies" (Wood 1991: 57).

It was the strength of the gentry's intricate web of personal relationships and skillful use of patronage that structured early American society. It was also the basis for the deferential politics that undermined the electoral independence of the very substantial component of the white male population that could vote.

Translating the personal, social, and economic power of the gentry into political authority was essentially what eighteenth-century politics was about. The process was self-intensifying: social power created political authority, which in turn created more social influence.

Everywhere it was the same: those who had the property and power to exert influence in any way—whether by lending money, doing favors, or supplying employment—created obligations and dependencies that could be turned into political authority. (Wood 1991: 88–89)

### Deferential Politics, Political Rhetoric, and Pluralistic Democracy: The Rise of Mass-Based Political Parties

The ominous beginnings of "popular" government in both England and her American colonies underscore the primacy of endogenous constraints on popular efficacy. The gravitational force exerted by these endogenous influences kept the people operating "within the orbit of the great landlords." However, one of the key points in Morgan's analysis of the emergence of popular government is that the gentry's "invention" of the people generated a dynamic that proved beyond their ability to control. Commoners took seriously the political rhetoric used by the colonial gentry in the revolutionary era to reshape traditional society. This rhetoric interacted with both the truncated nature of colonial society (it lacked the social extremes of traditional society) and important societal developments that began to unfold as early as the 1740s (increased social and physical mobility, religious upheavals, consumerism). This interaction proved to be instrumental in the demise of the society the founders desired to create, as well as their political domination of it (Wood 1991).

The revolutionary leaders' assault on traditional society and the dependencies that held it together was driven by a utopian vision. But the vision that spurred them was a republican vision, not a democratic one. One revolutionary leaders did not expect that commoners would fill the power vacuum created by the departures of thousands of prominent English loyalists. They believed that the profound changes they had engineered would generate a meritocracy that would govern with an enlightened view of the public interest. "For many of the revolutionary leaders this was the emotional significance of republicanism—a vindication of frustrated talent at the expense of birth and blood" (Wood 1991: 180). Such leaders would naturally command the respect of commoners, which would provide the basis for the legitimate exercise of political authority.

It was not long after the end of the war that the revolutionary leaders realized that the people were not as virtuous as they had thought—or as their republican vision of society demanded. The movement for a new constitution was a reaction to the excesses of state legislatures, which were viewed as more committed to serving local interests than to pursuing an enlightened view of the public good. While the republican vision of the American future prevailed in the Constitutional Convention, it ultimately failed in practice. Traditional society was ultimately replaced by a pluralistic, liberal democratic society, not a homogenous republican society.

> Instead of creating a new order of benevolence and selflessness, enlightened republicanism was breeding social competitiveness and individualism; and there seemed to be no easy way of stopping it. . . . The Revolution was the source of its own contradictions. . . .
>
> [Thus,] by the early nineteenth century, America had emerged as the most egalitarian, most materialistic—and most evangelical Christian—society in Western history. In many respects this new democratic society was the very opposite of what the revolutionary leaders had envisioned (Wood 1991: 230).

The most radical concept that was articulated in the revolutionary era was equality. In the end, it made deference to republican leaders just as unpalatable as deference to traditional aristocrats. The reason for this is that equality came to mean moral equality, the notion that all citizens shared a common moral sense and that ordinary citizens could resolve moral dilemmas as well as gentlemen. This meant that selfishness and localism no longer tainted the judgments and desires of ordinary citizens. Their views merited the same consideration as those offered by the gentry. As a result, the notion spread that the public good was best promoted by the exertion of "each individual seeking his own good in his own way." This led ordinary citizens to the view that they were entitled not merely to a vote, but also to a voice. This, of course, changed the way in which politics was viewed. It could no longer be merely a "squabble among gentlemen." The notion of moral equality, combined with the social and commercial revolutions that began before the Revolution (and were reinforced by it), changed that forever. Ordinary citizens began to see politics as a game in which they could become legitimate players and in which they had legitimate interests.

To accommodate broader participation in politics, and the limitless demands that a pluralistic democratic society generated, more was required than just radical political rhetoric. If government in a pluralistic, liberal democratic society was to accommodate the diverse interests of diffuse publics, there had to be a mechanism to aggregate those interests. If ordinary citizens were to have a voice, and not merely a vote, in the new political order, a means had to be found to make that voice heard—lest it be drowned out by the voices emanating from the well-connected families in Boston, along the Hudson River valley, or from the Virginia tidewater. Thus, mass-based political parties became more than a *legitimate* component of the new political order. They became an *essential* component. The political parties of Hamilton and Jefferson were of a different era and did not have the reach or the organizational capacity to accommodate the issues, conflicts, or the actors embodied in the democratic political milieu that was beginning to emerge in the early-nineteenth century (Chambers 1963: 147).

In response to the "anti-democratic" forces that denied Andrew Jackson the presidency in 1824, Martin Van Buren began the process of building and institutionalizing a mass-based party organization in the prelude to the presidential election of 1828. The organization and discipline required for collective political action ran counter to the individualism that was central to the political thinking of the era. To counter this and to provide for the acceptance of party organizations, Silbey notes that

> Van Buren and his followers essentially "drew upon the argument [that] organization advanced democracy," making themselves the logical instruments to mobilize large numbers on behalf of desirable policies. . . .
>
> Some might find, one pamphleteer argued, "novelty" in collective action for political purposes. But such organization was necessary to achieve an "honest" expression of public sentiment. America had to remember that political conflict was inevitable and preferable to "the calm and quietude of despotism." Collective action was the only way to harness and manage that conflict; this would allow those "periodical and wholesome storms" to "purify the political elements and bring with them increased health and vigor." The ideological shift was striking. The conceptions fueling and shaping what was under way were altogether different from the earlier stress on social harmony and deference. (Silbey 1991: 19)

## POLITICAL PARTIES, ENDOGENOUS INFLUENCES, AND VOTING BEHAVIOR

### Political Parties as Endogenous Institutions

Contemporary students of democracy would agree with Van Buren that parties are indispensable to the type of competitive, pluralistic democracy that emerged in nineteenth-century America. Schattschneider set the tone for contemporary assessments of political parties with his oft-quoted assertion that "democracy is unthinkable save in terms of parties" (1942: 1). Two different democratic explanations have been offered to support the argument that political parties are essential for representative democracies. One derives from a "principled" (Burkean) conception of political parties; the other derives from a pluralist conception.[1]

Despite the centrality of these conceptions of political parties in democratic thought, a very different conception of parties emerges from an elitist perspective on democratic politics. Rather than viewing political parties as vehicles for democracy, elitist conceptions stress the dominance of elites in the management of party affairs. Thus, they conceive of parties as tools political elites use to achieve personal concerns and interests. Indeed, Schattschneider's above quoted comments echo an observation made decades earlier by Michels. In his classic study of European political parties and democracy Michels notes, "Democracy is inconceivable without organization" (1962: 61). Unlike Schattschneider, however, Michels reached a different conclusion. To him, democracy *was* inconceivable: "this politically necessary principle of organization, while it overcomes the disorganization of forces which would be favorable to the adversary, brings other dangers in its train. We escape Scylla only to dash ourselves on Charybdis. Organization is, in fact, the source from which the conservative currents flow over the plain of democracy, occasioning there disastrous floods and rendering the plain unrecognizable" (62).

Corcoran succinctly captures the essence of Michels's assertions: "The moving and profound irony expressed by Michels is that the very means by which . . . democratic parties endeavor to create a democratic society is the procedure through which it must necessarily be lost. There is a Pyrrhic victory when a popular party organizes itself successfully and forms a stable, effective leadership competent enough to master the complexities of policy formulation, electoral success, and governmental administration. It is a victory, not for democracy, but for a battle-hardened, professional elite" (1983: 18).

At the core of Michels's analysis is his observation that the leaders of political parties inevitably become detached from the party membership.

---

[1] The principled explanation derives from utilitarian conceptions of democracy (Corwin 1929: 571) and was succinctly expressed by Edmund Burke, who defined political parties as "A body of men united for promoting by their just endeavors the national interest upon some particular principle in which they all agree (1930 (1770): 82)." James Madison echoed this view in his Federalist no.10 and it is at the core of the widely cited, post–World War Two APSA report on responsible party government. Within this conception individuals are attracted to political parties because they agree with the principles they espouse and the policies they adopt; they maintain their party attachments as long as the party remains committed to its core principles. The pluralist explanation derives from pluralist conceptions of democracy (Ricci 1984: 157). Pluralist, or cleavage representation, conceptions of political parties view them as coalitions of groups who unite for the purpose of achieving electoral victory (Binkley 1943; Truman 1951; Lipset and Rokkan 1967; Petrocik 1981). Group leaders hold important party positions and represent the interests, views and preferences of their members.

That is, as the party's leaders become embroiled in the governance process they develop a set of interests that are tied to their status as professional politicians. Enjoying and retaining the accoutrements of political power along with the pursuit of their own interests (pecuniary gain, self-serving policy objectives, future employment opportunities, etc.) become the primary forces driving their political actions. The advocacy and representation of the interests of the party's membership assumes a secondary status. These prodigal leaders are not replaced by the party membership because of the membership's incompetence and disinterestedness, their "veneration" of the party and its leaders, their incapacity for independent action, and their corresponding "need" for direction. Thus, oligarchic tendencies are inherent in political parties, and they cannot act as democratic vehicles for organizing, aggregating, and representing the interests of commoners. In Michels's view parties inevitably become endogenous institutions used by professional politicians to control and direct the masses.

Aldrich (1995) makes a similar assertion about political parties in a more recent work, one that articulates a rational choice perspective on political parties. Within this framework political parties are the creations of ambitious politicians, designed to serve their needs and further their interests. The ambitious politicians who direct political parties are motivated by self-interest, broadly defined. While those interests include a long and successful public career, political power, and personal prestige, they can also include fundamental values, widely shared principles, and broad policy goals. This notwithstanding, political parties emerge, and persevere, because they can be of use to ambitious politicians in dealing with a set of problems they confront in pursuing their personal goals (organizing the competition for office, mobilizing mass publics, forging durable majorities in government). Aldrich goes on to argue that when the structure of parties interferes with the pursuit of those personal goals, they are reformed or abandoned. It is in this sense that he contends that political parties are "the creature of the politicians, the ambitious office seeker and officeholder. They have created and maintained, used or abused, reformed or ignored the political party when doing so has furthered their goals and ambitions. The political party is thus an 'endogenous' institution— an institution shaped by these political actors" (1995: 4).

Aldrich characterizes the relationship between citizens and parties as an exchange relationship. Voters "are not part of the political party at all . . . but are critical as targets of party activities. Parties 'produce' candidates, platforms, and policies. Voters 'consume' by exchanging their votes for the party's product" (21). In viewing voters as consumers, Aldrich provides a *potentially* more central role to democratic forces in driving and shaping the actions of ambitious politicians than does Michels. While asserting the essential endogeny of political parties, he recognizes potential linkages between the interests of mass publics and those of ambitious politicians. Building on the work of Downs (1957) and Schlesinger (1991) Aldrich observes:

> The genius of democracy, in this view, is rather like the genius Adam Smith found in the free market. In Smith's case individuals acting in their own self-interest turn out to be guided, as if by some unseen hand, to act in the interest of the collective. In Schlesinger's case ambitious politicians, seeking to have a long and successful career, are all led by the necessity of winning broad support in the face of stiff competition to reflect the desires of those citizens who support them. . . . Seeking popular support in the face of competition yields officeholders who find it in their self-interest to respond to the wishes of the public so that that public will continually reelect them, thereby satisfying their career ambition. All else flows from this Schumpeterian view. (13)

This view of political parties offers only a *potentially* important role for mass publics because their impact on the strategies and actions of ambitious politicians is a contingent one. "Politicians may be expected to give up some of their personal autonomy only when they face an imminent threat of defeat without doing so" (26). Stated metaphorically, politicians need be concerned about voters only if citizens are discriminating consumers shopping in a competitive marketplace. Stated in more abstract theoretical terms, in charting a course of action ambitious politicians must resolve the tensions emanating from a set of competing forces. These forces include their desire to pursue their personal interests and goals, the demands of benefits seekers, and the perceived concerns and welfare of their constituents. The key vector—from the perspective of democratic theory—is the force ambitious politicians associate with the perceived desires of their electoral base. The force associated with this "democratic vector" is determined by the capacity of voters for electoral independence and the competitiveness of electoral settings.

If party elites are effective in shaping, managing, and controlling the behavior of the members of their electoral base, then the incidence of disequilibrating electoral jolts will be low—especially if electoral settings are not competitive. As a result, these elites will learn, over time, that there is little need to weigh popular concerns heavily in their political calculations. Ordinary citizens can be dealt with around election time with symbolic gestures and organizational efforts designed to mobilize the party faithful and attract the support of "unaligned" components of the electorate. If electoral decisions are less susceptible to control by political parties (i.e., electoral independence and electoral competitiveness are high), then strategic party elites will learn that it is important to weigh popular concerns more heavily.

## Partisanship and Voting Behavior

Unsurprisingly, given the history of endogenous influences in the Anglo-American democratic experience, much of what we know about electoral politics in the United States suggests that partisan attachments have exerted strong centripetal pulls on voting behavior since the beginnings of mass suffrage. Critics of political parties lamented their role within the electoral arena throughout the nineteenth century (Silbey 1991: chap. 11, esp.). Around the turn of the twentieth century the perceived electoral dominance of political parties was such that a key aim of Progressive reformers was to loosen the political parties' grip over voters through various electoral and party reforms (secret ballot, voter registration systems, literacy tests, elimination of patronage, etc.).

Gaetano Mosca was one of the first political scholars to incorporate the role of partisan attachments into an overarching analysis of democracy. At the core of his critique is the relationship between the masses and political parties. Drawing parallels between religious and political organizations he notes:

> Outside the directing nucleus comes the throng of proselytes. While this group constitutes the stronger element numerically, and supplies the church or party with its material strength and its economic basis, it is the most negligible factor intellectually and morally. A number of modern sociologists declare that the masses are conservative and "misoneistic"—chary of novelties. That means that the masses are hard to win to a new faith. However, once they are won to it, they abandon it with the greatest reluctance, and when they do drop away, the fault lies almost always with the promoting nucleus. . . .
>
> For many people, political, religious, or philosophical opinions are, at bottom, very secondary matters, especially when the first flush of youth has passed and the age of practical occupations, of "business," comes. So, to some extent through indolence, to some extent through habit, partly again through mistaken pride and respect for so-called consistency of character, a man often ends, when no strong conflict with his interests is involved, by keeping all his life long a doctrine that he embraced in a moment of youthful impulse, devoting to it such little energy and activity as the practical man is wont to set apart for what is called "the ideal." (1939: 171, 172)

The mid-twentieth-century work of V. O. Key—building on the insights of philosophers such as Mosca, "empiricists" dating to Wallas (1909), and analyses of aggregate election returns—elaborated on the psychological aspects of party attachments. Key likened the value of the party name to that of a trademark that had accumulated "good will" among voters. The party's nomination entitled a candidate to the "habitual party vote." He went on to note, "Once established, party allegiance and loyalty seem to have a remarkable persistence. Party attitudes seem to be transmitted from father to son, not biologically to be sure; community, family, and environmental influences play a part in the fixing of partisan attitudes" (1947: 596). While Key relied on rather crude data to support his views, the importance of partisan identifications emerged as the conceptual centerpiece of an innovative mid-twentieth-century approach to understanding voting behavior, the social-psychological approach. This approach is embedded in what is often referred to as the Michigan model of voting behavior. This model emerged from a pioneering collaboration that began in the late 1940s and has received strong empirical support from survey research.

Empirical findings generated by repeated applications of the Michigan model have had significant implications for our understanding of popular efficacy and American democracy. And for good reason. Rather than being based on the unstructured speculations of political observers, pundits, and reformers, these findings emerge from a broad theoretical framework that was empirically examined using survey data derived from random samples of the national electorate. This theoretical framework has dominated the field of electoral behavior for decades, and its key tenets have received empirical support from survey data derived from nearly a half-century of national elections. The literature on American voting behavior contains some of the most sophisticated and highly regarded analyses in behavioral political research. Indeed, in a recent review of the voting literature, Dennis asserts that "[t]he Michigan voter studies are undoubtedly the most remarkable and successful collective research effort ever mounted in political science, and are indeed unique among the annals of all social disciplines. . . . the subdiscipline has attracted some of the best minds and the largest resources of any in the discipline" (1991: 76, 84).

Understanding the theoretical structure of the Michigan model, along with its central empirical results, is key to understanding the role of endogenous influences on mass political behavior since the politics of partisanship replaced the politics of deference. Of particular importance here is the Michigan model's theoretical treatment of partisan influences on voting. Also important are the implications of partisan attachments for the evaluative capacities of citizens.

THE ROLE AND IMPACT OF PARTISAN INFLUENCES

The Michigan model of voting behavior recognizes a broad range of influences on vote choice and uses a "funnel of causality" metaphor to convey the sense that some plausibly relevant factors (religion, ethnicity, socioeconomic status, etc.) are more distant from the voting decision. They primarily exert indirect influence through more immediate factors. The most immediate causes of vote choice are a set of psychological predispositions or orientations toward three central political objects: political parties, candidates, and issues. Within this framework, the voter's orientations toward the political parties constitute the long-term component of the vote, while orientations toward candidates and issues constitute the short-term component of the vote.

In developing the metaphor of a funnel of causality, we located events and states within either of two broad classes, political and non-political. . . . It is common to explain voting behavior in terms of roots that are in the first instance relatively contemporary, and, in the second, largely non-political. In the traditional view, democratic elections are periodic reviews of governmental conduct. Hence roots of behavior are sought within the time interval since the preceding election.

We have chosen instead to devote our initial attention to the purely political roots of the proximal attitudes and the voting act. For we find that the individual's current choice tends to have simple and direct roots in time prior to the current era, and that this past is, in no small measure, a *political* past. . . . If we were to trace the roots of behavior deep enough in time past to encounter important apolitical sources of current behavior, we would frequently be forced to search into previous generations. Initial selection of a party may often be a response to non-political pressures; but once made, partisan choice tends to be maintained long after its non-political sources have faded into oblivion. Current pressures arising outside the political order continue to affect the evaluation process, and from time to time they may contribute to a critical margin of political victory. *Yet for most of the people most of the time such contemporary forces turn out to be minor terms in the decision equation.* (Campbell, Converse, et al. 1960: 117, 119, emphasis added)

Thus, while the actual vote decision is the result of the interplay between these long-term (endogenous) and short-term (exogenous) factors, partisan identifications enjoy a dominant role in the Michigan model. This generates a good deal of electoral stability, the type of stability that leads to the conclusion that it would be rational for strategic political elites to discount electoral pressures in their decisional calculus. "A general observation about the political behavior of Americans is that their partisan preferences show great stability between elections. Key speaks of the 'standing decision' to support one party or the other, and this same phenomenon soon catches the eye of any student of electoral behavior. Its mark is readily seen in aggregate election statistics. For virtually any collection of states, counties, wards, precincts, or other political units one may care to examine, the correlation of the party division of the vote in successive elections is likely to be high" (Campbell, Converse, et al. 1960: 121).

The dominant role ascribed to long-term partisan attachments was supported by initial empirical analyses reported in *The American Voter,* and its dominance has been reaffirmed in subsequent national surveys of voters. Indeed, in response to scholarly challenges to the impact of partisan identifications on vote choice as well as their temporal stability, Miller (1991) examined the National Election Study data for all presidential elections between 1952 and 1988. In assessing the *dominance* of partisan attachments, Miller conducted a set of correlation analyses. The average bivariate correlation between party identification and vote choice is .67 and it seems to be become stronger in post-1972 elections.[2] The average partial correlation (controlling for basic demographic characteristics) is .60 (Miller 1991: 565, table 2). With respect to the *stability* of partisan attachments, Miller examines changes in the distribution of partisan attachments for a variety of subgroups (North/South; men/women; blacks/whites). He concludes that for Northern whites a "steady state" period of relatively unchanging party identifications exists for most of the period between 1952 and 1988. In a subsequent work, Miller and Shanks engage in an even more in-depth analysis of these concerns. While their analyses suggest that there have been shifts in the partisan alignments for African Americans, Southerners, and Evangelical Christians, they go on to note that

> For two-thirds of the voters, changes in partisan identification have been very limited in scope for at least forty years. The noted exceptions aside, we have documented continuity in the party identifications of the remainder of the electorate that is akin to the stability we have observed in the correlates of voter turnout.
>
> As a long-term stable predisposition, party identification is not only a point of departure for electoral analysis; it is the most important of several predispositions that provide continuity across electoral epochs. We are very much in accord with the formulations of the *American Voter* which saw partisan loyalties limiting the frequency and magnitude of shifts in electoral preferences, *an inertial force against change and a magnet drawing defectors back to a habitual partisan point of departure in time for the next election* [emphasis added]. Party identification is only one of a host of themes relevant to vote choice, but year after year it is the dominant predisposition in providing continuity in voters' perspectives and behaviors from one election to the next. (512).

It is only when Miller and Shanks's observations are joined with some speculation made in *The American Voter* that the full import of their

---

[2] Bartels, using a different approach and extending the analysis through 1996 and to congressional elections, confirmed these results (2000).

conception of partisan attachments for electoral behavior can be appreciated. In that seminal work the authors note that

The distribution of partisan attachments in the nation today, a century after the Civil War, follows the same regional lines laid down at that time. The South, despite its occasional desertions of the Democratic presidential candidate, is still the citadel of the Democratic Party, with the Republican Party offering hardly more than token opposition in most parts of the area. The Northeast, including New England and the Middle Atlantic states, which was the center of the abolitionist movement, is now the strongest Republican area of the country. The Far West, which was both geographically and psychologically removed from the conflict in the Southern states, is at present the most Democratic region outside the South.

We do not wish to suggest that these regions are still preoccupied with the issues of the Civil War. The participants in that conflict now have long since passed from the scene, and slavery and secession now have only historic interest. But as Key has made clear, community patterns of party affiliations have a remarkable capacity to persist long after "the disappearance of the issues that created the pattern." (Campbell, Converse, et al. 1960: 152)

### PARTISAN IDENTIFICATIONS AND THE EVALUATIVE CAPACITY OF CITIZENS

The stability of partisan identifications and their dominance in electoral decisions are troublesome from the perspective of popular efficacy for two reasons. The first concerns how these identifications are formed and what these origins mean for the relationship between partisan attachments and core political desires. The second has to do with their role in coloring and interpreting short-term factors dealing with the performance of political parties and their leaders. The joint impact of these factors has profound implications for the conception of democratic citizens as discerning voters. It suggests that the evaluative capacities of citizens are muted and dulled by the centrality of endogenous (partisan) influences.

Partisan attachments are defined as the long-term component of the vote because

most citizens tend to locate themselves in a political party at an early point in their adult life, and . . . this identification typically gains strength throughout life. The party that wins favor appears to depend predominantly upon social transmission from the family or early reference groups. The critical initial decision appears to be taken most frequently under strong social influence early in life, when involvement in politics is at low ebb, and, presumably, political information is most scanty as well. Thus if involvement and background are preconditions for the establishment of meaningful links between basic values and party preference, then we must suppose that in the bulk of cases, the individual is committed to a party at a time when he is least likely to have the wherewithal to bring ideological considerations of this sort into play. Thereafter, the self-reinforcing aspects of a psychological identification progressively reduce the probability of change in partisan allegiance. If the crucial identifications were postponed until the individual had observed the parties for some time with the modest but more active involvement and fuller information of the middle-aged adult, we would expect that ultimate partisanship would show more convincing relationships with underlying values of this sort. (Campbell, Converse, et al. 1960: 212–13)

Compounding the effects of the "early onset" of partisanship is its role in coloring voters' interpretations of short-term factors, thus dulling their evaluative capacities. Stokes elaborates upon this aspect of partisanship by noting that

party identification and voting should not be regarded as a simple disposition to vote for one party or the other. To be sure, there is some totally unadorned persistence voting. But for most people the tie between party identification and voting behavior involves subtle processes of perceptual adjustment by which the individual assembles an image of current politics consistent with this partisan allegiance. With normal luck, the partisan voter will carry to the polls attitudes toward the newer elements of politics that support his long-standing bias. . . .

Therefore, the capacity of party identification to color perceptions holds the key to understanding why the unfolding of new events, the emergence of new issues, the appearance of new political figures fails to produce wider swings of party fortune. To a remarkable extent these swings are damped by processes of selective perception. Because the public so easily finds in new elements of politics the old partisan vice and virtues, our electoral history, as so much else, shows that *plus ca change, plus c'est la meme chose.* (1966: 127).

Thus, while partisan affiliations help the ordinary citizen to make sense out of politics, they also serve "to insulate him from non-political pressures that might otherwise push him to more frequent partisan re-evaluation" (Campbell, Converse et al. 1960: 119).

## Summary

The conclusions that flowed from the basic tenets of, and the empirical findings derived from, the Michigan model seemed to confirm some of the worst fears expressed by late-nineteenth-century critics of democracy. These scholars were the first to study critically the operations of a broadly based democracy operating in a nation-state within an industrial society.

They argued that the emergence of professional politicians, at the helm of powerful political machines, could control the electoral behavior of the masses. This, of course, interfered with the operation of social processes that were essential to refresh and renew societal leadership. As Mosca noted, "[N]ever have the many, especially if they were poor and ignorant, ruled the few, especially if they were rich and intelligent. The so-called dictatorship of the proletariat, therefore, could never be anything more than the dictatorship of a very restricted class exercised in the name of the proletariat" (1939: 392).

The fact that more recent research seems to confirm the dismal assessments that were made nearly a century ago has dire implications for popular efficacy. Two are most noteworthy. The first concerns the magnitude and nature of the forces embodied in the "democratic" revolution that took place in nineteenth-century America. Wood contends that the forces unleashed by the struggle with England forged a social revolution that destroyed aristocracy as it had been understood in the Western world for at least two millennia (1991: 8). That forces of this magnitude transformed endogenous influences, but were unable to eliminate them, is a testament to their durability. The second point is that the nineteenth-century American experience seems to be an illustration of a more general pattern. This pattern was captured by the work of a group of early-twentieth-century political theorists such as Mosca, Pareto, and Michels who had studied the European experience as it evolved from aristocracy to democracy. Michels, for example, concluded that

> society cannot exist without a "dominant" or "political" class, and . . . while its elements are subject to a frequent partial renewal, [they] nevertheless constitutes the only factor of sufficiently durable efficacy in the history of human development. According to this view, the government . . . cannot be anything other than the organization of a minority. . . . The majority is thus permanently incapable of self-government. Even when the discontent of the masses culminates in a successful attempt to deprive the bourgeoisie of power, this is after all, so Mosca contends, effected only in appearance; always and necessarily there springs from the masses a new organized minority which raises itself to the rank of a governing class. ([1915]1962: 353–54)

## REFERENCES

Aldrich, J. H. 1995. *Why Parties? The Origin and Transformation of Party Politics in America.* Chicago, University of Chicago Press.

Bartels, L. M. 2000. "Partisanship and Voting, 1952–1996." *American Journal of Political Science* 44 (1): 35–50.

Binkley, W. E. 1943. *American Political Parties: Their Natural History.* New York, Alfred A. Knopf.

Burke, E. [1770] 1930. "Thoughts on the Cause of the Present Discontent." In the *Collected Works of Edmund Burke.* Oxford, Oxford University Press.

Campbell, A., P. E. Converse, et al. 1960. *The American Voter.* New York, John Wiley and Sons.

Chambers, W. N. 1963. *Political Parties in a New Nation: The American Experience, 1776–1809.* New York, Oxford University Press.

Corcoran, P. E. (1983). "The Limits of Democratic Theory." In the *Democratic Theory and Practice*, edited by G. Duncan. Cambridge, Cambridge University Press.

Corwin, E. S. 1929. "The Democratic Dogma and the Future of Political Science." *American Political Science Review* 23 (3): 569–92.

Dalton, R. J. and M. P. Wattenberg. 1993. "The Not So Simple Act of Voting." In *Political Science: The State of the Discipline*, edited by A. W. Finifter. Washington, DC, *American Political Science Review.*

Dennis, J. 1991. "The Study of Electoral Behavior." In *Political Science: Looking to the Future*, edited by W. Crotty. Evanston, IL, Northwestern University Press.

Downs, A. 1957. *An Economic Theory of Democracy.* New York, Harper and Row.

Key, V. O. 1947. *Politics, Parties, and Pressure Groups.* New York, Thomas Crowell.

Lindblom, C. E. 1977. *Politics and Markets.* New York, Basic Books.

Lipset, S. M., and S. Rokkan. 1967. *Party Systems and Voter Alignments.* New York: Free Press.

Michels, R. [1915] 1962. *Political Parties: A Sociological Study of the Oligarchical Tendencies of Modern Democracy.* New York, Free Press.

Miller, W. E. 1991. "Party Identification, Realignment, and Party Voting: Back to the Basics." *American Political Science Review* 85 (2): 556–68.

Miller, W. E., and J. M. Shanks. 1996. *The New American Voter.* Cambridge, Harvard University Press.

Montesquieu, B. D. 1949. *The Spirit of the Laws.* New York, Franz Neumann.

Morgan, E. S. 1988. *Inventing the People: The Rise of Popular Sovereignty in England and America.* New York, W. W. Norton and Co.

Mosca, G. 1939. *The Ruling Class.* New York, McGraw Hill.

Niemi, R. G., and H. Weisberg, eds. 1993a. *Classics in Voting Behavior.* Washington, DC, Congressional Quarterly Press.

Ostrogorski, M. 1902. *Democracy and the Organization of Political Parties.* New York, Haskell House Publishers.

Petrocik, J. R. 1981. *Party Coalitions: Realignments and the Decline of the New Deal Party System.* Chicago, University of Chicago Press.

Poggi, G. 1978. *The Development of the Modern State: A Sociological Introduction.* Stanford, CA, Stanford University Press.

Ricci, D. M. 1984. *The Tragedy of Political Science*. New Haven, Yale University Press.

Schattschneider, E. E. 1942. *Party Government*. New York, Rinehart.

Schlesinger, J. A. 1991. *Political Parties and the Winning of Office*. Chicago, University of Chicago Press.

Silbey, J. H. 1991. *The American Political Nation, 1838–1893*. Stanford, CA, Stanford University Press.

Stokes, D. E. 1966. "Party Loyalty and the Likelihood of Deviating Elections." In *Elections and the Political Order*, edited by A. Campbell, P. E. Converse, W. E. Miller, and D. E. Stokes. New York, John Wiley and Sons.

Truman, D. B. 1951. *The Governmental Process*. New York, Alfred Knopf.

Wallas, G. 1909. *Human Nature in Politics*. London, Archibald Constable.

Williamson, C. 1960. *American Suffrage from Property to Democracy, 1760–1860*. Princeton, Princeton University Press.

Wood, G. S. 1991. *The Radicalism of the American Revolution*. New York, Vintage Books.

# CHAPTER FIVE

# Conceptual and Methodological Foundations
# for a Reexamination of Popular Efficacy

> [T]he nation's response to a changing political world is
> not wholly governed by fixed partisan loyalties. Some
> elements of political reality not agreeing with these loyal-
> ties will get through the perceptual screen raised in the
> partisan voter. A war, a sharp recession, a rash of scandal
> will leave their mark on all shades of partisans, though
> the mark will not be deep enough to change the votes
> of more than some. As they become relevant to politics,
> identifications of a racial or national or religious or class
> nature may counter the perceptual effects of long-term
> partisan loyalties in large segments of the electorate.
>     The interplay of basic orientations and transient fac-
> tors underlies the voters' decisions on election day. What
> is the relative weight of these influences in determining
> the total vote? What is the freedom of short-term forces
> to modify the influence of basic dispositions?
>     —DONALD E. STOKES, "Party Loyalty and the
>     Likelihood of a Deviating Election," in *Elections
>     and the Political Order*

THE DURABILITY of the image of citizens as manageable fools—that is to
say, the dominance of endogenous influences within the electoral arena—
derives from the fact that the inferences drawn from the seminal work
in political behavior confirmed the less systematic observations that had
accumulated since the onset of the Industrial Revolution. Beginning in the
late 1960s a number of revisionist scholars began to challenge this enduring image of democratic citizens. Much of this revisionist work was done
in the field of voting behavior, and most of it fit comfortably within the
framework of the Michigan model that guided so much of the early work.[1]

---

[1] The most important exceptions include spatial models derived from the rational choice
tradition and the emerging work in political psychology. Also relevant is the earlier literature
on partisan realignments. The literature on partisan realignments is not a challenge to the
Michigan model as much as it is a set of studies that focus on the consequences an extreme
set of conditions for partisan attachments. Moreover, much of this literature is based on
macro-level data and/or theorizing. A more current set of macro-level work that qualifies

Most revisionist scholars have challenged neither the model's core concepts nor the individual-level, survey research paradigm that has dominated voting research since the late 1940s. Rather, they have merely used innovative approaches to the analysis of survey data to reassess the significance of exogenous factors on voting. Or they have used survey data to question the strength ascribed to, or the interpretation given to the role of, partisan identification.[2]

That these revisionist scholars have been largely unsuccessful in dislodging the conventional wisdom concerning popular efficacy is aptly demonstrated by Fiorina's reflections (1981: 10), the more recent observations of Lupia and McCubbins (1998: 1) as well as the preface to *The Macro Polity* (Erikson, MacKuen, et al. 2002). The durability of the "manageable fools" conception of voters may reflect the fact that the scholarly consensus on this point is empirically well grounded. If so, we need to look elsewhere to explain the paradox of elected officials (i.e., to the psychological makeup and belief systems of public office seekers). On the other hand, the inability of revisionists to dislodge the conventional wisdom on popular efficacy may be due to theoretical and methodological shortcomings.

While the Michigan model has been at the core of much work on voting behavior, it is unlikely to have adversely affected research bearing on popular efficacy. The Michigan model is a broad, inclusive, and adaptable conceptual framework that has undergone extensive empirical examination. Moreover, despite the inferences drawn from repeated applications of the model, it is inherently agnostic on matters most relevant to popular efficacy: the durability of endogenous factors and the relative importance of endogenous and exogenous influences on electoral decisions. The authors of *The American Voter* unquestionably conclude that an endogenous factor, party identification, is the most important determinant of voting behavior. However, their discussions of party identification's role in voting are replete with equivocations that give rise to musings such as those included in the epigraph to this chapter.

More problematic with respect to inferences about popular efficacy is the individual-level, survey research paradigm that underlies most re-

---

as an exception here is the recent longitudinal work that uses aggregated survey data (Wright, Erikson et al. 1985; Wright, Erikson, et al. 1987; MacKuen, Erikson, et al. 1989; MacKuen, Erikson, et al. 1992; Erikson, Wright, et al. 1993; Erikson, MacKuen, et al. 2002).

[2] For example, the minimal role ascribed to short-term factors in voting has been challenged by the literature on issue voting, economic voting, and the impact of candidate evaluations (see Niemi and Weisberg, 1993a and 1993b for citations to, and a review of, these bodies of literature). The strength of partisanship, and its conceptualization as the "unmoved mover," has been challenged in a series of works that view self-designated partisan identifications as being influenced by short-term factors (Jackson 1975; Page and Jones 1979; Fiorina 1981; Franklin and Jackson 1983).

search on voting. Its reliance on survey instruments administered to random samples of the national electorate is extremely valuable for some purposes. But surveys have glaring deficiencies when it comes to studying electoral change. This is problematic because, as noted in chapter 1, the dynamics of electoral change are an important source of inferences about popular efficacy. While survey designs optimize the researcher's capacity to collect data on individual respondents and gauge individual-level relationships, *most of the factors that drive electoral change lie outside the individual* (see figure 3–2).

A related point here is that survey designs do not do a good job in gauging the dimensions of electoral change that are essential to generating inferences about popular efficacy: magnitude, duration, and geographic scope. To illustrate this point it is helpful to use a camera metaphor. Survey research, like a high-quality 35mm camera, can produce a refined snapshot of a set of voters at a point in time. But a 35mm camera is not a movie camera, and its capacity to capture change cannot compare with that of a movie camera. Indeed, unless a survey instrument is deployed in a panel study, it cannot accurately detect departures from normal voting behavior, much less gauge the magnitude, duration, or geographic scope of those departures. Moreover, unless a panel study covers decades, it is unlikely to include sufficient variation in exogenous events to generate a meaningful assessment of their electoral impact.

Another problem with using survey designs to study electoral change derives from their relatively recent vintage: the number of snapshots that can be assembled to craft an image of electoral change is limited to the post–World War Two era. Moreover, the longest series of quality survey snapshots available to portray electoral change has a national focus. This inhibits the identification of crosscutting trends and offsetting electoral pulses at the subnational level, thereby obscuring variations in the geographic scope of electoral change that were so central in the transformational model presented in chapter 3.

These problems combine to seriously compromise the utility of survey-based research to detect electoral change and to gauge accurately the relative importance of exogenous and endogenous factors in the generation of electoral change. These methodological deficiencies have affected scholarly judgments about the ability of voters to overcome the centripetal pulls of partisanship, which has had profound implications for the inferences that have been drawn about popular efficacy. Bartels captures the essence of these methodological deficiencies in some recent comments on the contributions of the survey research paradigm to electoral research:

> While this scholarly development has produced an unusually rich and technically proficient body of political research, it has also encouraged a sort of

provincialism, in which the totality of electoral politics is sometimes too readily equated with the psychology of voting behavior in the dozen U.S. presidential elections since 1952. Apparent changes within this fairly narrow compass are taken as reflections of momentous social or political transformations, while apparent continuities are taken as evidence of the way things have always been and will always be. What is one to make of a scholarly literature in which successive decades have witnessed the unveiling of *The American Voter* (Campbell, Converse et al. 1960), *The Changing American Voter* (Nie, Verba et al. 1976), *The Unchanging American Voter* (Smith 1989), and *The New American Voter* (Miller and Shanks 1996)? (Bartels 1998: 302)

Because the deficiencies of survey-based research compromise a potentially important source of inferences about popular efficacy, I use a very different research design. It is a longitudinal, subnational design that uses local electorates as the unit of analysis. The approach developed here is not intended to supplant survey designs in the study of electoral behavior, only to supplement them. Macro-level analyses of political behavior using a long time frame have their own shortcomings, which are rooted in the ecological fallacy and data limitations. These problems notwithstanding, political scientists have not been sufficiently aggressive in developing the potential of aggregate time-series data in addressing questions that are at the core of the discipline. Many inferences about key issues in empirical democratic theory can be drawn without committing the ecological fallacy. Moreover, diligent archival research and creative measurement techniques can generate empirical measures of key concepts that, in many cases, are of comparable quality to measures produced by survey techniques. In some cases the availability of a historical dimension can generate better measures.

The next section introduces the conceptual and methodological foundations of the approach used here. The second section presents some illustrative data generated by this approach. These data are used to demonstrate the connection between the research design developed here and the study of popular efficacy.

REEXAMINING THE CONVENTIONAL WISDOM CONCERNING POPULAR EFFICACY: A THEORETICAL AND METHODOLOGICAL REFORMULATION

To overcome the methodological deficiencies of the reigning paradigm in electoral research, it is necessary to operate outside of that paradigm, but not independently of it. Thus, the macro-level empirical analyses rest on conceptual foundations derived from the Michigan model, an individual-level model of voting behavior that has withstood substantial empirical scrutiny by survey researchers for nearly half a century. The Michigan model is essential to this reevaluation. It provides the conceptual basis for dealing with the most powerful endogenous influence within the electoral arena during the time frame of this study: voters' partisan attachments.

As argued in earlier chapters, these partisan influences dull the evaluative capacities of citizens by tainting the information shortcuts they use in processing data on exogenous events. To integrate the effects of these exogenous phenomena into a macro-level analysis, I incorporate core Michigan concepts into a *model of the local electorate*. I operationalize this model using a longitudinal, subnational research design. The structure of this research design is as important to this reassessment of popular efficacy as the Michigan-based model of the local electorate. *Its capacity to produce a more precise estimate of the relative importance of exogenous and endogenous influences on electoral behavior is the key to generating new, empirically based insights into popular efficacy.*

The study time frame adopted in this design, 1828–2000, is the longest time frame that could have been used while holding constant the primary source of endogenous influences on voting behavior, mass-based political parties. As such, it maximizes the likelihood of capturing exogenous events capable of overcoming the inertial inattention of citizens, piercing their perceptual barriers, and overpowering endogenous influences. Included within this time frame are several major societal transformations (the rise of a commercial economy, religious reawakenings, transportation revolutions, the integration of the frontier, the industrial revolution, waves of immigration, urbanization, the emergence of postindustrial society, the beginnings of a global economy, etc.). It also includes a variety of more discrete transformative events (a civil war, two world wars, a major depression, the civil rights movement, etc.) and a number of presidential scandals and missteps.

Another important feature of 1828–2000 time frame is its inclusiveness. It spans virtually the entire "democratic era" in American politics (i.e., the period characterized by more inclusive suffrage, broader popular participation, and mass-based political parties). This inclusiveness will strengthen the inferences drawn from the empirical analyses. Finally, the lengthy time frame adopted here produces important methodological benefits. It is far easier to generate accurate estimates of normal voting patterns using forty-four elections than fifteen or twenty elections. This advantage, of course, is important in differentiating between exogenous and endogenous influences on electoral behavior.

The methodological benefits derived from the longitudinal design used here are enhanced by its subnational focus. The adoption of a subnational focus was motivated by skepticism that national electoral patterns can accurately reflect electoral realities in a geo-politically diverse nation such as the United States. As noted in the discussion of the transformational model presented in chapter 3, exogenous events are likely to interact with the diverse constituencies that makeup the U.S. body politic, producing electoral reactions that differ across spatial units. This means that a national focus will dilute subnational effects, mask crosscutting electoral trends, and obscure offsetting deviations from those trends. Correspondingly, "unpacking" national electoral data offers the potential for new insights into popular efficacy. The potential for enduring and well-grounded insights is enhanced by the fact that the spatial reach of this study is as encompassing as its temporal reach. It includes all counties and most major cities in the continental United States (over 3,000 local units across 44 elections; over 110,000 observations).

In the next section I introduce a model of the local electorate. Then I describe the data archive I used to operationalize it. In the last section I outline the approach used to capture the impact of endogenous influences on local electoral behavior.

## A Model of the Local Electorate

The model of the local electorate I use to structure the empirical analyses derives from a view of individual-level voting behavior in which habit plays a dominant role during periods of political normalcy. This view of political behavior dates to the turn of the century (Wallas 1909) and is at the heart of the Michigan model of voting. Its basic tenets have been supported by decades of NES analysis. Habitual behavior within the electoral arena affects both the decision to vote as well as vote choice. This leads to the expectation that temporal electoral patterns for local electorates will be both well structured and relatively stable.

The role of habit in shaping the decision to vote is articulated in the earliest and most influential work in the Michigan tradition, *The American Voter* (Campbell et al., 1960: chap. 5). "It is plausible to think of voting as a type of conduct that is somewhat habitual and to suppose that as the individual develops a general orientation toward politics he comes to incorporate either voting or non-voting as part of his normal behavior. Certainly we have found a pronounced association between what people tell us their past behavior has been and whether they vote in the elections we have studied"(1960: 92). Miller and Shanks, in one of the most exhaustive analyses of the presidential data produced by the NES, suggest that the view of the electorate initially articulated in *The American Voter* has been unshaken by subsequent empirical research:"We have concluded that the population of the United States includes a range of citizens extending from the regular voters (I never miss an election even if I have to

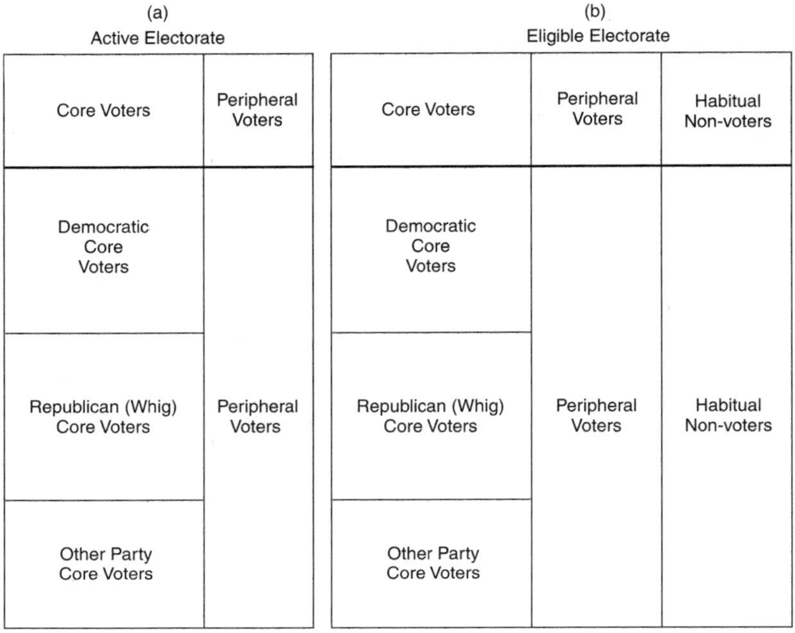

|  | (a)<br>Active Electorate |  |  | (b)<br>Eligible Electorate |  |
|---|---|---|---|---|---|

| Core Voters | Peripheral<br>Voters | Core Voters | Peripheral<br>Voters | Habitual<br>Non-voters |
|---|---|---|---|---|
| Democratic<br>Core<br>Voters |  | Democratic<br>Core<br>Voters |  |  |
| Republican (Whig)<br>Core Voters | Peripheral<br>Voters | Republican (Whig)<br>Core Voters | Peripheral<br>Voters | Habitual<br>Non-voters |
| Other Party<br>Core Voters |  | Other Party<br>Core Voters |  |  |

Figure 5–1. Components of the Local Electorate 1828–2000

vote absentee) to persistent non-voters who have never voted—and include some in between who are erratic, sometime-participants across any series of elections" (1996:17).

Voting research in the Michigan tradition suggests that the habitual component to electoral behavior is as strong in the case of vote choice as it is in the decision to vote. The most basic and stable political attitude among U.S. voters is their partisan identification, and party identification is the strongest determinant of the vote. Thus, the core electorate (that component comprised of citizens who "never miss an election") can usefully be thought of as being composed of well-structured partisan constituencies. The stability in temporal voting patterns generated by habitual behavior forms the basis for the concept of a normal vote (Converse 1966).

The basic categorizations of citizens that flow from the Michigan model can be extended to the counties and cities that form the units of analysis for this study. The eligible voters within these local electoral units can be divided into three groups: core voters, peripheral voters, and habitual nonvoters (see figure 5–1). It is expected that core voters have both stronger partisan attachments and deeper convictions about the importance and utility of voting than do habitual nonvoters and peripheral voters. Peripheral voters, along with the less committed partisans, make up a good deal of the "swing vote" that produces electoral perturbations. Core voters can be further subdivided into partisan constituencies that form a party's electoral base. It is also important to think about these basic voter groups in terms of both the active electorate (core voters and peripheral voters), which is depicted in figure 5–1(a); and the total electorate (core voters, peripheral voters, habitual nonvoters), which is depicted in figure 5–1 (b). This differentiation is important for the purpose of deriving normal vote estimates and for understanding the dynamics of electoral change (Anderson 1979).

### Profiling Local Electorates: The Historical Data Archive

To capitalize on the analytic potential of a longitudinal, subnational design I collected, cleaned, and assimilated a large amount of data on local electorates. I organized them by electoral unit for each year in which there was a presidential election (Westchester County, New York in 1856; Chicago, Illinois in 1972, etc.). The most important data collected fell into one of four categories: electoral, demographic, performance, and partisan. Electoral data for all of the elections and electoral units encompassed in this study were required to operationalize the various voter categories embodied in figure 5–1. Data were needed on the social composition of local electorates to help understand variations, over time or across electoral units, in the electoral partitions reflected in figure 5–1 (the core electorate, the Democratic electoral base, the Republican electoral base, etc.). Performance data on matters that affect core political desires (economic growth, price stability, years of peace, war deaths, crime, etc.) were needed to gauge electoral reactions to political stewardship. Finally, data on partisan settings and activities are important in understanding the interplay between exogenous and endogenous influences. In order to integrate these diverse bodies of data into a common archive a set of identifier variables had to be collected (county or city, state, year, etc.).

Data on presidential voting are available for the entire period, as are a good deal of demographic data (population, age distributions, immigrant populations, racial and gender breakdowns, etc.). Also, data are available for part of the 1828–2000 time frame on the distribution of religious affiliations (twenty-one religions, mostly since 1850) and ethnicities (twenty-eight ethnicities, mostly since 1870).[3] The availability of data on

---

[3] With the exception of population and voting age population, the data on the demographic variables ends with the 1990 census. I have had to extrapolate these variables to generate values beyond 1990; all other year-estimates are the result of interpolations. While I am comfortable with extrapolating the 1990 data to 1992, I am not comfortable going beyond 1992.

stewardship varies by domain (economic performance, war and peace, personal security). But, with one exception, some data sources exist for the entire time frame. Finally, data on partisan settings and activities are available from 1835 on. Detailing the procedures used to assemble the historical data archive (data sources, missing data problems, integration and interpolation problems, estimation of city data, etc.) would be quite tedious and too disruptive to report in the text. Hence, I describe the structure of the data archive in appendix I, available at *http://www.pol .uiuc.edu/nardulliresearch.html*. The core variables available in the archive are reported in table 5–1; chapter 8 discusses the data on performance and partisan settings and activities in more detail.

### *Habitual Behavior and Normal Voting Patterns: Gauging Endogenous Influences*

Capturing the inertial effects of habitual behavior and the centripetal pulls of enduring partisan attachments is central to this effort. These theoretical constructs lie at the heart of the various electoral partitions embodied in figure 5–1. These partitions can be operationalized using the concept of a normal vote (Converse 1966) in conjunction with the electoral time-series outlined above. Following Converse (13), the approach I adopt to estimating normal voting patterns relies on the use of multielection averages. Thus, the average proportion of the eligible electorate that actually votes across a series of elections is assumed to provide a good estimate of the size of a local electorate's *core voter partition*; the average proportion of the core electorate that supports the Democrats is assumed to provide a good estimate of the size of the Democrats' electoral base; the average proportion of the core electorate that supports the Republicans is assumed to provide a good estimate of the size of the Republicans' electoral base, and so forth.

The normal partisan vote estimates derived here will be used to represent endogenous influences upon electoral behavior.[4] When examined over time and compared with the actual votes, the normal voting patterns of local electorates will provide the basis for gauging the impact of, and interplay between, endogenous and exogenous factors on electoral behav-

---

[4] This is somewhat at odds with corollary C1, which holds that "*Citizens' existing political predispositions, including their normal voting behavior, are grounded in satisficing judgments that these predispositions are serving their core political desires.*" Conceding here that normal voting routines are determined by endogenous influences, rather that asserting that these routines are grounded in updated judgments about party positions and actions, is part of a conscious strategy to be conservative in drawing inferences about popular efficacy from the macro-level empirical analyses. Thus, inferences about popular efficacy will be drawn only on the basis of departures from normal voting patterns, viewing these patterns as being the manifestation of endogenous influences. More will be said about this inconsistency in chapter 6, which sheds some light on why this is a conservative strategy.

TABLE 5.1
Summary of Historical Data Archive

| Variable Category | Variable Name |
|---|---|
| **Electoral Variables** | |
| Raw Presidential Vote Variables | ELIGIBLE VOTERS |
| | TOTAL VOTES |
| | DEMOCRATIC VOTES |
| | REPUBLICAN VOTES |
| | OTHER VOTES |
| Derivative Vote Variables Based on the Total Number of Votes Cast | DEMOCRATIC PROPORTION$^V$ |
| | REPUBLICAN PROPORTION$^V$ |
| | OTHER PROPORTION$^V$ |
| | MARGIN OF VICTORY (DEMOCRATIC PROPORTION$^V$– REPUBLICAN PROPORTION$^V$) |
| Derivative Vote Variables Based on the Total Number of Eligible Voters | DEMOCRATIC PROPORTION$^E$ |
| | REPUBLICAN PROPORTION$^E$ |
| | OTHER PROPORTION$^E$ |
| | TURNOUT (TOTAL VOTES/ ELIGIBLE VOTERS) |
| **Identifier and Place Variables** | |
| Identifier Variables | STATE POSTAL CODE, STATE FIPS CODE, STATE ICPSR CODE, COUNTY NAME, COUNTY FIPS CODE, COUNTY ICPSR CODE |
| Place Variables | LOCALE TYPE: URBAN$_1$, URBAN$_2$, SUBURBAN$_1$, SUBURBAN$_2$, SMALL TOWN, RURAL |
| | SECTION: NEW ENGLAND, MIDDLE ATLANTIC, SOUTH, BORDER, MIDWEST, PLAINS, MOUNTAIN, WEST COAST |
| **Demographic Variables** | |
| Basic Demographic Characteristics (measured as a percentage of the total unit population; most available since 1828) | POPULATION, DENSITY, WHITE, AFRICAN AMERICAN, OTHER RACE, FEMALE, FOREIGN BORN, FOREIGN BORN PARENTS |
| Religious Affiliation (Measured as a percentage of the total unit population; most available since 1850) | ADVENTIST, BAPTIST, CHRISTIAN SCIENTIST, DISCIPLES OF CHRIST, DUTCH REFORMED, ORTHODOX, EPISCOPALIAN, JEWISH, LUTHERAN, MENNONITE, METHODIST, MORAVIAN, MORMON, OTHERS, PENTECOSTAL, PRESBYTERIAN, QUAKER, ROMAN CATHOLIC, SPIRITUALIST, CONGREGATIONALIST, UNITARIAN |
| Ethnic Composition (Measured as a percentage of the total unit population; most available since 1870) | AUSTRIA, BELGIUM/LUXEMBURG, CANADA/ENGLISH, CANADA/FRENCH, CUBA/WEST INDIES, CZECHSLOVAKIA, DENMARK. ENGLAND, FINLAND, FRANCE, GERMANY, GREECE, HUNGARY, IRELAND, ITALY, MEXICO, NETHERLANDS, NORWAY, POLAND, ROMANIA, SCOTLAND, SOUTH AMERICA, SPAIN, SWEDEN, SWITZERLAND, TURKEY, USSR, WALES |
| Summary Ethnic Composition Variables | NORTHERN EUROPEAN, SOUTHERN EUROPEAN, EASTERN EUROPEAN, SCANDINAVIAN |
| Performance Indicators | Δ RGDP, DEFLATION RATE$_0$, INFLATION RATE$_0$, WAR DEATHS, UNPOPULAR WAR, YEARS OF PEACE, UCR CRIME INDEX, Δ UCR CRIME INDEX |
| Derivative Political Setting Variables | STATE PARTY DOMINANCE, STATE PARTY COMPETITIVENESS |

ior. Because of the theoretical centrality of endogenous influences on voting, the averaging procedures used to estimate normal voting patterns are crucial to the validity of the inferences drawn from the empirical analyses. In adopting an averaging process to generate normal vote estimates, three types of exogenously generated threats to inertial and centripetal forces had to be considered: electoral perturbations, secular changes in voting trends, and critical changes in normal voting patterns.

*Electoral perturbations* are election-specific blips in long-term voting trends. Exogenous factors such as economic fluctuations, crime rates, wars, and scandals can generate these perturbations, as can endogenous factors such as partisan campaign tactics and strategies. As noted in chapter 3, *secular changes* in voting trends are slow, incremental shifts in central tendencies. They can be generated by a wide variety of factors: diffuse reactions to exogenous events and/or the drift of party platforms; differences in generational replacement rates (Democratic families with higher birth rates than Republican families); population migration patterns (greater mobility on the part of Republican adherents); the differential experiences of emerging voter cohorts (younger voters coming of age in a Democratic era); and life-cycle changes in the habitual behavior of some members of the local electorate (moving from labor to management, becoming unemployed). *Critical changes* in normal voting patterns are sharp, enduring changes that fundamentally reconfigure local electorates. These changes are generated only by a series of related and reinforcing exogenous events rooted in a common exogenous development, such as a fundamental societal transformation, a major economic crisis, or a deeply rooted moral conflict.

For reasons developed in chapter 3, all three of these factors had to be considered in the derivation of normal voting patterns. The reconfigurations that accompany critical change define distinct electoral eras in the history of local electorates. It is only possible to define normal voting patterns within these electoral eras; the definition of "normal" varies across the discontinuities that define them. Within those electoral eras secular change is possible and electoral perturbations are likely. Thus, to identify normal voting patterns within electoral eras, the electoral returns must be shorn of the effects of electoral perturbations, without obscuring whatever secular change may be unfolding. If this is done properly, normal voting patterns should reveal (1) clearly demarcated electoral eras and (2) smooth trends within electoral eras.

To address these theoretical/methodological considerations, I devised a modified, multistage moving average procedure. I applied it to two sets of electoral proportion variables: DEMOCRATIC PROPORTION$^V$, REPUBLICAN (WHIG) PROPORTION$^V$, OTHER PARTY PROPORTION$^V$ and DEMOCRATIC PROPORTION$^E$, REPUBLICAN (WHIG) PROPORTION$^E$, OTHER PARTY PROPOR-

TION[E], TURNOUT[5]. This procedure generated normal vote estimates for the various partitions depicted in figure 5–1. A *moving average* procedure was adopted to allow for the possibility of within-era secular change. A *modified* moving average process was used because the moving average process had to deal with the effects of outlier elections and it had to be conducted within electoral eras (i.e., time frames demarcated by critical elections). A *multistage process* was used to insure that the specification of electoral orders (outlier elections, critical elections) used in the moving average procedure was comparable across units.

It was a significant methodological challenge to derive both valid and reliable normal vote estimates for over 3,000 electoral units across a 172-year period, a challenge that required nearly 15,000 executions of the moving average program. To meet this challenge I had to use both existing knowledge about electoral history and interim results produced by the moving average procedure (statistics, graphic displays). Results from earlier iterations of the procedure made it possible to create concrete criteria to use in specifying electoral orders (i.e., how big a perturbation had to be in order to be considered an outlier; how large an enduring break had to be to be considered a realignment). These criteria were used in generating the final version of the normal vote estimates. The details of the moving average procedure for local electorates are described in appendix II, which is available at *http://www.pol.uiuc.edu/nardulliresearch.html*. Appendix II also includes validity and reliability analyses. The normal vote variables derived from the moving average procedure map onto the partitions of the local electorate as depicted in figure 5–2. State and national normal vote estimates were produced using essentially the same protocol used at the local level.[6]

## NORMAL VOTING PATTERNS AND THE STUDY OF POPULAR EFFICACY

This section introduces the normal vote estimates produced by the moving average procedure and demonstrates how they relate to the study of popular efficacy. The first section reports the results of an election-by-election analysis of the correspondence between actual votes and normal votes to show that the approach adopted here represents a conservative effort to

---

[5] Throughout this work I will frequently refer to the Whig/Republican component of local electorates as the Republican component. However, all entries prior to 1856 are the Whig proportion of the electorate.

[6] Because the state and national data were far less "noisy" than the local data, they required only two iterations of the moving average procedure; the local data required three. The only other difference in the protocols was that "outlier" elections were defined at those whose deviation from preliminary normal vote estimates was greater than or equal to .20, rather than .30. This, again, was due to the existence of less noise in the state and national data.

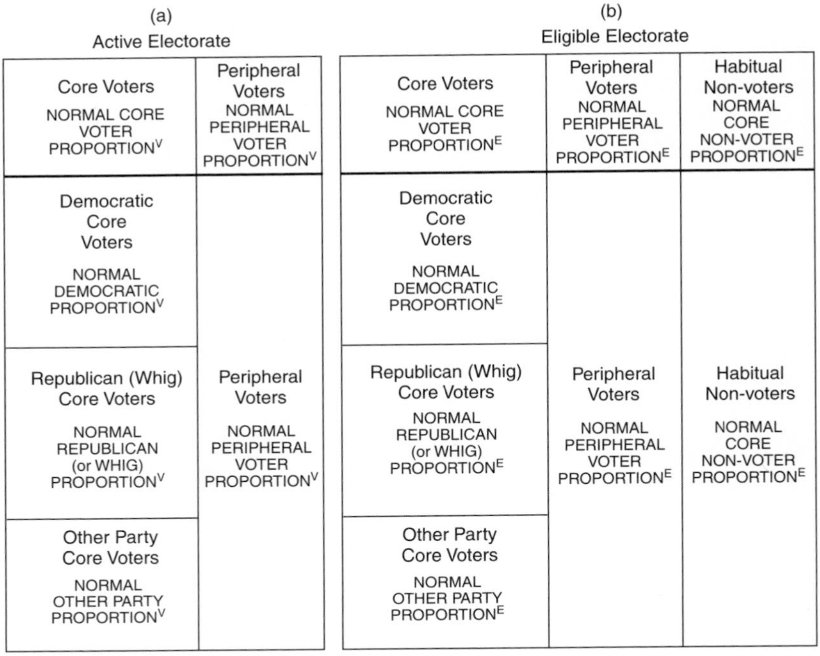

Figure 5–2. The Normal Vote Variables and the Components of the Local Electorate

reexamine the conventional wisdom about popular efficacy. The second section presents illustrative normal voting patterns from three counties with very different electoral histories. It uses these examples to introduce a set of variables that will be used in the empirical analyses and explains how they can be used to gauge electoral independence and electoral competitiveness. The third section uses the illustrative county data to provide a concrete discussion of how the data generated here can be used to generate fresh insights into popular efficacy.

## The Role of Partisan Influences in Historical Perspective: Normal Votes and Actual Votes

The averaging procedure described in appendix II maximizes the amount of variance in election returns that can be attributed to endogenous factors—while still providing a valid operationalization of the notion of a normal vote. Thus, it represents a decidedly conservative approach to challenging the conventional wisdom about popular efficacy (chap. 2, n.2). Because normal voting patterns are viewed as the manifestation of en-

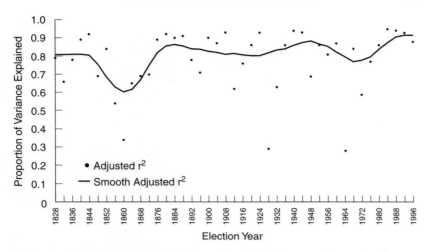

Figure 5–3. Correlation between Normal Partisan Balance and Margin of Victory

dogenous influences on voting, it is possible to demonstrate the dominant role of partisanship in by correlating MARGIN OF VICTORY with NORMAL PARTISAN BALANCE. Figure 5–3 reports this correlation (weighted by TOTAL VOTES) for each local election from 1828 to 2000. In addition to the $r^2$'s, figure 5–3 displays a moving average for the $r^2$'s.[7] The moving average is helpful in identifying both historical patterns and outlier elections.

As is evident in figure 5–3, the moving average is generally quite high. Indeed, it falls below .8 in only two time spans (1848 to 1872, 1972–76). The moving average hovers at around .8 in the pre-1848 period, then drops to the .6 to .75 range during the period around the Civil War (1848 to 1872). From 1876 to 1924, a period generally associated with the height of the party era, the moving average generally exceeds .8. There is a slight decline over the 1876–1924 period, but it is due solely to the effects of a handful of turbulent elections: 1892, 1896, 1912, and 1916. Excluding those four elections, the average correlation for the 1876–1924

[7] To capture the underlying patterns in the correlations I used a multiwave application of a moving average procedure, similar to the approach I used in the derivation of the normal vote variables (see chapter 4 and appendix II). Here I used a two-wave application. To smooth out the variations in the data, I used a five-election moving average in the first wave. In this first application I excluded the elections of 1928 and 1964 because they distorted the trend line in an egregious manner. I did not exclude 1860, even though it was almost as low as 1928 and 1964, because it was at the bottom of a trough; keeping it in the calculations did not misrepresent the distribution of the raw data. In the second wave I used a three-election moving average because it did a better job in preserving the period-specific contours that were evident after the first application of the moving average procedure.

period is .9. The correlations for 1928 and 1932 are significantly below the .9 level (.29 and .63, respectively). However, in the aftermath of the New Deal realignment, the $R^2$'s return to the .9 range. Beginning in 1948 the moving average shows a decline that continues through the 1970s, with outlier elections in 1948, 1964, and 1972. This decline reverses itself in 1980; the $r^2$'s average .94 for the elections held after 1980.

It is not a monumental achievement to calculate the moving average (NORMAL PARTISAN BALANCE) for a dependent variable (MARGIN OF VICTORY), correlate them, and generate high correlation coefficients—even correlations in the .9 range. The point of this exercise is simply to illustrate that the inferences to be drawn about popular efficacy using a macro-level, normal vote approach are not inconsistent with one of the most well established findings in survey-based voting research. Partisan influences are a strong determinant of voting behavior and have been for a long time. The argument here is simply that the documentation of strong partisan influences, by itself, is an insufficient basis for generating valid inferences about popular efficacy. The next section will illustrate the approach to be used in demonstrating how those inferences will be drawn. This conservative nature of this approach, in conjunction with the scope and reach of the empirical analysis, will enhance the strength and durability of the inferences that can be drawn from the empirical analyses reported in chapter 7 through chapter 9.[8]

### Normal Voting Patterns, Electoral Independence, and Electoral Competitiveness

Figures 5–4 through 5–6 illustrate electoral profiles for three counties with very different normal voting patterns: Greene County, Indiana; Oxford County, Maine; and Lewis County, New York. Displayed in these figures are two derivative variables that will be used throughout the remainder of this book: MARGIN OF VICTORY and NORMAL PARTISAN BALANCE.[9] The dark continuous lines in figure 5–4 through figure 5–6 are the

---

[8] I should also note that the definition of short-term effects used here is a conservative measure of these effects. It is not uncommon to measure short-term effects by calculating interelection swings. In the vast majority of cases the "interelection swing" approach will produce a short-term effect that is considerably larger than the "deviation from the normal vote" approach. Only in cases where two consecutive elections are above (or below) the normal vote trend line can the "interelection swing" approach possibly produce a smaller short-term effect than the approach adopted here.

[9] The derivation of these variables is as follows:

MARGIN OF VICTORY = DEMOCRATIC PROPORTION$^V$ – REPUBLICAN PROPORTION$^V$

NORMAL PARTISAN BALANCE = NORMAL DEMOCRATIC PROPORTION$^V$

NORMAL REPUBLICAN PROPORTION$^V$

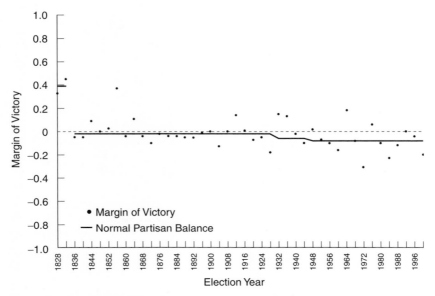

Figure 5–4. Normal Partisan Balance and Margin of Victory, Greene County, IN, 1828–2000.

values of the NORMAL PARTISAN BALANCE variable; they depict the normal vote trend lines. The dots are the values of the MARGIN OF VICTORY variable; they represent the actual returns for a given election. The breaks in the normal vote trend lines represent critical realignments; a critical election is the election that initiates a critical realignment. The more gradual changes in normal vote trend lines represent periods of secular change; flat trend lines indicate periods of electoral stability. The differences between the lines and the dots represent electoral perturbations.

The dashed line at the 0 point on the vertical axes in figures 5–4 through figure 5–6 separates the geometric space encompassed by the graph into a "Democratic" and a "Whig/Republican" sphere. Dots above the 0 line indicate a Democratic victory for a particular election; dots below the 0 line indicate a Whig/Republican victory. The greater the distance between the dots and the 0 line, the greater the victory. The normal vote trend lines above the dashed 0 line indicate a normally Democratic electorate;

The structure of this derivation means that positive values of MARGIN OF VICTORY indicate a Democratic plurality in a locale; negative values indicate a Republican or Whig plurality. Positive values of NORMAL PARTISAN BALANCE indicate a "normally" Democratic locale; negative values indicate a "normally" Republican or Whig locale.

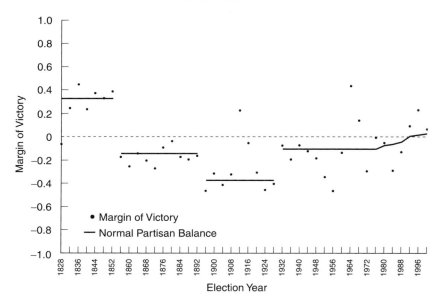

Figure 5–5. Normal Partisan Balance and Margin of Victory, Oxford County, ME, 1828–2000

those below the 0 line indicate a normally Republican electorate (Whig before 1856).

I rely heavily on the MARGIN OF VICTORY and NORMAL PARTISAN BALANCE variables for two reasons. The first is their efficiency; the second is their centrality to the study of popular efficacy. The MARGIN OF VICTORY and NORMAL PARTISAN BALANCE variables are efficient because they succinctly capture information on electoral outcomes and the partisan makeup of local electorates. For the vast majority of elections (i.e., those in which third parties do not capture a plurality of the vote), MARGIN OF VICTORY provides information on both the electoral outcome and the magnitude of the victory. NORMAL PARTISAN BALANCE captures the relative size of the two major party electoral bases (see figure 5–2 [a]). These variables are central to the study of popular efficacy because they can be used to gauge electoral competitiveness and two forms of electoral change that define electoral independence: enduring change in normal vote trend lines and electoral perturbations (election-specific deviations from normal voting patterns).

### ELECTORAL COMPETITIVENESS

The absolute value of NORMAL PARTISAN BALANCE is a measure of *electoral competitiveness*; the smaller the absolute value, the more competi-

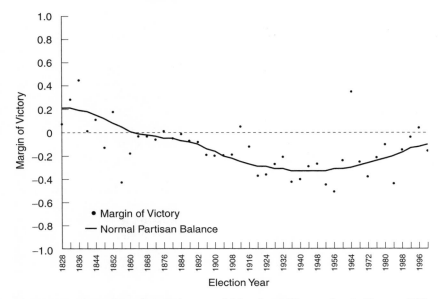

Figure 5–6. Normal Partisan Balance and Margin of Victory, Lewis County, NY, 1828–2000.

tive the electoral setting. Electoral competitiveness is depicted in figure 5–4 through figure 5–6 by the distance between the normal vote trend line and the 0 line: the smaller the distance, the greater the competitiveness of the electoral setting. The distance between these two lines can be thought of as either the dominant party's "comfort margin" or the minority party's "normal vote deficit." The political importance of shifts in and departures from normal vote trend lines is gauged in reference to these comfort margins and normal vote deficits because electoral shifts affect electoral outcomes only when they eliminate these margins/deficits. Moreover, when the absolute value of the NORMAL PARTISAN BALANCE variable is less than .03, a dominant party cannot be said to exist. That is, neither party can be said to enjoy an electoral advantage derived from the relative size of its electoral base. The rationale underlying this .03 criterion is outlined in chapter 9 (Table 9–1); it is rooted in the average size of electoral perturbations. Because of the tenuousness of small comfort margins, when the absolute value of the NORMAL PARTISAN BALANCE variable is less than .03, the electoral setting is said to be competitive.

### ELECTORAL INDEPENDENCE

As noted earlier, electoral independence is defined here by changes in and deviations from normal voting patterns. The first set of changes reflect enduring electoral change, the second reflect short-term electoral change. Enduring electoral change is defined as the interelection differences in NORMAL PARTISAN BALANCE. The incidence of enduring electoral change is a reflection of the durability of partisan forces.[10] The durability of partisan influences is less when the incidence of enduring electoral change is great. The flatter and more continuous the normal vote trend line, the greater the durability of local partisan attachments. There are two types of enduring electoral change that are relevant to the study of popular efficacy: critical changes (large, enduring shifts in normal voting patterns) and periods of secular change (small, incremental shifts in normal voting patterns).[11]

An electoral perturbation for a specific election is defined simply as the difference between NORMAL PARTISAN BALANCE and MARGIN OF VICTORY for that election.[12] Electoral perturbations speak to the power of centripetal partisan pulls in the electoral arena. Centripetal pulls are less powerful when large electoral perturbations are routine. The tighter the distribution of actual electoral returns around the normal vote trend line, the greater the centripetal pull of partisan attachments.

---

[10] The root measure of enduring electoral change I use throughout this work is a differenced version of NORMAL PARTISAN BALANCE:

$$\text{PARTISAN BALANCE}_{\text{DIF1}}^{\text{NORMAL}} = \text{PARTISAN BALANCE}_{\text{T1}}^{\text{NORMAL}} - \text{PARTISAN BALANCE}_{\text{T0}}^{\text{NORMAL}}$$

The NORMAL PARTISAN BALANCE$_{\text{DIF1}}$ variable is a continuous variable that captures temporal, interelection differences in NORMAL PARTISAN BALANCE. Its theoretical range is from $-1$ to $1$.

[11] The rule of thumb used to identify critical realignments was a 20-point break in the values of the NORMAL PARTISAN BALANCE variable. The procedures used to define critical changes are reported in tables II–2 and II–4 of appendix II, which is available at *http://www.pol.uiuc.edu/nardulliresearch.html*. The procedures used to identify periods of secular change and to create a categorical variable termed ENDURING CHANGE are described in appendix III, available at *http://www.pol.uiuc.edu/nardulliresearch.html*. The rule of thumb here was that five small, but directionally consistent, changes in the NORMAL PARTISAN BALANCE variable had to exist for a period of secular change to be defined. Each unit-election on the ENDURING CHANGE variable is coded as being (1) a critical election, (2) part of a period of secular change, or (3) part of a stable electoral period.

[12] To measure electoral perturbations I created a deviation variable:

$$\text{PARTISAN BALANCE}_{\text{DEV}}^{\text{NORMAL}} = \text{OF VICTORY}^{\text{MARGIN}} - \text{PARTISAN BALANCE}^{\text{NORMAL}}$$

The PARTISAN BALANCE$_{\text{DEV}}$ variable is a continuous variable that captures the differences between the actual margin of victory in a unit-election and the expected margin of victory. The absolute value of most of these deviations ranged between 0 and 20 points (80 percent); 90 percent ranged between 0 and 30 points. The mean is 13 points (SD = .14). However, there was a good deal of variation in the average size of these deviations across electoral units. Over 20 percent of the counties and cities had *average* deviations that were 10 points or smaller; almost 12 percent had *average* deviations that exceeded 16 points.

To further elucidate the concept of electoral independence, the data depicted in figures 5–4 through 5–6 will used to illustrate three types of disequilibrating elections: realigning elections, deviating elections, and endorsement elections. More rigorous definitions of these elections will be provided in chapter 9. For present purposes, however, they can be thought of in the following terms:

- *Realigning elections* are those critical elections in which the shift in the normal vote trend line is large enough to either create a new majority party or, at the very least, eliminate the electoral advantage of the ex ante majority party (i.e., create a competitive electoral setting). Thus, for a realigning election to occur, two conditions must be met. First, a critical election must occur (i.e., there must be a sharp, enduring break in the normal vote trend line). Second, the resulting critical shift must effect a change in the competitive standing of the major parties.
- *Deviating elections* are those elections that the majority party loses. For a deviating election to occur, two conditions must be met. First, a majority party must exist (i.e., the absolute value of NORMAL PARTISAN BALANCE must be greater than or equal to .03). Second, the majority party must get fewer votes than the minority party.
- *Endorsement elections* are those elections that involve the endorsement of the majority party and the rejection of the minority party. To qualify as an endorsement election at the local level, two conditions must be met. First, a majority party must exist. Second, a large deviation favoring the majority party must occur. Operationally a "large deviation" means that the absolute value of the NORMAL PARTISAN BALANCE$_{DEV}$ variable is at least .16. This value is twice the standard deviation of the NORMAL PARTISAN BALANCE$_{DEV}$ variable.

### *Normal Voting Patterns, Electoral Competitiveness, and Disequilibrating Elections: Selected Examples*

The normal vote data for Greene County, Indiana (figure 5–4) illustrate many of the electoral phenomena central to this analysis. While Greene County voters strongly supported Andrew Jackson in 1828 and 1832, the emergence of an organized alternative to the Jacksonians generated a sharp, steplike movement away from the Democrats in 1836. The Election of 1836 qualifies as both a critical and a realigning election. It embodies a 37-point shift that eliminated the Democrat's electoral advantage and generated a durable and highly competitive electoral setting. Indeed, from 1836 through 1928, the value of the NORMAL PARTISAN BALANCE variable remains constant, at −.02. Because no majority party existed during this time frame, there could be no deviating or endorsement elections.

The electoral setting in Greene County changes in 1932. It becomes decidedly more Republican as the value of the NORMAL PARTISAN BALANCE variable drops to –.06 in 1932 and –.08 in 1948. The electoral benefit of this partisan shift is somewhat offset, however, by the increasing independence of Greene County voters after 1900. The average size of the electoral perturbations almost doubles after 1900. Moreover, deviating elections occur in 1932, 1936, 1948, 1964, 1976, and 1992. The Election of 1972 qualifies as an endorsement elections, while the Election of 1984 just misses meeting the .16 criterion.

In sharp contrast to Greene County's electoral profile, which evidences very stable normal vote patterns after 1836, is that of Oxford County, Maine (figure 5–5). Its normal voting pattern evidences a series of large, enduring breaks. These occurred in 1856, 1896, and 1932. However, while each of these three elections represents a critical election, only 1856 is a realigning election. Oxford changes from a county that normally voted Democratic before 1856 to a Republican county after 1856. It never switches back to being a normally Democratic county. Oxford does, however, return Democratic pluralities in six elections (1912, 1964, 1968, 1992, 1996, and 2000). Only three of these qualify as deviating elections because by 1992 Oxford has a competitive electoral setting (i.e., the absolute value of the NORMAL PARTISAN BALANCE variable is less than .03). Oxford's voting history also reveals four endorsement elections: 1952, 1956, 1972, and 1984. It is clear from these data that the force of centripetal partisan pulls in Oxford County declines dramatically in the post–World War Two era. The average size of the electoral perturbations since 1952 is .20, almost four times the pre-1952 level.

The final county analyzed here, Lewis County, New York (figure 5–6), illustrates yet another pattern of electoral change. The normal vote trend line for Lewis shows a great deal of sustained electoral change. But no sharp, enduring breaks exist in its normal vote trend line. All of its enduring electoral change has come in the form of secular shifts. Lewis County was a Democratic county in the early part of the nineteenth century, with comfort margins in the 20-point range. However, it became quite competitive in 1860 and remained competitive through 1872. Republican secular changes led Lewis to become a normally Republican county beginning in 1876. It becomes increasingly Republican through 1952. After 1952 it begins to drift toward the Democrats; by 2000 the Republican's comfort margin had been cut by about 70 percent, from 33 points to 10 points.

Another unique aspect of Lewis's voting patterns concerns its pattern of electoral volatility. It is quite volatile in the pre–Civil War era, evidencing deviating elections in 1848 and 1856, no doubt reflecting the electorate's concern with the slavery issue. The Election of 1836 qualifies as an endorsement election. The electoral perturbations from 1864 through 1908 are markedly muted (mean =.03), reflecting the strength of both Civil War era partisan identifications and the Gilded Age party organizations. Beginning in 1912 the average size of electoral perturbations in Lewis increase considerably. Even excluding the elections of 1912 and 1964 (both of which are deviating elections), the average size of the perturbations for post-1908 elections is .09. The size of the Republicans' comfort margin throughout the twentieth century minimized the effects of this increased volatility. However, the Democrat's post-1952 secular gains have begun to change that; the Election of 1996 qualifies as a deviating election. Both 1956 and 1984 are endorsement elections in Lewis.

## Summary

In the epigraph to this chapter Donald Stokes articulates a set of concerns that has preoccupied political thinkers throughout the democratic era in American politics. These concerns speak to the efficaciousness of ordinary citizens in representative democracies dominated by organized political parties. The first part of this chapter argues that, despite the convergence of findings from nearly a century of research, much of the more systematic empirical work on popular efficacy has been hampered by methodological shortcomings endemic to the survey research paradigm. In an effort to generate a new set of inferences about the mass-elite linkages in American politics, I offer a longitudinal, subnational approach to the study of electoral behavior.

This approach focuses on electoral independence and electoral competitiveness. The temporal and spatial reach of the aggregated electoral data offers a unique set of insights into the relative importance of endogenous and exogenous influences on voting behavior. This, in turn, offers the potential for new insights into popular efficacy, as illustrated by the data displayed in figures 5–4 through 5–6. The conservative nature of the approach developed to derive normal voting patterns insures that the broadly based empirical insights produced here will be durable.

Chapter 5 is an important bridge in this work. It links, in a very concrete way, the themes, conceptualizations, and concerns identified in the preceding three chapters to the empirical analyses conducted in later chapters. It lays the groundwork for: (1) developing a better understanding of the meaning of partisan influences on electoral behavior (chapter 6); (2) providing a broad assessment of electoral independence (chapter 7 and chapter 8), and (3) gauging the effect of electoral independence on electoral settings and outcomes (chapter 9). While the electoral independence analyses speak to the capacity of citizens to be discriminating consumers of public goods, the effect of electoral independence on electoral settings and outcomes reveals what political elites have been taught about democratic politics. These analyses offer a unique set of insights into the incentives that elites have to be responsive to the core political desires of citizens in the world's longest-lasting representative democracy.

## References

Anderson, K. 1979. *The Creation of Democratic Majority 1928–1930*. Chicago: University of Chicago Press.

Bartels, L. M. 1998. "Electoral Continuity and Change, 1868–1996." *Electoral Studies* 17 (3):301–26.

Campbell, A., P. E. Converse, et al. 1960. *The American Voter*. New York, John Wiley and Sons.

Campbell, A., P. E. Converse, W. E. Miller, and D. E. Stokes. 1966. *Elections and the Political Order*. New York, John Wiley and Sons.

Converse, P. E. 1966. "The Concept of a Normal Vote." In *Elections and the Political Order*, edited by A. Campbell, P. E. Converse, W. E. Miller, and D. E. Stokes. New York, John Wiley and Sons.

Erikson, R. S., G. C. Wright, et al. 1993. *Statehouse Democracy: Public Opinion and Policy in the American States*. Cambridge, Cambridge University Press.

Erikson, R. S., M. B. Mackuen, et al. 2002. *The Macro Polity*. New York, Cambridge University Press.

Fiorina, M. P. 1981. *Retrospective Voting in American National Elections*. New Haven, Yale University Press.

Franklin, C. H., and J. E. Jackson. 1983. "The Dynamics of Party Identification." *American Political Science Review* 77:957–73.

Jackson, J. E. 1975. "Issues, Parties, and Presidential Votes." *American Journal of Political Science* 19:161–85.

Lupia, A., and M. D. McCubbins. 1998. *The Democratic Dilemma: Can Citizens Learn What They Need to Know?* New York, Cambridge University Press.

MacKuen, M. B., R. S. Erikson, et al. 1989. "Macropartisanship." *American Political Science Review* 83:1125–42.

———. 1992. "Peasants or Bankers? The American Electorate and the U.S. Economy." *American Political Science Review* 86:597–611.

Miller, W. E., and J. M. Shanks. 1996. *The New American Voter*. Cambridge, Harvard University Press.

Nie, N. H., S. Verba, et al. 1976. *The Changing American Voter*. Cambridge, Harvard University Press.

Page, B. I., and C. Jones. 1979. "Reciprocal Effects of Policy Preferences, Party Loyalties, and the Vote." *American Political Science Review* 73:1071–89.

Smith, E.R.A.N. 1989. *The Unchanging American Voter*. Berkeley and Los Angeles, University of California Press.

Stokes, D. E. 1966. "Party Loyalty and the Likelihood of Deviating Elections."
    In *Elections and the Political Order*, edited by A. Campbell, P. E. Converse,
    W. E. Miller, and D. E. Stokes. New York, John Wiley and Sons.
Wright, G. C., R. S. Erikson, et al. 1985. "Measuring State Partisanship and Ideol-
    ogy with Survey Data." *Journal of Politics* 47:469–89.
———. 1987. "Public Opinion and Policy Liberalism in the American States."
    *American Journal of Political Science* 31:980–1001.

# CHAPTER SIX

# The Roots of Partisanship: Party Elites, Exogenous Groups, and Electoral Bases

Jefferson as a veritable pioneer in American politics set the pattern of party leadership. No less than Jackson, Lincoln, or the two Roosevelts, he could lead the people only where they were willing to go. The hard facts of the history of party leadership in the United States play havoc with the Carlylean conception of heroes. More pertinent is the old story of the French Revolutionary leader who, hearing a tumult outside in the street, exclaimed excitedly to the group in the house where he happened to be at the time: "There goes the mob. I am their leader. I must follow them."

—WILFRED BINKLEY, *American Political Parties: Their Natural History*

[T]he major political party is the creature of the politicians, the ambitious office seeker and office holder. They have created and maintained, used or abused, reformed or ignored the political party when doing so has furthered their goals and ambitions. The political party is thus an "endogenous" institution—an institution shaped by these actors. Whatever its strength or weakness, whatever its form and role, it is the ambitious politicians' creation.

—JOHN ALDRICH, *Why Parties? The Origin and Transformation of Party Politics in America*

THE NORMAL voting patterns introduced in chapter 5 are at the heart of the quantitative analyses of electoral independence to be presented in the next three chapters. These normal voting patterns are viewed as macro-level manifestations of partisan influences on voting behavior. As such, they are viewed here as an endogenous influence on voting. By this I mean that partisan influences are centripetal forces rooted in the interests, concerns, and preferences of party elites. This conceptualization of partisan influences is inconsistent with corollary C1, which holds that citizens' normal voting routines are rooted in judgments that these routines serve *their* core political desires. I nevertheless adopt this interpretation of partisan influences because it is useful for analytic purposes: viewing them as endogenous provides for clean and conservative inferences about popular efficacy. Those inferences will be based solely on the capacity of voters to overcome the centripetal pulls and dulling effects of partisan allegiances, generating departures from normal voting patterns that impinge upon the core political interests of political stewards.

Despite the analytic value of viewing partisan influences on voting as endogenous, corollary C1 suggests that it is a contested interpretation. Because this contested interpretation is based on a conception of political parties that speaks to the core concerns of this book, it will be useful to pause here and examine it. To do this I introduce two models of political parties (the machine model and the pluralist model), develop a strategy to examine these different conceptions empirically, and use the historical data archive assembled here to conduct a set of multivariate analyses of the NORMAL PARTISAN BALANCE variable. These multivariate analyses will provide valuable background information for conducting and interpreting the results of the electoral independence analyses.

The next section compares the machine and pluralist conceptions of parties. It develops their implications for mass-elite linkages within parties and the meaning of partisan influences on voting. The second section lays out a strategy used to examine empirically these different conceptions of parties; the last two sections report the empirical results.

## MODELS OF POLITICAL PARTIES, MASS-ELITE LINKAGES, AND PARTISAN INFLUENCES ON VOTING

The machine model is a "special case" of Aldrich's (1995) more general theory of political parties, a theory that views parties as endogenous institutions (i.e., as tools of political elites). The machine model views party affairs as being dominated by a relatively small group of self-serving professional politicians. These insiders control the party's considerable political resources and use them to attract and maintain the loyalty of large blocs of voters. Within this model voters are viewed as "targets" of party activities; they are the focus of efforts by party insiders to capture their allegiance and loyalty.

The loyalty of voters to "their" party is the currency party elites use to further their personal and professional agendas. The latitude these elites enjoy in pursuing their personal goals and ambitions is determined by party loyalists' level of political discernment. If these partisans are informed and attentive, and political competition is keen, the latitude of party elites to engage in self-serving behavior is limited. However, if party loyalists are ill-informed and disengaged, and the electoral setting is not competitive, the opportunity for elites to engage in self-serving behavior is enhanced. Under these conditions it is possible to interpret partisan influences on voting as endogenous: rooted in the interests, concerns, and preferences of party elites.

As defined here the machine model is more reflective of how parties operated during the Gilded Age than how they operate in contemporary American politics. However, this limiting case of Aldrich's theory is indispensable to the conception of partisan influences on voting as endogenous. The reason the machine model does not resonate well with contemporary American politics is that the conceptualization of mass-elite linkages embedded in it fails to incorporate a potentially important source of mass influences within political parties: the activities of social group and interest leaders. The constraints emanating from these leaders are important in limiting the latitude of party professionals in defining and pursuing policy agendas. These leaders of exogenous groups and interests play a dominant role within the pluralist model of parties. Indeed, this model views political parties as loosely knit coalitions of diverse social groups and interests forged for the purpose of winning electoral office and maximizing the political influence of their constituent groups.[1]

---

[1] The pluralist model of political parties views them as electoral coalitions of disparate social groupings with varying degrees of cohesiveness. It rests on a long line of scholarly work that has spanned the disciplines of political science, sociology, and history. Charles Merriam's classic work on political parties, *The American Party System* (1922a) is a sophisticated, behaviorally oriented restatement of the logic and rhetoric first articulated by Martin Van Buren and his followers almost a century earlier. Perhaps the first comprehensive scholarly effort to outline the evolving social bases of American political parties is Wilford Binkley's *American Political Parties: Their Natural History* (1943). This conception of parties is reflected in the sociological tradition in voting studies (Lazarsfeld, Berelson et al. 1948; Berelson, Lazarsfeld et al. 1954) as well as in Lubell's *The Future of American Politics* (1952).

A theoretically more developed conception of American political parties as amalgams of social groups and interests is presented in Eldersveld's pioneering work on Detroit political parties (1964). The seminal work on party cleavages in a cross-national setting, *Party Systems and Voter Alignments*, was done by Seymour Martin Lipset and Stein Rokkan (1967). More recent work in the sociological tradition is reported in Knoke's *The Social Bases of Political Parties* (1976) and, most recently, Manza and Brooks's *Social Cleavages and Political Change: Voter Alignments and U.S. Party Coalitions* (1999). The latter work provides a fairly comprehensive theoretical and empirical review of work done in this tradition. Samuel Hays and Lee Benson pioneered a tradition among historians that highlighted the ethnoreligious makeup of American politics and political parties in the nineteenth century. Some of the key works in this tradition are: Kleppner 1970; Jensen 1971; Benson 1972; McSeveney 1972. James Wright provides a useful overview and critique of this literature (1973). Axelrod uses survey data to detail the recent social bases of parties (1972) as does Stanley, Bianco, and Niemi (1986). Petrocik provides a fairly comprehensive, but dated, bibliography of works that deal with specific periods and groups (1981: 183 n. 23).

Within the pluralist model, partisan influences on voting are conceptualized as a reflection of the core concerns of the various social groups and interests that make up the party's electoral base. During periods of political normalcy intermediary agents, social and interest group leaders who are congealed within the party hierarchy, articulate these core concerns. These leaders are active and influential participants in the forging of party affairs; they monitor and scrutinize party actions from the perspective of their constituents.

In the next section I develop the machine and the pluralist models of political parties more fully. I then use the differences between them to provide theoretical insights into the meaning of partisan influences on voting.

### The Machine Model

The most distinctive features of Aldrich's theory of political parties are the centrality it ascribes to the party's hierarchy and the motivations it ascribes to party elites. Rather than looking to exogenous forces and actors to understand party dynamics, Aldrich focuses primarily on the interests and ambitions of the party hierarchy. These party elites are motivated by an identifiable subset of selective incentives: *those that accrue from the attainment of elective office.* Their behavior is shaped by various institutional and historical constraints. Thus, Aldrich offers what he terms "a rational choice account of the party, an account that presumes that rational, elective office seekers and holders use the party to achieve their ends" (1995: 21). Correspondingly,

> [T]he fundamental syllogism for the theory of political parties to be offered here is just what Rhode and Shepsle (1978) originally offered as the basis for the rational-choice-based new institutionalism: political outcomes—here political parties—result from actors' seeking to realize their goals, choosing within and possibly shaping a given set of institutional arrangements, and so choosing within a given historical context.

> [T]he institutions that define the political party are unique, and as it happens they are unique in ways that make an institutional account especially useful. Their establishment and nature are fundamentally extralegal; they are non-governmental political institutions. Instead of statute, their basis lies in the actions of ambitious politicians that created and maintained them. They are, in the parlance of the new institutionalism, *endogenous institutions*—in fact the most highly endogenous institutions of any substantial and sustained political importance in American history.

> By endogenous, I mean it was the actions of political actors that created political parties in the first place, and it is the actions of political actors that

have shaped and altered them over time. . . . It is often the same set of actors who write the party's rules and then choose the party's outcomes, sometimes at nearly the same time and by the same method (6, 19).

In Aldrich's account political parties have two principal components: a hierarchy and a bureaucracy. The party hierarchy is the most important for understanding the dynamics of party affairs. It is composed of two types of actors: office seekers and benefit seekers. Office seekers include both incumbent office holders and candidates; they are at the top of the hierarchy. Benefit seekers are defined as "those for whom realization of their goals depends on the party's success in capturing office" (20). Benefit seekers are critical to office seekers because "they command the resources, whether money, expertise, and information or merely time and labor, that office seekers need to realize their ambitions. As a result activists' motivations shape and constrain the behavior of office seekers, as their own roles are, in turn, shaped and constrained by the office seekers" (21).

The key to Aldrich's view of political parties as endogenous institutions is his assertion that party elites are motivated by personal interests that can be achieved only by attaining elective office. However, in elaborating his model Aldrich defines personal interests broadly and acknowledges a variety of incentives that drive office seekers. It is possible, for example, that an office seeker may be motivated not by careerism but by deeply felt policy goals (21). These policy objectives may be derived from strong ideological commitments or by long-term affiliations with a variety of societal groups and interests. Moreover, in his discussion of contemporary parties (prologue to part III, chap. 6), Aldrich introduces a type of benefit seeker, the policy activist, who is quite different from a patronage benefit seeker. Policy activists are "motivated more by policy concerns than by the selective incentives of jobs, contracts, and the like typical of the machine age" (160).

By including office seekers and benefit seekers with strong ties to various social groups and interests within the party hierarchy, Aldrich makes his theory more resonant with the contemporary American experience. However, this inclusion also makes a political party much less of an "endogenous" institution. This can be illustrated by considering the case of policy activists, who do not fit comfortably within Aldrich's definition of a benefit seeker (i.e., "those for whom realization of their goals depends on the party's success in capturing office"). The source of this discomfort is that the most influential policy activists are closely tied to exogenous social and interest groups. Indeed, the source of policy activists' influence within the party lies in their ties to groups that form the party's electoral base (291).

The manner in which these external ties undermine the conceptualization of parties as endogenous institutions can be illustrated by developing the implications of one of the cornerstones of rational choice analysis: the primacy of self-interest. The personal interests of the most influential policy activists are rooted in their "home" organization. This is because the values they are likely to prize most—income, stature, visibility, and the like—derive from the group they represent, not the party they embrace. Moreover, their source of influence within the party derives from their ties to, and position within, groups external to the party.

Exogenous group leaders can enhance their standing by being effective advocates and having the views of "their" constituents represented in the policies of "their" party. Their image as a leader will be enhanced if the party they embrace endorses the views of the group they represent—*and wins sweeping electoral victories*. In contrast, if social group leaders are not effective advocates for their group's interests within the party, they will lose legitimacy and stature in the eyes of their constituents—*irrespective of electoral outcomes*. This will jeopardize their standing within their home organization and, ultimately, within the party.

If a policy activist's party wins elective office by repudiating the interests of the activist's constituents (advocating the repeal of civil rights legislation, abandoning the concerns of women, opening up fragile land for oil extraction, advocating steep increases in corporate taxes, enhancing the regulatory power of government over industry, etc.), then it is difficult to conceive of electoral victory furthering the long-term goals of the policy activist. Therefore, unlike benefit seekers motivated by selective incentives derived from the attainment of elective office, most policy activists would rather lose elections than sacrifice the interests of their constituents. Losing an election after abandoning the interests of a core constituency would underscore the electoral value of that group to the party, thereby strengthening the policy activist's position in the election's aftermath.

Thus, including political actors with strong ties to social groups and interests within the party hierarchy makes it difficult to conceive of parties as endogenous institutions. The more powerful the role of these actors within the party, and the stronger their ties to exogenous groups, the less the party can be driven by the personal concerns of party elites. This, of course, has important implications for how we interpret partisan influences on voting. Partisan influences can be interpreted as purely endogenous influences only when the party's hierarchy is dominated by actors who are motivated by selective benefits that accrue from elective office. Therefore, within the machine model the party hierarchy is posited to consist of only "pure office seekers" and "patronage benefit seekers."[2]

---

[2] Aldrich defines pure office seekers as ambitious politicians who are "motivated by the desire for holding office per se . . . who place no value on policy or other nonpersonal uses of the office they seek. . . . [T]he value of holding office as a member of one party or another

Limiting the party hierarchy to this subset of political actors makes it possible to conceive of partisan influences on voting as being endogenous influences.

## The Pluralist Model

The pluralist model derives from an intellectual tradition rooted in the seminal contributions of Arthur F. Bentley (1908) rather than Adam Smith. Within this model social groups and interests, along with their representatives, are an integral part of a political party. Indeed, within the pluralist model, political parties are, to a large extent, *a reflection of their external constituencies*. A party's electoral base is conceived of as an amalgam of social groups and interests; leaders and representatives of these groups and interests are influential members of the party's hierarchy.[3] Different social groups and interests are attracted to different parties for historical reasons, are congealed within them, and play an active role in shaping party affairs. Merriam and Gosnell captured the essence of the pluralist model a half-century ago: "Of great significance in the composition of any political party are the numerous types of social groupings. These are fundamental in any scientific study of the political party, and too great an emphasis cannot be placed upon them. Social scientists are just beginning to make an analysis of these groups, without a careful consideration of which we are likely to obtain an artificial picture of the political party, often far afield from the actual facts of party life . . . [These groups] formulate principles and policies; they create an environment out of which comes the "hereditary voter"; they are the material out of which come leaders and chiefs, as well as the organization and managing groups found in all permanent parties" (1949: 88–89).

Because of the salience of the party's social environment to its operation, pluralist scholars view the party hierarchy as a rather loose, unruly, and disjointed group of elected officials, aspiring office seekers, party pro-

---

is a matter of indifference to this pure office seeker. . . . The ambitious politician would choose to run for office in whichever party offers the most probable access to office" (1995: 137). Patronage benefit seekers are simply those party professionals motivated by selective benefits associated with political spoils (graft, power, favorable treatment for kin and friends, the prospect of future employment or preferment, etc.).

[3] The theoretical role of societal influences on party development is most fully developed in Lipset and Rokkan's cross-national analysis of party systems and voter alignments (1967). This work is probably the most ambitious account of the origins and structure of social cleavages as well as their implications for political parties. The role of the party's social environment in shaping and driving political parties is central in their work, in stark contrast to the machine model. The same contrast can be found in Wilfred Binkley's 1948 historical analysis of the role of groups, sections, and interests in American parties.

fessionals, and social and interest group leaders. Moreover, they see this hierarchy as a porous and continually evolving inner core, the makeup of which changes with electoral fortunes and societal developments. Thus, rather than viewing the party as a tool strategically wielded by party insiders striving to further their personal ambitions, pluralist theorists see a broader and more involved competition for the control and deployment of party resources. Eldersveld's work (1964) develops the implications of the party's social environment for how it operates and illustrates why this model of parties has been central to pluralistic accounts of American democracy (Truman 1951; Dahl 1956, 1961, 1971; Held 1987: 186–95; Ricci 1984: 156–57).

> The party must be understood as a clientele-oriented structure. . . . Singularly reliant on votes as the arithmetic of power, the party reflects structurally an inherent tendency toward joint advantage. The party is a mutually exploitative relationship—it is joined by people who would use it; it mobilizes for the sake of power those who would join it.
>
> The party, in this image, exists as an intermediary group representing and exploiting multiple interests for the achievement of direct control over the power apparatus of the society. . . . The party organization as a single enterprise "bargains" with these subgroups, enters into a coalitional agreement with them . . . and thus develops a "joint preference" ordering of organizational objectives. This, presumably, is the result of "side payments" to the subcoalitions, a subtle calculus of reciprocal strengths, \needs, and contributions to the total party structure. . . .
>
> [Further] these structures are not static or closed. They reveal a high degree of dynamic interaction with the social environment within which they recruit and function. . . . The party must, therefore, be perceived as in a state of continual, dynamic interaction with its social and political environment. The party is a competitive, constant, social-renewal group if it is at all success-minded. (Eldersveld 1964: 6–7; 533–34)

Despite the importance of exogenous factors in the pluralist model, it does not ignore the role party insiders play in shaping party affairs. What distinguishes the pluralist model from the machine model in this regard is that pluralist scholars see social and interest group leaders as party elites, making the party hierarchy, to a large extent, a reflection of its environment. Moreover, they place more emphasis on the external constraints upon, rather than the choices of, party elites. That is, they are far more likely to see these "choices" as being forced by electoral realities.

*Mass-Elite Linkages and Partisan Influences on Voting:*
*Machine and Pluralist Perspectives*

The machine and pluralist models have different conceptions of the origins and makeup of the party's electoral base, which give rise to distinctive views of the mass-elite dynamic within parties. Understanding these different conceptions of mass-elite linkages is the key to understanding the contested interpretations of partisanship. Within the machine model core voters are viewed as "brand name" loyalists whose partisan affinities are forged by the efforts of party professionals, whether nineteenth-century ward heelers or twenty-first-century media and polling consultants. Within the pluralist model, the most important source of core voters is their identity with the social groups and interests aligned with the party. Developing these two points will illustrate their implications for the meaning of partisan influences on normal voting behavior.

Central to the conception of mass-elite linkages within the machine model is an exchange relationship between voters and the party. The primary concern of political parties within the electoral arena is to market their "products" (candidates and policies), doing whatever it takes to sell them and establish long-term loyalties among voters. If voters were political sophisticates who were fully informed about policy matters, this would be a fruitful exchange relationship from the perspective of democratic theory. But most voters are neither politically sophisticated nor well informed. Consequently, there are serious normative problems with this exchange-oriented view of mass-elite linkages. Unchecked by knowledgeable elites with strong ties to external groups, self-serving party professionals can pursue a number of strategies to sell the party's products and transform voters into brand name loyalists.

The party's marketing efforts can include the skillful manipulation of political symbols and gestures, as well as timely, but largely symbolic, overtures to key constituencies. Waving the "bloody shirt," sponsoring family picnics on Labor Day, and participating in marches on St. Patrick's Day can also generate brand name loyalty and electoral support. Other effective marketing tools include fixing traffic tickets or juvenile delinquency cases, providing turkeys on Thanksgiving, and arranging jobs for newly arrived immigrant relatives. More contemporary variants of efforts by parties to sell their products include slick media campaigns prepared by advertising agencies, unsettling commercials, smear campaigns, and catchy slogans pretested in carefully selected focus groups. The skillful deployment of these marketing strategies by self-serving party elites is the basis for viewing partisan influences on voting as endogenous influences: electoral heuristics tainted by elected officials and their associates.

Central to the conception of mass-elite linkages within the pluralist model is the existence of strenuous intraparty advocacy within a diverse party hierarchy. Intense bargaining and compromise takes place and results in the party's policy commitments reflecting some amalgam of constituent group preferences. While no constituent group is likely to be entirely satisfied, such compromises are the stuff of pluralistic democracy. Self-interested party professionals are willing to accommodate the demands of social group leaders to forestall the type of constituent discontent that the defection of a visible and respected leader would generate. Discontent on the part of these opinion leaders may lead important components of the party's electoral base to question the party's continuing value as an electoral heuristic. The interests and preferences of social groups and interests aligned with the party are essential to the vital interests of the party because they constitute its electoral base. And maintaining the loyalty of a party's electoral base is the starting point for any successful electoral strategy.

Selling party images, candidates, and platforms to diffuse publics is profoundly different from dealing with, and being held accountable by, sophisticated, informed, and influential representatives of important electoral constituencies. Thus, if the mass-elite dynamic within parties corresponds more closely to the pluralist model than the machine model, then partisan influences on voting cannot be viewed as endogenous. Rather than being rooted in the personal goals and ambitions of party insiders, these influences must be seen as reflecting the preferences and interests of the party's core constituencies. The driving force behind these preferences and interests is the dynamic engagement of interest group leaders in party affairs, as Merriam and Gosnell (1949), Key (1947), Eldersveld (1964), and others, noted long ago. An apt analogy is the difference between *consumer groups* being represented on a corporate board versus *consumers* being relegated to the domain of the advertising and/or the public relations departments.

Thus, the pluralist model suggests that the powerful centripetal force exerted by partisanship derives from the ties maintained though an ongoing dialogue between social group leaders and political parties. The active, continual, and effective engagement of social group leaders in party affairs suggests that the party can serve as a valuable heuristic to voters. That is, the party label can provide low cost, but valuable, information concerning electoral choices. The dynamic engagement in party affairs of social group leaders provides for the updating of party positions. This periodic updating undermines some of the criticism that has been leveled at the role of long-standing, intergenerational party loyalties since the seminal work of Mosca and Michels.

The dynamic engagement of social group leaders in party affairs suggests that "democratic" influences exist on party elites quite independently of Election Day jolts provided by voters. This, in turn, suggests that the party heuristic is not necessarily, or entirely, tainted by endogenous influences. Put differently, the pluralist perspective suggests that the structure of mass-elite linkages within political parties roots partisanship in factors that are exogenous to the party. Within the pluralist model, these linkages are an integral component of electoral accountability during periods of normalcy. They serve as exogenous constraints on the latitude of party elites even when most members of the party's electoral base are not politically engaged.

## PARTISAN INFLUENCES ON VOTING: THE STRUCTURE OF THE EMPIRICAL ANALYSES

Because of the implications of these differing accounts of mass-elite linkages for popular efficacy, empirically based insights into the meaning of partisanship could make important contributions to democratic theory. A direct and rigorous empirical examination of the machine and pluralist accounts would entail a truly monumental undertaking, especially for the period covered by this study. While such an effort is beyond the scope of this work, an indirect examination can be conducted. The focus of this examination is on the factors that affect the relative size of local electoral bases. It employs regression analysis to examine three theses, the *machine thesis*, the *pluralist thesis,* and a corollary to the pluralist thesis, the *patterned change thesis*. These various theses should not be viewed as mutually exclusive, and the analyses conducted here will not be able to "prove" one account or the other. They will, however, allow us to reject one or both models, modify them, or make some judgment about their relative merits.

The machine thesis derives from the view of political parties as powerful, elite-dominated political institutions. It asserts that parties are capable of forging and maintaining electoral bases simply on the basis of aggressive and well-conceived strategies engineered by committed professional politicians. What accounts for differences in electoral bases across locales are differences in the institutional strength of parties. Partisan loyalties cannot be created overnight. Over time, however, determined and organized efforts by party activists can forge a viable electoral base. The more determined, organized, and well-funded the efforts of party activists, the larger the electoral base. Party activists will invest resources in activities that affect the size of their electoral base because they are crucial to their desire for electoral success, as posited in chapter 3 (A2).

The pluralist thesis is premised on the view of political parties as a loosely knit coalition of social groups and interests. It follows from this premise that variance in the size of electoral bases across locales should be determined largely by the geographic distribution of social groups and interests. While this thesis does not reject the importance of institutional factors in forging electoral bases, it does suggest that the impact of these strategic efforts is constrained by exogenous factors. Nonetheless, because of the core political interests of political elites posited in chapter 3, they will forge as large and cohesive an electoral base as possible (A2).

The patterned change corollary to the pluralist thesis is based on the view of partisan allegiances as dynamic rather than unthinking or unalterable commitments. Pluralists view group-based partisan loyalties as being dependent upon the party espousing values that resonate with its members and promoting policies that enhance their welfare. Depending on the fidelity of the party to their interests and concerns, group ties to a party will vary over time—in a manner consistent with the set of corollaries posited in chapter 3 (C1, C2, C2.1). Thus, the patterned change thesis asserts that we are likely to find patterned temporal changes in the electoral support social groups and interests provide political parties.

### Examining the Machine Thesis

The key to examining the machine thesis is adequately measuring the institutional strength of the major political parties and the resources they invest in forging local electoral bases. These are extraordinarily difficult things to measure, particularly for the number of local electorates and the time period analyzed here. Because direct measures of institutional strength and resources are not available, I employ a surrogate measure, STATE PARTY DOMINANCE. As noted in chapter 5 and appendix I, STATE PARTY DOMINANCE is the average of eight lags of a measure of the partisan composition of the state legislature. Thus, not only is this measure not a multidimensional measure of parties and their electoral activities (i.e., it ignores such things as the size of the party's permanent staff, budget, numbers of committed volunteers, etc.), it is a *state level* measure that is incapable of picking up locale-specific variations.

Despite this, as noted in appendix I (*http://www.pol.uiuc.edu/nardulliresearch.html*) the STATE PARTY DOMINANCE variable is a plausible surrogate for institutional strength and resources. Empirical evidence for this assertion can be found in figure 6–1. It reports two sets of results ($r_2$'s) from bivariate regressions between NORMAL PARTISAN BALANCE and STATE

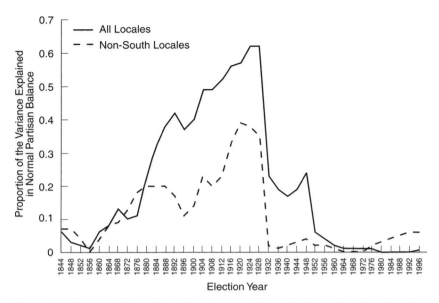

Figure 6–1. Impact of State Party Dominance with and without Southern Locales

PARTY DOMINANCE for each election from 1844 through 1992. As seen in the legend for figure 6–1, one set of results is for all locales; the other excludes the South. The South was excluded for one set of regressions because a persuasive argument can be made that including Southern states, at least during the Jim Crow era, artificially inflates the results. The argument is that the high correlation between NORMAL PARTISAN BALANCE and STATE PARTY DOMINANCE for Southern states during this time frame is driven by issues of race and has nothing to do with party strength.

While it is difficult to rebut this argument, figure 6–1 demonstrates that even excluding the South there is still a strong relationship between these two variables, enough to justify using the STATE PARTY DOMINANCE as a surrogate for party strength and resources. The $r_2$'s for both analyses are quite low for the pre–Civil War period but begin to rise steadily in the 1870s—the period most associated with the rise of machine politics in the United States. While STATE PARTY DOMINANCE explains only 10 percent of the variance in NORMAL PARTISAN BALANCE in the 1870s, it explains between 30 percent and 40 percent in the last two decades of the nineteenth century (about half as much if the South is excluded). By 1904 STATE PARTY DOMINANCE explains half the variance in NORMAL PARTISAN BALANCE and the $r_2$'s rise steadily until 1928, when they peak at .62. Outside the South $r_2$'s peak at .39. After the New Deal realignment the $r_2$'s plummet for locales outside the South; they plummet everywhere after 1948, rising slightly outside the South after 1972.[4]

The bivariate effects of the STATE PARTY DOMINANCE variable reported in figure 6–1 conform to the picture sketched by Aldrich (and others before him), both for the Gilded Age and the post–World War Two era. Moreover, they answer part of the basic query concerning mass-elite linkages within political parties: the machine model does not seem to apply to most of American political history. This cannot be said, however, for the half-century between 1880 and 1932. The powerful effect of the STATE PARTY DOMINANCE variable on the NORMAL PARTISAN BALANCE variable during that period suggests that well-entrenched political parties may well be capable of forging and maintaining cohesive electoral bases.[5]

### The Pluralist Thesis and the Spatial Distribution of Social Groups and Interests

The results reported in figure 6–1 suggest that the STATE PARTY DOMINANCE variable may be an adequate surrogate for the institutional strength of parties. However, they do not yield convincing empirical support for the machine thesis in the 1880–1928 era: they are bivariate results that are amenable to a pluralist interpretation. From a pluralist perspective, the impact of STATE PARTY DOMINANCE during this era is simply a reflection of the geographic distribution of social groups and interests aligned with the major parties. That is, a state party dominates the state legislature in the eight-year period before a presidential election for the same reason that its presidential candidate receives strong support among the state's voters: the characteristics of social groups and interests within the state.

This ambiguity can be resolved only by a multivariate analysis containing both STATE PARTY DOMINANCE and a set of "pluralist" variables.

---

[4] The scatter plots between NORMAL PARTISAN BALANCE and STATE PARTY DOMINANCE do not reveal any nonlinearities. Thus, the $r_2$'s reported here capture this relationship fairly well.

[5] While the results reported in figure 6–1 are the result of a very simple empirical test, they are plausible in light of the size, strength, and discipline of parties during this era. For example, Charles Merriam (1922: 69), citing estimates from Ostrogorski and doing some of his own calculations, estimates that there were between 600,000 and 900,000 party workers in the United States during the heyday of the party system. Most of these workers relied upon the party for their livelihood and "did politics 365 days in the year." The size of these "partisan armies" is all the more impressive when they are considered in light of the number of votes cast in presidential elections during this period, especially before the onset of women's suffrage. These totals ranged from around 9 million in 1880 to 18 million in 1916 and then jump to the 26 million to 30 million range after 1920.

Pluralist variables are those that capture the distribution of social groups and interests across local electorates. For the pluralist thesis to receive empirical support a strong and enduring relationship must exist between the distribution of social groups and interests in local electorates and NOR-MAL PARTISAN BALANCE. To examine this thesis, multivariate analyses involving several sets of pluralist variables were conducted for all elections between 1872 and 1992.[6] While the available data provide for only a limited test of this thesis, an analysis of them can yield important insights into the meaning of partisan influences on voting.[7]

The variables available to examine the pluralist thesis (see table 5–1 and appendix I) include both ethnocultural variables (gender, race, religion, and ethnicity) and two sets of dummy geo-political variables (the section and locale type variables).[8] While these variables constitute only a subset of the variables needed to examine the pluralist thesis comprehensively, conducting the analysis was a formidable task. Nearly seventy variables had to be examined across thirty-one elections.[9] This required a good deal of preliminary analysis to reduce the number of

[6] A complete set of data for the relevant variables is not available before 1870, and the last set of census data available was 1990. While I felt comfortable in extrapolating to 1992, I did not feel comfortable in extrapolating beyond it. Consequently, I ended the empirical analysis with the Election of 1992.

[7] The unavailability of data on income, education, union membership, and occupation for most of the study time frame means that an important set of variables relevant to the pluralist model cannot be included in the multivariate analyses. In addition, the fact that the ethnocultural variables used reflect data for the entire population in an electoral unit, not just its eligible voters, means that they are not as precise as would be desirable. Both of these factors will limit the explanatory power of the pluralist variables.

[8] The ethnocultural variables measure the distribution of specific social groups, such as Catholics, African Americans, Germans, women, etc., in local electorates. Over the course of American political history these groups have had distinctive political interests and concerns to which political parties have appealed, with differing degrees of effort and success. Similarly, the section and locale type variables depict geophysical spaces (the South, the West, large cities, rural areas, etc.) that have had distinct political interests; at different points in time political parties have formulated policies to address these concerns.

Racial, religious, and ethnic groups have been distributed differently across sections and locale types. But, net of their ethnocultural makeup, the fact that local electorates are located within a particular geophysical space has political implications that can be manifested in partisan allegiances. The importance of agriculture, shipping, mining, manufacturing, banking, etc. has varied across sections of the nation as well as locales within those sections. The same can be said for issues such as slavery, internal improvements, states' rights, concern for the environment, law and order, gun control, etc. Thus, while the use of dummy geo-political variables is a clumsy way to capture these matters, these variables are expected to have an independent effect on the size of local electoral bases.

[9] I am enormously indebted to my research assistant, David Darmofal, for his contributions in conducting the multivariate analyses upon which this chapter is based. His commitment, thoroughness, and care made an otherwise unbearable task manageable.

variables to a more manageable subset and to check for nonlinearities and heteroscedastity.[10]

The preliminary analyses suggested that the following sets of variables had the most consistent and enduring impact on NORMAL PARTISAN BALANCE: (1) FEMALE (after 1920 only); (2) AFRICAN AMERICAN$_{LN}$ and AFRICAN AMERICAN$_{LN}$ X URBAN$_1$; (3) five variables reflecting the unit's religious makeup (BAPTIST, EPISCOPALIAN, METHODIST, PRESBYTERIAN, ROMAN CATHOLIC); (4) four variables that capture the unit's ethnic makeup (ENGLAND, GERMANY, SOUTHERN EUROPEAN, SCANDINAVIAN); and (5) a set of dummy variables that depict the section of the nation within which the unit is located (NEW ENGLAND, MIDDLE ATLANTIC, SOUTH, MIDWEST, PLAINS, MOUNTAIN, WEST COAST).[11] Hence, the pluralist thesis will be tested by examining the relationship between these variables and NORMAL PARTISAN BALANCE for each election from 1872 through 1992.

### The Patterned Change Thesis:
### Examining the Durability of Voter Alignments

The patterned change thesis asserts that partisan allegiances are not unalterable commitments. To examine this thesis the analytic focal point must shift from the explanatory power of the pluralist variables to temporal changes in their B-coefficients. Invariant or randomly fluctuating B-coefficients for a pluralist variable would lead to the rejection of the patterned change thesis; *temporally patterned changes* in those B-coefficients would be consistent with it. By temporally patterned changes I mean either a set of secular changes or a critical break in the level of B-coefficients. If more pluralist variables evidence patterned changes in their B-coefficients than would be expected by chance, then the patterned change thesis cannot be rejected. Additional empirical support for this thesis would be garnered to the extent that *realigning changes* in the pluralist variables occurred more than would be expected by chance. By a realigning change I mean a patterned change that results in the sign of a pluralist variable's B-coefficient being reversed.

---

[10] I eliminated many variables simply because they had no consistent impact on NORMAL PARTISAN BALANCE across the thirty-one elections. Nonlinearity and heteroscedastity were not a problem except with respect to the AFRICAN AMERICAN variable. Thus, I had to use a logarithmic transformation of this variable (AFRICAN AMERICAN$_{LN}$) and I had to use it in conjunction with an interaction term (AFRICAN AMERICAN$_{LN}$ X URBAN$_1$). This interaction term reflects the fact that voting patterns for African American differed for the largest urban areas.

[11] The BORDER variable was used as the residual or baseline category for the section dummy variables.

To determine whether patterned changes in B-coefficients existed, I was guided by the procedures used to define secular and critical changes in local voting patterns (see chapter 5 as well as appendix II and appendix III, which are available at *http://www.pol.uiuc.edu/nardulliresearch .html*). Thus, for a series of secular changes in B-coefficients to qualify as a "patterned change," it had to contain at least five directionally consistent, contiguous changes. In detecting critical changes, however, I could not specify a minimum threshold; the scale of the B-coefficients for the pluralist variables simply varied too much. As lamentable as this is, it is not a crippling problem. Large, enduring changes in the levels of the B-coefficients proved to be rare events that stand out in graphical displays, as an examination of table 6–1 suggests.

It is possible to define realigning changes in B-coefficients with more precision. The criteria differ for secular and critical changes. For a series of secular changes in B-coefficients to qualify as a realigning change it had to meet four criteria: (1) the series must qualify as a patterned change; (2) the sign of the B-coefficients must change at some point in the series; (3) the change in sign must endure for at least five elections; and (4) statistically significant B-coefficients must exist in both the positive and the negative series. A critical change in B-coefficients qualifies as a realigning change as long as it yields a statistically significant B-coefficient with a different sign.[12]

### THE MACHINE AND PLURALIST THESES: A LONGITUDINAL, MULTIVARIATE ANALYSIS

The examination of the machine and pluralist theses involves a comparison of the explanatory power of the STATE PARTY DOMINANCE variable and the pluralist variables across the thirty-one elections held from 1872

---

[12] An example using the ROMAN CATHOLIC variable will illustrate these decision rules. A series of B-coefficients that was constant over a series of elections, or fluctuated randomly, would suggest that there was no patterned change in the ROMAN CATHOLIC variable. However, if the B-coefficients declined steadily over a series of at least five elections, then it would be impossible to reject the patterned change thesis for the ROMAN CATHOLIC variable. If the B-coefficients for ROMAN CATHOLIC declined steadily from .50 to −.10 over a series of ten elections, it would be evidence of both secular change and realigning change as long as two other conditions are met. They are: (1) the series of negative coefficients would have to endure for at least five elections; and (2) the entire series would have to include *statistically significant* B-coefficients that were both *positive and negative*. A sudden drop in B-coefficients (i.e., a B-coefficient of .50 in 1892 to −.10 in 1896) would qualify as a critical change as long as the B-coefficients remained in the −.10 range for at least five elections. Because the drop in B-coefficients also involves a change in sign (i.e., from .50 to −.10), this qualifies as a realigning change.

through 1992. To conduct this examination I constructed a stepwise regression model for each of these elections; the unit of analysis is the local electorate. As a measure of explanatory power, I use the change in $r_2$'s attributable to the variables entered at different stages of the analysis. In conducting the regressions I adopted a uniform model specification. The order in which the variables were entered into the analysis is as follows: (1) FEMALE, (2) the variables used to capture the effects of race (AFRICAN AMERICAN$_{LN}$, URBAN$_1$, AFRICAN AMERICAN$_{LN}$ X URBAN$_1$), (3) the religion variables (BAPTIST, EPISCOPALIAN, METHODIST, PRESYBTERIAN, ROMAN CATHOLIC), (4) the ethnicity variables (ENGLAND, GERMANY, SOUTHERN EUROPEAN, SCANDINAVIAN), (5) the sectional dummy variables (NEW ENGLAND, MIDDLE ATLANTIC, SOUTH, MIDWEST, PLAINS, MOUNTAINS, WEST COAST), and (6) STATE PARTY DOMINANCE.

The gender and race variables were entered first because they represent the most fundamental and immutable demographic traits. The religion variables preceded the ethnicity variables because several of the ethnicities included here are multidenominational (ENGLAND, GERMANY), and I wanted to determine the effect of ethnicity net of religion. The four sets of ethnocultural variables precede the sectional variables because, as noted earlier, the latter are crude indicators of social and economic interests. Their impact should only be gauged "net" of the social composition of local electorates. The STATE PARTY DOMINANCE variable is entered last because it cannot be considered causally prior to any of the pluralist variables. For the machine thesis to receive empirical support, the regression analyses must demonstrate that dominant parties can assemble larger electoral bases than would be expected by the social composition and geopolitical setting of a local electorate.

The B-coefficients for the regression models produced by this analysis are reported in table 6–1; the statistically significant coefficients (using the .001 criterion) are bolded. The results of the analysis itself are displayed in figure 6–2, which the report changes in the $r_2$'s for each set of variables. Table 6–2 reports the data used to construct figure 6–2, along with the adjusted $r_2$'s for each model.[13]

---

[13] The model $r_2$'s ranged from .26 in 1872 to .69 in 1928. The makeup of local partisan constituencies becomes progressively more structured after 1872, with the $r_2$'s rising in every election until 1932. The $r_2$'s decline from .62 in 1932 to .48 in 1952, then begin to rise. They reach a post-1932 peak of .61 in 1988 and 1992. The main reason for the decline in $r_2$'s after 1932 is the deterioration in the effects of the STATE PARTY DOMINANCE variable. The impact of the pluralist variables reaches historically high levels after 1932 but their impact begins to decline in 1940. This post-1940 decline is due largely to a drop in the strength of section, religion, and race. After 1952, however, the impact of the pluralist variables begins to rise again, largely due to the emergence of a gender gap, the increasing significance of race in large urban areas, and the increasing importance of the ethnicity variables.

TABLE 6.1
Mass-Elite Dynamics Regression Coefficients

| Year | Constant | Female | African American$_{LN}$ | Urban$_1$ | African American$_{LN}$ X Urban$_1$ | Baptist | Episcopalian | Methodist | Presbyterian | Roman Catholic | English |
|------|----------|--------|-------------------------|-----------|-------------------------------------|---------|--------------|-----------|--------------|----------------|---------|
| 1872 | −0.07 |  | −0.01 | 0.01 | 0.06 | 0.05 | −0.66 | 0.13 | 0.11 | 0.08 | −1.12 |
| 1876 | −0.16 |  | −0.02 | −0.08 | 0.10 | 0.04 | −0.87 | 0.14 | 0.10 | 0.14 | −1.20 |
| 1880 | −0.25 |  | −0.02 | −0.06 | 0.05 | −0.04 | −0.60 | 0.07 | −0.01 | 0.21 | −1.23 |
| 1884 | −0.31 |  | −0.05 | −0.08 | 0.01 | −0.14 | −0.36 | 0.06 | 0.00 | 0.19 | −1.03 |
| 1888 | −0.33 |  | −0.02 | −0.03 | −0.03 | −0.18 | −0.21 | 0.00 | 0.03 | 0.20 | −1.13 |
| 1892 | −0.31 |  | 0.00 | −0.05 | −0.03 | −0.06 | −1.55 | 0.20 | −0.12 | 0.40 | −1.51 |
| 1896 | −0.24 |  | 0.01 | 0.06 | −0.13 | 0.07 | −2.42 | 0.58 | −0.34 | 0.40 | −2.06 |
| 1900 | −0.25 |  | 0.00 | 0.08 | −0.12 | 0.05 | −1.21 | 0.81 | −0.39 | 0.33 | −2.48 |
| 1904 | −0.34 |  | −0.01 | 0.05 | −0.13 | 0.40 | 0.01 | 1.07 | −0.75 | 0.33 | −2.84 |
| 1908 | −0.26 |  | −0.01 | 0.06 | −0.11 | 0.48 | −0.46 | 0.93 | −0.75 | 0.34 | −3.05 |
| 1912 | −0.25 |  | 0.04 | 0.05 | −0.05 | 0.38 | −1.10 | 0.61 | −0.96 | 0.21 | −2.95 |
| 1916 | −0.34 |  | 0.03 | 0.03 | −0.04 | 0.36 | −1.22 | 0.42 | −0.95 | 0.14 | −2.65 |
| 1920 | −0.63 | 0.44 | 0.01 | 0.06 | −0.07 | 0.28 | −0.49 | 0.53 | −0.75 | 0.23 | −4.13 |
| 1924 | −0.49 | 0.14 | 0.01 | 0.08 | −0.09 | 0.30 | −0.46 | 0.64 | −0.83 | 0.23 | −4.47 |
| 1928 | −0.46 | 0.08 | 0.03 | 0.13 | −0.07 | 0.40 | −1.18 | 0.80 | −0.96 | 0.24 | −1.57 |
| 1932 | 0.26 | −0.40 | 0.22 | 0.11 | 0.32 | 0.51 | −4.48 | −0.20 | −1.13 | 0.36 | 1.54 |
| 1936 | 0.12 | −0.17 | 0.20 | 0.04 | 0.35 | 0.56 | −4.49 | −0.18 | −1.19 | 0.35 | 2.49 |
| 1940 | 0.15 | −0.33 | 0.21 | 0.00 | 0.39 | 0.51 | −4.50 | −0.25 | −1.00 | 0.32 | 2.31 |
| 1944 | 0.03 | −0.12 | 0.21 | −0.09 | 0.39 | 0.33 | −4.71 | −0.33 | −0.76 | 0.29 | 2.48 |
| 1948 | −0.08 | 0.12 | 0.22 | −0.20 | 0.42 | 0.18 | −4.54 | −0.41 | −0.60 | 0.27 | 2.32 |
| 1952 | 0.20 | −0.43 | 0.22 | −0.10 | 0.41 | 0.34 | −3.94 | −0.33 | −0.58 | 0.30 | 1.67 |
| 1956 | −0.30 | 0.50 | 0.21 | −0.16 | 0.40 | 0.30 | −3.83 | −0.36 | −0.38 | 0.34 | 1.26 |
| 1960 | −0.48 | 0.79 | 0.16 | −0.33 | 0.43 | 0.28 | −3.54 | −0.38 | −0.09 | 0.36 | −0.31 |
| 1964 | −0.54 | 1.06 | 0.13 | −0.31 | 0.37 | 0.22 | −3.22 | −0.32 | 0.06 | 0.32 | −1.02 |
| 1968 | −0.35 | 0.83 | 0.11 | −0.38 | 0.37 | 0.18 | −2.61 | −0.26 | 0.20 | 0.25 | −1.26 |
| 1972 | −0.57 | 1.17 | 0.09 | −0.39 | 0.34 | 0.09 | −2.02 | −0.25 | 0.28 | 0.22 | −1.01 |
| 1976 | −1.07 | 2.04 | 0.08 | −0.31 | 0.29 | −0.02 | −1.42 | −0.12 | 0.26 | 0.17 | −0.91 |
| 1980 | −1.24 | 2.30 | 0.07 | −0.55 | 0.34 | −0.10 | −0.96 | 0.00 | 0.27 | 0.12 | −0.80 |
| 1984 | −1.32 | 2.49 | 0.05 | −0.68 | 0.35 | −0.19 | −0.93 | 0.06 | 0.43 | 0.08 | −0.71 |
| 1988 | −1.55 | 2.93 | 0.05 | −0.76 | 0.36 | −0.26 | −0.89 | −0.02 | 0.57 | 0.05 | −0.64 |
| 1992 | −0.85 | 1.65 | 0.01 | 0.32 | 0.36 | −0.32 | −0.21 | −0.15 | 0.55 | 0.09 | −0.53 |

TABLE 6.1 (*cont'd*)
Mass-Elite Dynamics Regression Coefficients

| Year | German | Scandi- navian | Southern European | New England | Mid Atlantic | South | Midwest | Plains | Mountain | West Coast | State Party Dominace |
|------|--------|--------|--------|--------|--------|--------|--------|--------|--------|--------|--------|
| 1872 | 0.98 | −1.74 | −1.55 | −0.18 | −0.12 | 0.03 | −0.16 | −0.09 | −0.02 | −0.12 | 0.29 |
| 1876 | 1.02 | −1.87 | −1.94 | −0.09 | −0.03 | 0.18 | −0.08 | −0.03 | 0.05 | −0.04 | 0.31 |
| 1880 | 0.82 | −1.66 | 3.43 | 0.01 | 0.04 | 0.22 | −0.03 | −0.02 | 0.10 | −0.04 | 0.42 |
| 1884 | 0.77 | −1.35 | 3.96 | 0.07 | 0.04 | 0.17 | 0.00 | 0.03 | 0.16 | −0.03 | 0.56 |
| 1888 | 0.66 | −0.97 | 3.34 | 0.08 | 0.04 | 0.17 | 0.00 | 0.03 | 0.05 | −0.02 | 0.59 |
| 1892 | 0.50 | −1.03 | 3.68 | 0.02 | 0.04 | 0.20 | −0.02 | 0.01 | 0.08 | 0.02 | 0.48 |
| 1896 | −0.15 | −1.48 | 6.26 | −0.16 | −0.08 | 0.21 | −0.04 | 0.04 | 0.09 | 0.00 | 0.33 |
| 1900 | −0.09 | −1.47 | 4.67 | −0.14 | −0.11 | 0.22 | −0.03 | 0.06 | 0.13 | 0.03 | 0.34 |
| 1904 | 0.17 | −1.28 | 3.68 | −0.10 | −0.10 | 0.24 | −0.01 | 0.07 | 0.15 | 0.04 | 0.40 |
| 1908 | −0.17 | −1.32 | 2.74 | −0.17 | −0.15 | 0.27 | −0.05 | 0.02 | 0.11 | −0.04 | 0.27 |
| 1912 | −0.25 | −1.13 | 2.22 | −0.19 | −0.14 | 0.27 | −0.07 | −0.02 | 0.08 | −0.07 | 0.29 |
| 1916 | −0.18 | −0.97 | 1.40 | −0.13 | −0.09 | 0.30 | −0.08 | −0.02 | 0.09 | −0.03 | 0.40 |
| 1920 | 0.13 | −0.50 | 1.54 | −0.12 | −0.08 | 0.26 | −0.11 | −0.03 | 0.04 | −0.01 | 0.50 |
| 1924 | 0.10 | −0.69 | 1.31 | −0.10 | −0.06 | 0.21 | −0.06 | 0.00 | 0.01 | −0.01 | 0.57 |
| 1928 | 0.48 | −0.95 | 1.33 | −0.10 | −0.09 | 0.25 | −0.05 | 0.01 | 0.03 | −0.06 | 0.49 |
| 1932 | −2.01 | 1.09 | 2.88 | −0.18 | −0.20 | 0.36 | −0.17 | −0.11 | 0.00 | −0.06 | −0.07 |
| 1936 | −2.54 | 1.34 | 2.85 | −0.17 | −0.19 | 0.34 | −0.15 | −0.10 | 0.00 | −0.06 | −0.05 |
| 1940 | −3.06 | 1.82 | 2.94 | −0.13 | −0.15 | 0.31 | −0.13 | −0.07 | 0.01 | −0.04 | 0.04 |
| 1944 | −3.23 | 2.11 | 4.27 | −0.13 | −0.15 | 0.30 | −0.14 | −0.06 | 0.00 | −0.08 | 0.04 |
| 1948 | −3.51 | 2.34 | 3.47 | −0.11 | −0.14 | 0.30 | −0.15 | −0.07 | 0.00 | −0.11 | 0.02 |
| 1952 | −3.14 | 1.01 | 2.45 | −0.08 | −0.13 | 0.05 | −0.15 | −0.13 | −0.05 | −0.09 | −0.12 |
| 1956 | −2.63 | 0.63 | 1.65 | −0.09 | −0.15 | 0.03 | −0.15 | −0.11 | −0.07 | −0.09 | −0.10 |
| 1960 | −1.70 | 1.08 | 0.76 | −0.07 | −0.13 | −0.01 | −0.10 | −0.06 | −0.09 | −0.08 | −0.04 |
| 1964 | −1.53 | 0.86 | −0.20 | −0.04 | −0.07 | −0.04 | −0.07 | −0.03 | −0.09 | −0.07 | −0.03 |
| 1968 | −1.16 | 0.64 | −0.66 | 0.00 | −0.05 | −0.05 | −0.05 | −0.02 | −0.09 | −0.07 | −0.05 |
| 1972 | −0.82 | 0.62 | −0.86 | 0.04 | −0.01 | −0.08 | −0.03 | 0.01 | −0.08 | −0.06 | 0.05 |
| 1976 | −0.67 | 0.61 | −0.87 | 0.04 | 0.02 | −0.11 | 0.00 | 0.04 | −0.06 | −0.03 | 0.16 |
| 1980 | −0.55 | 0.50 | −0.74 | 0.06 | 0.04 | −0.12 | 0.01 | 0.05 | −0.03 | −0.01 | 0.23 |
| 1984 | −0.49 | 0.39 | −0.67 | 0.07 | 0.05 | −0.12 | 0.02 | 0.06 | 0.00 | 0.01 | 0.25 |
| 1988 | −0.42 | 0.32 | −0.58 | 0.09 | 0.07 | −0.12 | 0.03 | 0.08 | 0.03 | 0.04 | 0.28 |
| 1992 | −0.37 | 0.20 | −0.40 | 0.06 | 0.05 | −0.12 | 0.03 | 0.07 | 0.00 | 0.00 | 0.30 |

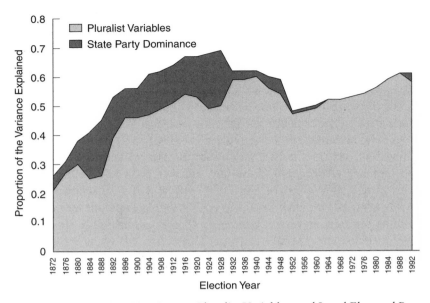

Figure 6–2. State Party Dominance, Pluralist Variables, and Local Electoral Bases

This analysis is admittedly a rough test of the machine and pluralist perspectives on mass-elite linkages. However, the multivariate results summarized in figure 6–2 reveal a fundamentally different picture from that depicted in figure 6–1. It suggests that the machine model is not merely temporally limited: the STATE PARTY DOMINANCE variable does not exert a powerful, independent effect on the size of local electoral bases at any point in time. The results of the multivariate analyses show that much of the explanatory power of the STATE PARTY DOMINANCE variable depicted in figure 6–1 is, in fact, attributable to ethnocultural and geo-political factors. Once these variables are controlled, the change in $r_2$ due to STATE PARTY DOMINANCE never amounts to more than 19 percent of the variance, less than a third of its largest value in the bivariate analyses. Moreover, the STATE PARTY DOMINANCE variable explains 19 percent of the variance in only three elections; it adds more than 10 percent in only ten elections—less than one-third of those studied. None of these were before 1884 or after 1928.

The pluralist model offers a far more persuasive account of mass-elite linkages, particularly in the twentieth century. On average, the pluralist variables account for 55 percent of the variance in NORMAL PARTISAN BALANCE after 1900. Moreover, the pluralist variables, on average, account for 95 percent of the variance explained by the regression models during the twentieth century. In contrast, STATE PARTY DOMINANCE ac-

TABLE 6.2
Change in $r_2$'s by Categories of Variables

| Year | Gender | Race | Religion | Ethnicity | Locale | Section | Party Dominance | Model $r_2$ |
|------|--------|------|----------|-----------|--------|---------|-----------------|-------------|
| 1872 |        | 0.08 | 0.02     | 0.06      | 0      | 0.05    | 0.05            | 0.26        |
| 1876 |        | 0.1  | 0.03     | 0.06      | 0      | 0.08    | 0.04            | 0.31        |
| 1880 |        | 0.13 | 0.02     | 0.07      | 0      | 0.08    | 0.08            | 0.38        |
| 1884 |        | 0.12 | 0.02     | 0.07      | 0      | 0.04    | 0.16            | 0.41        |
| 1888 |        | 0.15 | 0.01     | 0.07      | 0      | 0.03    | 0.19            | 0.45        |
| 1892 |        | 0.19 | 0.09     | 0.06      | 0      | 0.05    | 0.14            | 0.53        |
| 1896 |        | 0.18 | 0.14     | 0.08      | 0      | 0.06    | 0.1             | 0.56        |
| 1900 |        | 0.17 | 0.14     | 0.07      | 0      | 0.08    | 0.1             | 0.56        |
| 1904 |        | 0.17 | 0.2      | 0.04      | 0      | 0.06    | 0.14            | 0.61        |
| 1908 |        | 0.17 | 0.23     | 0.02      | 0      | 0.07    | 0.13            | 0.62        |
| 1912 |        | 0.19 | 0.23     | 0.02      | 0      | 0.07    | 0.13            | 0.64        |
| 1916 |        | 0.18 | 0.26     | 0.02      | 0      | 0.08    | 0.13            | 0.67        |
| 1920 | 0.02   | 0.19 | 0.24     | 0.03      | 0      | 0.05    | 0.14            | 0.67        |
| 1924 | 0.01   | 0.16 | 0.28     | 0.02      | 0      | 0.02    | 0.19            | 0.68        |
| 1928 | 0.01   | 0.16 | 0.29     | 0.01      | 0      | 0.03    | 0.19            | 0.69        |
| 1932 | 0.01   | 0.15 | 0.21     | 0.04      | 0      | 0.18    | 0.03            | 0.62        |
| 1936 | 0.04   | 0.14 | 0.2      | 0.05      | 0      | 0.16    | 0.03            | 0.62        |
| 1940 | 0.04   | 0.14 | 0.19     | 0.05      | 0      | 0.18    | 0.02            | 0.62        |
| 1944 | 0.04   | 0.14 | 0.18     | 0.04      | 0      | 0.16    | 0.04            | 0.6         |
| 1948 | 0.03   | 0.13 | 0.16     | 0.04      | 0      | 0.18    | 0.05            | 0.59        |
| 1952 | 0.04   | 0.08 | 0.11     | 0.04      | 0      | 0.2     | 0.01            | 0.48        |
| 1956 | 0.07   | 0.09 | 0.12     | 0.03      | 0      | 0.17    | 0.01            | 0.49        |
| 1960 | 0.09   | 0.08 | 0.11     | 0.04      | 0      | 0.17    | 0.01            | 0.5         |
| 1964 | 0.1    | 0.09 | 0.1      | 0.07      | 0      | 0.16    | 0               | 0.52        |
| 1968 | 0.11   | 0.1  | 0.09     | 0.08      | 0.01   | 0.13    | 0               | 0.52        |
| 1972 | 0.13   | 0.09 | 0.07     | 0.09      | 0.01   | 0.14    | 0               | 0.53        |
| 1976 | 0.18   | 0.09 | 0.06     | 0.1       | 0      | 0.11    | 0               | 0.54        |
| 1980 | 0.18   | 0.11 | 0.05     | 0.11      | 0.01   | 0.1     | 0               | 0.56        |
| 1984 | 0.19   | 0.12 | 0.04     | 0.11      | 0.02   | 0.11    | 0               | 0.59        |
| 1988 | 0.16   | 0.13 | 0.07     | 0.11      | 0.02   | 0.12    | 0               | 0.61        |
| 1992 | 0.17   | 0.07 | 0.13     | 0.12      | 0.06   | 0.03    | 0.03            | 0.61        |

counts for as much as 5 percent of the variance in only one election after 1928. At the height of its explanatory power (1884 to 1928) the STATE PARTY DOMINANCE variable accounts for about 40 percent of the variance explained by all of the independent variables in two elections (1884 and 1888), but the normal range for this period is between 20 percent and 25 percent of the variance explained by the regression models.

The results of the multivariate analyses presented thus far provide important insights into mass-elite linkages within political parties. They suggest that parties have some ability to enlarge their electoral bases, but it peaked during the late-nineteenth century and has declined markedly throughout the latter half of the twentieth century. On the other hand, the ability of party elites to forge local electoral coalitions is bounded by important exogenous constraints. Institutional characteristics have never been as important to the forging of local electoral bases as the distribution of social groups and interests. Thus, the pluralist perspective on mass-elite linkages within political parties seems closer to the mark than the machine perspective. This, of course, suggests that the political actions and strategies of party elites are guided and constrained by the demographic makeup of their locales. While this may not be surprising to pluralists, it has important implications for the interpretation of partisan influences on voting.

## THE PATTERNED CHANGE THESIS: THE DURABILITY OF VOTER ALIGNMENTS

Examining the patterned change thesis can generate additional insights into the meaning of partisan influences on voting. The argument that social and interest group leaders are important members of party hierarchies is an important part of the pluralist perspective on mass-elite linkages. Central to the pluralist perspective is the assertion that major social groups and interests will adjust their partisan affiliations if parties are insensitive to their needs. The lessons learned from these periodic ruptures of group ties become part party elites' education into democratic politics. However, if social groups have not regularly demonstrated the capacity to switch partisan affiliations, party professionals would learn a different set of lessons about democratic politics. Threats by social and interest group leaders to "bolt" would not be taken seriously, and party elites would have more latitude to pursue personal agendas. As a consequence, the influence of those leaders within party councils would be considerably reduced.

For these reasons, the examination of the patterned change thesis focuses on the temporal distribution of B-coefficients for the pluralist variables reported in table 6–1. If these B-coefficients do not reveal patterned changes, then the data would be inconsistent with the assertion that social groups and interests have demonstrated the capacity to realign their loyalties. And the patterned change thesis would have to be rejected. Table 6–3 summarizes the results of the patterned change analysis. Table 6–4 displays the patterned changes in the B-coefficients reported in table 6–1. A blue background indicates patterned Democratic changes; a red background indicates patterned Republican changes. Critical changes in B-coefficients are bolded and bordered; an asterisk indicates realigning changes.

The summary data reported in table 6–3 show that the patterned change thesis cannot be rejected. Overall, nearly half of the B-coefficients (45 percent) evidence some form of patterned change (secular or critical). This aggregate figure masks a good deal of variance across the pluralist variables, as is evident in column 2 of table 6–3. For example, the B-coefficients for the MOUNTAIN variable evidence no patterned changes, while more than 70% of the B-coefficients for PRESBYTERIAN, SCANDINAVIAN, GERMAN, and ENGLISH evidence patterned changes. Overall, the B-coefficients for the ethnicity variables reveal much more patterned change (67 percent) than those for the section variables (34 percent), or for the race, gender, and religion variables (32 percent). The vast majority of patterned changes are secular. Indeed, only eight instances of critical changes in B-coefficients were uncovered (table 6–3, column 4). Seventeen instances of realigning changes were uncovered (table 6–3, column 5). Only six variables did not yield an instance of realigning change (FEMALE, AFRICAN AMERICAN$_{LN}$, ROMAN CATHOLIC, MIDWEST, MOUNTAIN, WEST COAST).

Examining table 6–4 demonstrates that there is an underlying temporal structure to the patterned changes summarized in table 6–3. Nearly all of the critical changes in B-coefficients (7 of 8) occur in one of two elections: 1932 and 1952. As will be seen in chapter 7, these two elections represent two of the most important critical elections in U.S. political history (see figure 7–2). It is also clear the bulk of the secular changes in B-coefficients occur in one of two periods. The first is around the turn of the twentieth century. These changes correspond to two realignment eras identified in chapter 7 identifies as the Jim Crow Era and the Industrial Era (see map 7–3 and 7–4; figure 7–6 and 7–7). Table 6–4 shows that there was a clear ethnocultural structure to the electoral shifts that took place in those eras, in addition to the geo-political structure displayed in map 7–3 and map 7–4. During this period the data suggest that locales with high concentrations of several ethnocultural groups (Baptists, Presbyterians, English, Germans, Scandinavians, Southern Europeans) modified their partisan leanings, as did major sections of the United States. (New England, Middle Atlantic States, South).

The second period of widespread partisan change among important social groups and interests corresponds to what chapter 7 identifies as the Civil Rights Era (see map 7–6 and figure 7–9). The second half of the twentieth century has seen a major reshuffling of the electoral bases that emerged from the New Deal Era (see map 7–5 and figure 7–8). Locales with higher concentrations of women and African Americans evidence sustained movements into the Democratic camp, along with several Protestant denominations (Episcopalians, Methodists, Presbyterians) and Northern Europeans (English, Germans). Also, locales in New England, the Middle Atlantic States, the Midwest, the Plains States, and the West Coast shifted from net Republican leanings to net Democratic leanings during this period. In contrast, locales with high concentrations of Baptists, Roman Catholics, Scandinavians, and Southern Europeans have moved toward the Republicans during this period. So too has the South.

## Summary

The data presented here, while crude and indirect, provide important insights into the nature of mass-elite linkages within political parties. These data suggest that the machine model seems plausible for only a brief interlude in American political history, the tail end of the nineteenth century. On the other hand, neither the pluralist thesis nor the patterned change thesis could be rejected. The examination of the pluralist thesis shows that, even during the Gilded Age, the pluralist variables "outperformed" STATE PARTY DOMINANCE by a considerable margin. The empirical support for the pluralist thesis is even stronger in the twentieth century. After 1900 ethnocultural and geo-political factors explain, on average, more than half of the variance in the NORMAL PARTISAN BALANCE variable and most (95 percent) of the variance explained by the regression models.

These findings lend little credence to the view that political parties are capable of forging and maintaining electoral coalitions simply on the basis of aggressive and well-conceived organizational strategies. Strategic efforts by strong local party organizations may be sufficient to sway swing voters in some elections, and these shifts may be sufficient to generate electoral victories in competitive electoral settings. But there is no support for the view that the actions and strategies of party insiders trump the group loyalties of voters. Instead, the findings reported here suggest that party elites have important incentives to be attentive to the concerns and demands of the social groups and interests that form their electoral base. The examination of the patterned change thesis produced results that reinforced this inference. Looking at group-based partisan allegiances over time, it is clear that they have regularly demonstrated the capacity to adjust their partisan loyalties.

TABLE 6.3
Summary of Data on Patterned Changes in B-coefficients

| Pluralist Variable | Proportion of B-coefficients Evidencing Patterned Changes | Secular Changes | Critical Changes | Realigning Changes |
|---|---|---|---|---|
| FEMALE | 0.56 | 1956–1988 (Democratic) | None | None |
| AFRICAN AMERICAN$_{LN}$ | 0.37 | 1956–1992 (Republican) | None | None |
| AFRICAN AMERICAN$_{LN}$ X URBAN$_1$ | 0.03 | None | 1932 (Democratic) | 1932 (Democratic) |
| BAPTIST | 0.37 | 1956–1992 (Republican) | 1904 (Democratic) | 1904 (Democratic); 1976 (Republican) |
| EPISCOPALIAN | 0.43 | 1948–1992 (Democratic) | 1932 (Republican) | None |
| METHODIST | 0.27 | 1964–1984 (Democratic) | 1932 (Republican) | 1932 (Republican) |
| PRESBYTERIAN | 0.70 | 1892–1912 (Republican); 1940–1992 (Democratic) | None | 1964 (Democratic) |
| ROMAN CATHOLIC | 0.23 | 1964–1988 (Republican) | None | None |
| ENGLISH | 0.80 | 1888–1924 (Republican); 1948–1968 (Republican); 1972–1992 (Democratic) | 1928–1932 (Democratic) | 1932 (Democratic); 1960 (Republican) |
| GERMAN | 0.73 | 1880–1900 (Republican); 1932–1948 (Republican); 1952–1992 (Democratic) | 1932 (Republican) | 1932 (Republican) |
| SCANDINAVIAN | 0.70 | 1900–1928 (Democratic); 1932–1948 (Democratic); 1964–1992 (Republican) | 1932 (Democratic) | 1932 (Democratic) |
| SOUTHERN EUROPEAN | 0.47 | 1900–1916 (Republican); 1948–1976 (Republican) | None | 1964 (Republican) |
| NEW ENGLAND | 0.47 | 1936–1988 (Democratic) | None | 1896 (Republican); 1972 (Democratic) |
| MID-ATLANTIC | 0.47 | 1936–1988 (Democratic) | None | 1896 (Republican); 1976 (Democratic) |
| SOUTH | 0.63 | 1892–1916 (Democratic); 1936–1980 (Republican) | 1952 (Republican) | 1960 (Republican) |
| MIDWEST | 0.26 | 1960–1988 (Democratic) | None | None |
| PLAINS | 0.30 | 1956–1988 (Democratic) | None | 1972 (Democratic) |
| MOUNTAIN | 0.00 | None | None | None |
| WEST COAST | 0.27 | 1960–1988 (Democratic) | None | None |

TABLE 6.4
Patterned Changes in Regression Coefficients for the Pluralist Variables

| Year | Female | African American$_{LN}$ | African American$_{LN}$ X Urban$_1$ | Baptist | Episcopalian | Methodist | Presbyterian | Roman Catholic | English |
|------|--------|------------------------|------------------------------------|---------|--------------|-----------|--------------|----------------|---------|
| 1872 |       | −0.01 | 0.06 | 0.05 | −0.66 | 0.13 | 0.11 | 0.08 | −1.12 |
| 1876 |       | −0.02 | 0.10 | 0.04 | −0.87 | 0.14 | 0.10 | 0.14 | −1.20 |
| 1880 |       | −0.02 | 0.05 | −0.04 | −0.60 | 0.07 | −0.01 | 0.21 | −1.23 |
| 1884 |       | −0.05 | 0.01 | −0.14 | −0.36 | 0.06 | 0.00 | 0.19 | −1.03 |
| 1888 |       | −0.02 | −0.03 | −0.18 | −0.21 | 0.00 | 0.03 | 0.20 | −1.13 |
| 1892 |       | 0.00 | −0.03 | −0.06 | −1.55 | 0.20 | −0.12 | 0.40 | −1.51 |
| 1896 |       | 0.01 | −0.13 | 0.07 | −2.42 | 0.58 | −0.34 | 0.40 | −2.06 |
| 1900 |       | 0.00 | −0.12 | 0.05 | −1.21 | 0.81 | −0.39 | 0.33 | −2.48 |
| 1904 |       | −0.01 | −0.13 | 0.40* | 0.01 | 1.07 | −0.75 | 0.33 | −2.84 |
| 1908 |       | −0.01 | −0.11 | 0.48 | −0.46 | 0.93 | −0.75 | 0.34 | −3.05 |
| 1912 |       | 0.04 | −0.05 | 0.38 | −1.10 | 0.61 | −0.96 | 0.21 | −2.95 |
| 1916 |       | 0.03 | −0.04 | 0.36 | −1.22 | 0.42 | −0.95 | 0.14 | −2.65 |
| 1920 | 0.44 | 0.01 | −0.07 | 0.28 | −0.49 | 0.53 | −0.75 | 0.23 | −4.13 |
| 1924 | 0.14 | 0.01 | −0.09 | 0.30 | −0.46 | 0.64 | −0.83 | 0.23 | −4.47 |
| 1928 | 0.08 | 0.03 | −0.07 | 0.40 | −1.18 | 0.80 | −0.96 | 0.24 | −1.57 |
| 1932 | −0.40 | 0.22 | 1.32* | 0.51 | −4.48 | −0.20* | −1.13 | 0.36 | 1.54* |
| 1936 | −0.17 | 0.20 | 0.35 | 0.56 | −4.49 | −0.18 | −1.19 | 0.35 | 2.49 |
| 1940 | −0.33 | 0.21 | 0.39 | 0.51 | −4.50 | −0.25 | −1.00 | 0.32 | 2.31 |
| 1944 | −0.12 | 0.21 | 0.39 | 0.33 | −4.71 | −0.33 | −0.76 | 0.29 | 2.48 |
| 1948 | 0.12 | 0.22 | 0.42 | 0.18 | −4.54 | −0.41 | −0.60 | 0.27 | 2.32 |
| 1952 | −0.43 | 0.22 | 0.41 | 0.34 | −3.94 | −0.33 | −0.58 | 0.30 | 1.67 |
| 1956 | 0.50 | 0.21 | 0.40 | 0.30 | −3.83 | −0.36 | −0.38 | 0.34 | 1.26 |
| 1960 | 0.79 | 0.16 | 0.43 | 0.28 | −3.54 | −0.38 | −0.09 | 0.36 | −0.31* |
| 1964 | 1.06 | 0.13 | 0.37 | 0.22 | −3.22 | −0.32 | 0.06* | 0.32 | −1.02 |
| 1968 | 0.83 | 0.11 | 0.37 | 0.18 | −2.61 | −0.26 | 0.20 | 0.25 | −1.26 |
| 1972 | 1.17 | 0.09 | 0.34 | 0.09 | −2.02 | −0.25 | 0.28 | 0.22 | −1.01 |
| 1976 | 2.04 | 0.08 | 0.29 | −0.02* | −1.42 | −0.12 | 0.26 | 0.17 | −0.91 |
| 1980 | 2.30 | 0.07 | 0.34 | −0.10 | −0.96 | 0.00 | 0.27 | 0.12 | −0.80 |
| 1984 | 2.49 | 0.05 | 0.35 | −0.19 | −0.93 | 0.06 | 0.43 | 0.08 | −0.71 |
| 1988 | 2.93 | 0.05 | 0.36 | −0.26 | −0.89 | −0.02 | 0.57 | 0.05 | −0.64 |
| 1992 | 1.65 | 0.01 | 0.36 | −0.32 | −0.21 | −0.15 | 0.55 | 0.09 | −0.53 |

TABLE 6.4 (*cont'd*)
Patterned Changes in Regression Coefficients for the Pluralist Variables

| Year | German | Scandi-navian | Southern European | New England | Mid Atlantic | South | Midwest | Plains | Mountain | West Coast |
|------|--------|--------|--------|--------|--------|--------|--------|--------|--------|--------|
| 1872 | 0.98 | −1.74 | −1.55 | 0.18 | −0.12 | 0.03 | −0.16 | −0.09 | −0.02 | −0.12 |
| 1876 | 1.02 | −1.87 | −1.94 | −0.09 | −0.03 | 0.18 | −0.08 | −1.03 | 0.05 | −0.04 |
| 1880 | 0.82 | −1.66 | 3.43 | 0.01 | 0.04 | 0.22 | −0.03 | −0.02 | 0.10 | −0.04 |
| 1884 | 0.77 | −1.35 | 3.96 | 0.07 | 0.04 | 0.17 | 0.00 | 0.03 | 0.16 | −0.03 |
| 1888 | 0.66 | −0.97 | 3.34 | 0.08 | 0.04 | 0.17 | 0.00 | 0.03 | 0.05 | −0.02 |
| 1892 | 0.50 | −1.03 | 3.68 | 0.02 | 0.04 | 0.20 | −0.02 | 0.01 | 0.08 | 0.02 |
| 1896 | −0.15 | −1.48 | 6.26 | −0.16* | −0.08* | 0.21 | −0.04 | 0.04 | 0.09 | 0.00 |
| 1900 | −0.09 | −1.47 | 4.67 | −0.14 | −0.11 | 0.22 | −0.03 | 0.06 | 0.13 | 0.03 |
| 1904 | 0.17 | −1.28 | 3.68 | −0.10 | −0.10 | 0.24 | −0.01 | 0.07 | 0.15 | 0.04 |
| 1908 | −0.17 | −1.32 | 2.74 | −0.17 | −0.15 | 0.27 | −0.05 | 0.02 | 0.11 | −0.04 |
| 1912 | −0.25 | −1.13 | 2.22 | −0.19 | −0.14 | 0.27 | −0.07 | −0.02 | 0.08 | −0.07 |
| 1916 | −0.18 | −0.97 | 1.40 | −0.13 | −0.09 | 0.30 | −0.08 | −0.02 | 0.09 | −0.03 |
| 1920 | 0.13 | −0.50 | 1.54 | −0.12 | −0.08 | 0.26 | −0.11 | −0.03 | 0.04 | −0.01 |
| 1924 | 0.10 | −0.69 | 1.31 | −0.10 | −0.06 | 0.21 | −0.06 | 0.00 | 0.01 | −0.01 |
| 1928 | 0.48 | −0.95 | 1.33 | −0.10 | −0.09 | 0.25 | −0.05 | 0.01 | 0.03 | −0.06 |
| 1932 | −2.01* | 1.09* | 2.88 | −0.18 | −0.20 | 0.36 | −0.17 | −0.11 | 0.00 | −0.06 |
| 1936 | −2.54 | 1.34 | 2.85 | −0.17 | −0.19 | 0.34 | −0.15 | −0.10 | 0.00 | −0.06 |
| 1940 | −3.06 | 1.82 | 2.94 | −0.13 | −0.15 | 0.31 | −0.13 | −0.07 | 0.01 | −0.04 |
| 1944 | −3.23 | 2.11 | 4.27 | −0.13 | −0.15 | 0.30 | −0.14 | −0.06 | 0.00 | −0.08 |
| 1948 | −3.51 | 2.34 | 3.47 | −0.11 | −0.14 | 0.30 | −0.15 | −0.07 | 0.00 | −0.11 |
| 1952 | −3.14 | 1.01 | 2.45 | −0.08 | −0.13 | 0.05 | −0.15 | −0.13 | −0.05 | −0.09 |
| 1956 | −2.63 | 0.63 | 1.65 | −0.09 | −0.15 | 0.03 | −0.15 | −0.11 | −0.07 | −0.09 |
| 1960 | −1.70 | 1.08 | 0.76 | −0.07 | −0.13 | −0.01* | −0.10 | −0.06 | −0.09 | −0.08 |
| 1964 | −1.53 | 0.86 | −0.20* | −0.04 | −0.07 | −0.04 | −0.07 | −0.03 | −0.09 | −0.07 |
| 1968 | −1.16 | 0.64 | −0.66 | 0.00 | −0.05 | −0.05 | −0.05 | −0.02 | −0.09 | −0.07 |
| 1972 | −0.82 | 0.62 | −0.86 | 0.04* | −0.01 | −0.08 | −0.03 | 0.01* | −0.08 | −0.06 |
| 1976 | −0.67 | 0.61 | −0.87 | 0.04 | 0.02* | −0.11 | 0.00 | 0.04 | −0.06 | −0.03 |
| 1980 | −0.55 | 0.50 | −0.74 | 0.06 | 0.04 | −0.12 | 0.01 | 0.05 | −0.03 | −0.01 |
| 1984 | −0.49 | 0.39 | −0.67 | 0.07 | 0.05 | −0.12 | 0.02 | 0.06 | 0.00 | 0.01 |
| 1988 | −0.42 | 0.32 | −0.58 | 0.09 | 0.07 | −0.12 | 0.03 | 0.08 | 0.03 | 0.04 |
| 1992 | −0.37 | 0.20 | −0.40 | 0.06 | 0.05 | −0.12 | 0.03 | 0.07 | 0.00 | 0.00 |

The group-based patterns of electoral change documented here have important implications for our understanding of popular efficacy. They provide the stuff of party lore and are part of the political education of party elites. Stories about the missteps that led to the alienation of the women's vote, the Catholic vote, the ethnic vote, the South, and so forth, are part of the legacy that is disseminated across generations of party elites. Thus, the findings reported here underscore pluralist claims about the primacy of group loyalties by suggesting that core constituencies can, and do, desert parties with some regularity. These findings cast doubt on the conception of parties as endogenous institutions and underscore the importance of social and interest group leaders within party hierarchies, providing some insight into elites' incentives to be responsive to the concerns of their party's electoral base.

These findings have important implications for our understanding of partisan influences on voting. At a minimum, the multivariate findings presented here suggest that the interpretation of partisanship as an endogenous influence on voting is an extremely conservative one. A more generous view of these findings provides empirical support for three key corollaries posited in chapter 3 (C1, C2, C2.1). This view suggests that the party is not wholly tainted as a political heuristic, one that largely reflects the personal interests and strategic manipulations of party insiders. Rather, party may, in fact, be a low cost but valuable source of information during times of political normalcy, one that is continually updated by the dynamic engagement of pluralistic group leaders.

## REFERENCES

Aldrich, J. H. 1995. *Why Parties? The Origin and Transformation of Party Politics in America*. Chicago, University of Chicago Press.

Axelrod, R. 1972. "Where the Voters Come From: An Analysis of Electoral Coalitions: 1952–1968." *American Political Science Review* 66 (March): 11–21.

Benson, L. 1972. *The Concept of Jacksonian Democracy*. Princeton, Princeton University Press.

Bentley, A. F. 1908. *The Process of Government*. Cambridge, Harvard University Press.

Berelson, B. R., P. F. Lazarsfeld, et al. 1954. *Voting: A Study of Opinion Formation in a Presidential Campaign*. Chicago, University of Chicago Press.

Binkley, W. E. 1943. *American Political Parties: Their Natural History*. New York, Alfred A. Knopf.

Dahl, R. A. 1956. *A Preface to Democratic Theory*. Chicago, University of Chicago Press.

Dahl, R. A. 1961. *Who Governs? Democracy and Power in an American City.* New Haven, Yale University Press.

———. 1971. *Polyarchy: Participation and Opposition.* New Haven, Yale University Press.

Eldersveld, S. J. 1964. *Political Parties: A Behavioral Analysis.* Chicago, Rand McNally.

Held, D. 1987. *Models of Democracy.* Stanford, CA, Stanford University Press.

Jensen, R. 1971. *The Winning of the Midwest: Social and Political Conflict, 1888–1896.* Chicago, University of Chicago Press.

Key, V. O. 1947. *Politics, Parties, and Pressure Groups.* New York, Thomas Crowell.

Kleppner, P. 1970. *The Cross of Culture: A Social Analysis of Midwestern Politics, 1850–1900.* New York, Free Press.

———. 1979. *The Third Electoral System, 1853–1892: Parties, Voters, and Political Cultures.* Chapel Hill, University of North Carolina Press.

Knoke, D. 1976. *The Social Bases of Political Parties.* Baltimore, Johns Hopkins University Press.

Lazarsfeld, P. F., B. Berelson, et al. 1948. *The People's Choice.* New York, Columbia University Press.

Leiserson, A. 1958. *Parties and Politics: An Institutional and Behavioral Approach.* New York, Alfred A. Knopf.

Lipset, S. M., and S. Rokkan. 1967. *Party Systems and Voter Alignments: Cross-National Perspectives.* New York, Free Press.

Lubell, S. 1952. *The Future of American Politics.* New York, Harper and Row.

Manza, J., and C. Brooks. 1999. *Social Cleavages and Political Change: Voter Alignments and U.S. Party Coalitions.* Oxford, Oxford University Press.

McSeveney, S. T. 1972. *The Politics of Depression: Voting Behavior in the Northeast, 1893–1896.* New York, Oxford University Press.

Merriam, C. E. 1922. *The American Party System: An Introduction to the Study of Political Parties in the United States.* New York, Macmillan.

Merriam, C. E., and H. F. Gosnell. 1949. *The American Party System.* New York, MacMillan Company.

Petrocik, J. R. 1981. *Party Coalitions: Realignments and the Decline of the New Deal Party System.* Chicago, University of Chicago Press.

Ricci, D. 1984. *The Tragedy of Political Science.* New Haven, Yale University Press.

Stanley, H. W., W. T. Bianco, et al. 1986. "Partisanship and Group Support over Time: A Multivariate Analysis." *American Political Science Review* 80 (September): 969–76.

Truman, D. B. 1951. *The Governmental Process.* New York, Alfred Knopf.

Wright, J. 1973. "The Ethno-Cultural Model of Voting: A Behavioral and Historical Critique." *American Behavioral Scientist* 6 (May–June): 653–74.

# CHAPTER SEVEN

# Partisan Realignments and Electoral Independence: The Incidence, Distribution, and Magnitude of Enduring Electoral Change

The House of Commons in the 1640s apparently intended to speak for a sovereign but silent people much as the king had hitherto spoken for a sovereign but silent God. The people, however, proved more vocal than anticipated. . . . The history of popular sovereignty in both England and America after 1689 can be read as a history of the successive efforts of different generations to bring the facts into closer conformity with the fiction, efforts that have gradually transformed the very structure of society.
—EDMUND S. MORGAN, *Inventing the People*

[N]ew complexities, which the Jacksonians did not have to face, were weakening the faith of even some democrats in the efficacy of the radical democratic solution. . . . Starting on a large scale in the eighteen-forties, thousands of Europeans, ill-educated, tractable, used to low economic standards, unused to political liberty, began flocking to American shores. . . . The political consequences of the rise of this new population were plain and terrifying. The "masses," huddled together in the slums, seemed no longer, in any real sense, to be free. As voters they were either at the beck and call of their employers, or else the dupes of unscrupulous demagogues. "Bread and circuses" appeared to be once more the formula for political success.
—ARTHUR M. SCHLESINGER, JR., *The Age of Jackson*

THE OBJECTIVE of the next three chapters is to generate inferences about popular efficacy that will speak to the disparate assessments articulated by Morgan and Schlesinger in the epigraphs to this chapter. To do this I examine the data on macro-level normal voting patterns introduced in chapter 5 in light of the approach to mass-elite linkages presented earlier.

At the core of this approach is role of exogenous events that generate disequilibrating electoral jolts. Consequently, the focuses of the following empirical analyses are on electoral jolts and their impact on the core political interests of elites.

The first two sets of analyses deal largely, but not exclusively, with electoral independence: this chapter focuses on partisan realignments; chapter 8 deals with electoral perturbations. These analyses will be used to generate inferences about the level of political discernment within the U.S. electorate, as well as elite perceptions of citizens as efficacious political actors. Chapter 9 combines the data on enduring changes and perturbations and addresses their impact on political elites' prospects for electoral success. The analyses presented in chapter 9 will be used to generate inferences about what the distribution of competitive electoral settings and disequilibrating elections has taught elites about the role of citizens in democratic politics. Together these analyses will provide fresh insights into mass-elite linkages, shedding new light on electoral accountability and democratic responsiveness.

## Enduring Electoral Change and Electoral Independence: Generating Inferences About Popular Efficacy

The approach to mass-elite linkages driving this analysis yields certain expectations about the incidence, distribution, and magnitude of enduring electoral change. At the core of the operative political dynamics introduced earlier are exogenous events that impinge upon citizens' core political desires; these critical events stimulate interludes of intensive information processing, reassessments of political stewardship, and departures from normal voting behavior. These dynamics lead to two key expectations about the data on enduring electoral change. First, these data should be patterned in ways suggested by the transformational model presented in figure 3–2. Second, the impact of these enduring electoral shifts upon prevailing voting patterns must be large enough to teach elites that citizens are efficacious political actors, a force to be reckoned with in democratic politics.

These expectations are central to the plan of analysis in this book. If the data are not consistent with them, then the individual-level dynamics posited above cannot be used to generate inferences about popular efficacy. The macro-level analyses cannot "prove," or even provide direct empirical support for, the individual-level dynamics posited earlier. But these analyses can be used to reject those individual-level dynamics, making inferences about popular efficacy problematic. If the enduring electoral change data are consistent with the expectations laid out above, then these data can provide indirect support for the approach to mass-elite linkages offered here. And the findings can be used in conjunction with that theoretical approach to generate inferences about popular efficacy.

The centrality of these expectations for the empirical analysis leads to the use of a two-pronged approach, the results of which will be presented in the next two sections of this chapter. The first prong tests a proposition derived from the transformational model presented in figure 3–2, the *patterned change thesis*, which follows from assumption A1 and corollaries C2 and C2.1. The patterned change thesis posits that citizens have the capacity to respond to the radiated effects of a series of related and reinforcing critical events by making lasting changes in their normal voting behavior. Moreover, because these critical events are happenings, most have a temporal and a spatial dimension, leading to enduring electoral changes that will be structured both temporally and spatially. Thus, if these changes are randomly distributed over time or space, it is unlikely that they would have been generated by the dynamics embodied in figure 3–2.

The second prong in this analysis examines the *magnitude* of enduring electoral changes; it speaks to the likely impact of these changes on elite perceptions of the electorate. In order to yield fresh insights on mass-elite linkages, patterned enduring shifts in normal voting routines must be of sufficient magnitude to lead political elites to view citizens as a potent force within democratic politics.

To illustrate the logic underlying this two-pronged approach to generating inferences about popular efficacy, consider the data on critical change. If critical elections at the local level are evenly distributed across elections and randomly distributed across locales, it will be impossible to interpret them as popular responses to a series of related and reinforcing critical events rooted in a more fundamental societal development, as posited in chapter 3. Thus, the magnitude of these random critical shifts will be irrelevant. However, if the data on critical elections do not refute the patterned change thesis, then it is also necessary to show that they have a sizable impact on normal voting patterns. If the magnitude of these enduring shifts is not great, then it will be difficult to argue that they are capable of educating elites about the importance of popular concerns in democratic politics.

## THE PATTERNED CHANGE THESIS

### Testing the Patterned Change Thesis

In an effort to refute the patterned change thesis, I test for the existence of temporal and spatial patterns in the enduring electoral change data. Testing for the existence of *temporal patterns* in these data is complicated by the fact that there are two forms of enduring electoral change, critical and secular. However, because the electorate's capacity to generate sharp electoral jolts is central to the notion of popular efficacy, I begin the temporal order analysis by focusing on critical elections. I then show how the results of this analysis can be used to provide a more comprehensive examination of the temporal structure of both critical and secular change. I then outline the procedures used to conduct the spatial order analysis, which builds on the temporal order analysis.

### THE TEMPORAL ORDER ANALYSIS

To test whether the data on critical elections are temporally ordered, I employ dummy variable probit analysis. In this analysis:

- The dependent variable is CRITICAL ELECTION, a dummy variable that captures the incidence of a critical break in local normal voting patterns
- The independent variables are a set of 44 election-specific dummy variables.
- The unit of analysis is the unit-election.

In this probit analysis I am testing the null hypothesis, that there is no systematic variance in the incidence of critical breaks in normal vote patterns across elections. If systematic deviations from the global mean of the CRITICAL ELECTION variable occurred no more frequently than would be expected by chance, then the patterned change thesis must be rejected.[1] If systematic deviations from the global mean of the CRITICAL ELECTION variable occurred more frequently than would be expected by chance, then it can be said that the incidence of critical elections is temporally structured. The larger the pseudo $R^2$, the stronger the temporal order of the data on critical elections—and the firmer the basis will be for making inferences about popular efficacy.

As will be demonstrated below, the temporal order analysis shows that the incidence of critical elections is temporally ordered. Moreover, the results of this analysis make it possible to identify a set of six realignment eras. These realignment eras are used to extend the temporal order analysis to incorporate the data on secular change by determining the proportion of all enduring electoral change that falls within one of these six eras.

### THE SPATIAL ORDER ANALYSIS

This analysis employs the global version of Moran's I (Moran 1950a, 1950b), a standard measure of spatial autocorrelation, to detect the exis-

---

[1] I am indebted to Professor Brian Gaines of the University of Illinois for his insights on how to structure this analysis.

tence of spatial order in each of the six realignment eras detected in the temporal order analysis. In the spatial order analysis:

- The variables analyzed are a set of era dummy variables depicting whether a local electorate experienced enduring electoral change in a realignment era.
- The unit of analysis is the unit-election.

The global version of Moran's I tests for the existence of correlations among geographically proximate units for the variable being analyzed. In the absence of spatial autocorrelation, the expected value of Moran's I is 0 for large $n$'s. A 0 value for Moran's I means that the spatial clustering of incidents of enduring electoral change is no greater than would be expected by chance. A negative, statistically significant Moran's I means that *dissimilar* values are geographically clustered. A positive, statistically significant Moran's I means that geographically proximate units have *similar* values. Thus, I am positing positive and statistically significant Moran's I's for each of the six realignment eras analyzed. If a positive and statistically significant Moran's I is not produced for a given era, then it cannot be said that the realignments that occurred in that era were spatially ordered. And the patterned change thesis must be rejected.

## The Patterned Change Thesis: An Empirical Test

### THE TEMPORAL ORDER ANALYSES

The results of the temporal order probit analysis are strongly supportive of the patterned change thesis. The likelihood ratio chi-square is 17914, which indicates that the null hypothesis can be rejected with a level of confidence that exceeds .0001. Thus, the distribution of critical elections is not randomly distributed across time. Indeed, these elections have a well-defined temporal order. The pseudo $R^2$ for the probit analysis is .56. The strength of this relationship is confirmed by a dummy variable regression analysis. The adjusted $R^2$ for this analysis is .57 (n = 111,871), which is virtually identical to the pseudo $R^2$ produced by the probit analysis.

The temporal order of critical elections suggested by the results of the probit and regression analyses can be seen clearly in figure 7–1. It displays the weighted proportion of critical elections by partisan direction and election year (weight = TOTAL VOTES). The data reported in figure 7–1 show that that five critical elections stand out as the most significant: 1836, 1856, 1896, 1932, and 1952. Moreover, 97 percent of all the critical realignments fall within one of six electoral sequences: 1836 and 1840, 1856 to 1864, 1872 to 1904 (in the South), 1884 to 1900 (in the West and the Northeast), 1932, and 1952. When these critical elections are

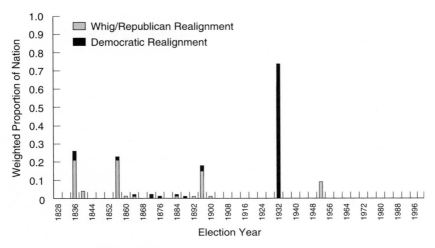

Figure 7–1. The Distribution of Critical Changes, by Year

joined with the temporal distribution of secular changes, and examined geographically, six well-defined realignment eras emerge. These six eras incorporate 90 percent of all secular changes in local normal voting patterns,[2] suggesting a highly structured temporal order to these data.

The realignment eras detected here are important in understanding the temporal order of these data and in structuring the spatial order analysis. They are also important in providing some concrete illustrations to the theoretical dynamics discussed in chapter 2 and chapter 3. Therefore, I briefly discuss each. While a detailed historical analysis is not possible here, historians have studied these eras extensively. In the following discussions I merely try to suggest the series of related and reinforcing events that are likely to have given rise to them, along with the emotional triggers that were crucial to their emergence.

### EXOGENOUS EVENTS, EMOTIONAL TRIGGERS, AND REALIGNMENT ERAS

I label the first realignment era the *Jacksonian Era*. While the Jacksonian Era is often referred to as the "Second Party System," it is the first mass-based partisan alignment in United States history. Indeed, it is probably the first mass-based partisan alignment in the modern history of democ-

---

[2] More than 95 percent of all incidents of enduring change uncovered here involved secular changes in normal voting patterns, and they account for 35 percent of all of the enduring electoral change that has occurred in the U.S. since 1828. The procedures used to define periods of secular change are reported in appendix III, Procedures Used to Define Periods of Enduring Change: http://www.pol.uiuc.edu/nardulliresearch.html.

racy. The contours of the Jacksonian Era were shaped by the critical elections of 1836–40, which I will refer to as the Whig realignment. The Whig Party represented the solidification of an organized opposition to the Jacksonians, and the Whig realignment is defined in reference to the partisan alignment that made possible Jackson's historic victories in 1828 and 1832. Critical changes favoring the Whigs account for approximately 65 percent of the enduring electoral change that unfolded during the Jacksonian Era; the remaining 35 percent are the result of secular changes favoring the Whigs.

The Whig realignment was rooted in some fundamental changes taking place in American society that generated different reactions from different segments of the electorate. Perhaps the most important of these was the emergence of a commercial economy and the opportunities and challenges that accompanied the settlement of the frontier. However, while these developments gave rise to different ideas about the role of government in the antebellum period, and set the stage for the Whig realignment, they were not the proximate cause of it.

The emotional triggers that initiated intensive reevaluations of political allegiances during this period were a series of events rooted in an economic decline that diffused through much of the United States in the mid 1830s. Real per capita gross domestic product declined by almost 8 percent between 1835 and 1837. In addition to impacting the well-being of individuals and businesses, the economic decline embarrassed many state governments that had invested heavily in internal improvements (roads, canals) to capitalize on the opportunities that the nation's commercial expansion seemed to provide. The impact of these events on citizens' assessments of their economic well-being, as well as their future prospects, was almost certainly a major factor contributing to the 1836 critical elections depicted in figure 7-1.

To put the 1835–36 decline in historical perspective, it must be noted that this was the biggest two-year drop in productivity between the War of 1812 and 1907–8—with the exception of 1865. A dismal economic performance in 1840—a 7 percent drop in prices and a 3.4 percent decline in productivity—cemented the realignment and provided the Whigs with their first presidential victory. It also should be mentioned that the economic decline of the 1830s was the first that occurred in the democratic era of American politics. The electoral response of the newly democratized electorate established a precedent that has been repeated with some regularity since then.

The Jacksonian Era lasted until 1856. The issues that defined partisan allegiances in the 1830s (the tariff, the Bank of the United States, internal improvements) had become less salient by the 1850s and the party coalitions were strained by a series of exogenous events rooted in some fundamental societal developments. These included a rapid increase in immigration, which generated a surge in anti-Catholicism and nativism, and an incipient temperance movement. The political significance of these developments notwithstanding, however, it was the reemergence of slavery as a national political issue that brought the Jacksonian Era to an abrupt end. It generated a set of critical realignments that began in 1856 and gave rise to what I will refer to as the *Slavery Era*.

The slavery issue had plagued the nation since its founding. It was not until a series of events began to unfold in the late 1840s, however, that the latent emotional power of slavery was unleashed within the electoral arena. These developments were rooted in the acquisition of new territories after the Mexican American War. The acquisition of these territories reopened the debate over admitting slave states into the union and gave rise to confrontational strategies by activists on both sides of the slavery debate. The resulting conflicts peaked with violent confrontations in Kansas and Nebraska.

This series of violent events served as the emotional trigger that generated political reevaluations that reconfigured electoral politics in the United States in the 1850s. As seen in figure 7–1, these reevaluations generated a series of critical elections that first appeared at the presidential level in 1856. These critical changes were accompanied by a wave of Republican secular changes. Critical changes account for about 62 percent of the Republican gains during the Slavery Era, with the remaining 38 percent resulting from secular changes. The net national effect of these Republican gains was reduced somewhat by a smaller set of Democratic gains. Secular changes account for approximately 84 percent of all the Democratic gains during the Slavery Era; the remaining 16 percent were generated by critical changes.

Despite the existence of modest Democratic gains in the Slavery Era, most of their electoral gains from the reignited slavery controversy came after Reconstruction. A set of events rooted in the slavery issue and the Civil War, and unprecedented in American history, served as emotional triggers that initiated intensive reassessments of political allegiances within the South after the Civil War. The electoral effect of these reassessments transformed the South from an electorally competitive region to a stronghold of the Democratic Party, the "Solid South." Civil war, a humiliating military defeat, economic dislocation and devastation, occupation by triumphant union forces, the enfranchisement of the freed slaves, the disenfranchisement of many confederates, the machinations of the carpetbaggers, scalawags, and the like, had a devastating impact on white Southerners, especially those who had dominated Southern society before the Civil War.

The enduring Democratic gains produced by these developments were manifested in what I refer to as the *Jim Crow Era*. The realities of Reconstruction delayed the electoral effects of the developments noted above. But their emotional impact was so profound and widely shared that they were reinforced throughout the South and intensified over time. Ultimately, the electoral effects of these developments proved irrepressible. Thus, the Jim Crow electoral shifts diffused steadily through most of the South after the Union troops departed. Like the Democratic gains in the Slavery Era, the dominant mode of change in the Jim Crow Era was secular: secular changes account for 68 percent of the Democratic gains. The electoral force of the events rooted in the slavery issue and the Civil War began to manifest itself in isolated Southern locales in the Election of 1872; it continued through the Election of 1908.

While white Southern political elites were preoccupied with reasserting the South's sovereignty and preserving its norms, mores, and political hierarchy, the rest of the nation resumed some of the tasks that were interrupted by the Civil War. These included the settlement of the West and the solidification of the Northeast as the nation's industrial and financial center. The geo-political conflicts generated by these developments interacted with ongoing ethnocultural conflict. Moreover, a series of economic difficulties that unfolded in the 1880s and 1890s underscored the incongruities between the Eastern center and the Western periphery. These ongoing economic difficulties, rooted in the Industrial Revolution, acted as the emotional trigger that ultimately generated a set of enduring electoral shifts that once again transformed the contours of presidential politics.

A long period of deflation following the Civil War returned price levels close to their prewar level by 1880, and the 1880s represented a period of fairly steady economic growth for the nation as a whole. But that economic growth was accompanied by another sustained period of deflation that began around 1883. Over the course of a decade price levels dropped by nearly 20 percent, a development that was devastating to farmers and other debtors. Then, in 1893, a sharp depression gripped much of the nation and initiated a set of critical changes that reconfigured the nation's electoral landscape outside the South. I will refer to this reconfiguration as the *Industrial Era*.

The Industrial Era is composed of two distinct sets of electoral shifts. One is the Populist movement in the West.[3] These electoral shifts began

---

[3] There was also a potent Populist Movement in the parts of the South. However, because of the race issue and the emphasis on maintaining the dominance of the Democratic Party, the electoral effects of the Southern Populist Movement were muted. The only shifts I detected occurred in the 1880s. Only 129 rural counties realigned, mostly in the upland region of the South. Because these were independent movements, they could not easily be integrated with the Western Populist movement, which ultimately favored the Democrats. Thus,

to surface in the Election of 1884 but peaked in 1896. About 69 percent of the Democratic gains during this era were the result of critical realignments, and by 1896 the Democratic Party was dominated by agricultural and pietistic groups. This transformation was underscored by William Jennings Bryan's famous "Cross of Gold" speech. The ideological and geo-political reconfiguring of the Democratic Party, in conjunction with the 1893 depression, contributed to a wave of critical and secular shifts in the Northeast and Midwest favoring the Republicans. Approximately 77 percent of these Republican gains were secular; most of the critical gains occurred in 1896.

The Industrial Era was brought to an abrupt end in 1932 by the most sweeping set of enduring electoral changes in the democratic era of American politics. I will refer to these electoral shifts as the *New Deal Era*. The emotional trigger that produced this electoral sea change was the stock market crash of 1929 and the unfolding economic deterioration that followed for nearly a decade. As suggested in figure 7–1, the vast majority of the Democratic gains in the New Deal Era (98 percent) were the result of critical realignments that occurred in 1932. However, the tact that Roosevelt used in assembling his "New Deal" alienated a small subset of the electorate. Their unease initiated enough intensive reevaluations to generate an electoral backlash that tempered the overall Republican losses. Many regions that did not shift toward the Democrats in 1932 experienced secular changes that favored the Republicans. While there were a handful of Republican critical changes in the 1940s, almost 100 percent of the Republican gains in the New Deal Era were realized from secular changes.

The final realignment era detected here is termed the *Civil Rights Era*. While the roots of this realignment can be traced to the Emancipation Proclamation, the more proximal causes almost certainly lie in the Great Depression and World War Two. The New Deal era realignment led many African Americans to reject the party of Lincoln and embrace the Democrats. The emergence of a strong Northern urban electoral base made the Democrats less dependent on the South and gave rise to policy demands that were incompatible with the beliefs and interests of Southern political elites. These political strains were exacerbated in the aftermath of World War Two. Many African American soldiers returned from the war with heightened expectations concerning their role and stature in American society. No longer willing to tolerate the strictures of Jim Crow norms and prohibitions, they breathed new life into an incipient civil rights

---

I do not deal with them here. The small size of these rural counties is such that this does not have much of an impact on the analysis.

movement. By the late 1940s the Truman administration, backed by a
new breed of Democratic leaders, began to embrace this movement.

The electoral reaction to the Civil Rights Movement and the Democrat's embrace of it was initially manifested in the Dixiecrat Revolt in
1948, even though white Southerners did not shift decisively to the Republican Party at the presidential level until 1952. The unfolding of the
Civil Rights Movement in the 1950s and 1960s—the dismantling of Jim
Crow by the federal courts, sit-ins, marches, nationally telecast battles
between Southern sheriffs and civil rights activists, landmark civil rights
legislation, and so forth—reinforced the cognitive reassessments many
Southerners began in the late 1940s. Moreover, their realignment was
nurtured and encouraged by a series of Republican policy shifts that
began to unfold in the 1960s. This series of reinforcing and related events
undermined the strongest and most enduring set of ties between a region
and a national political party in United States history.

The enduring Republican shifts during the Civil Rights Era came largely
in the form of a set of critical changes in 1952. But there was also a modest
amount of secular change favoring the Republicans, about 11 percent of
the total. These secular changes had a discernible impact on normal voting
patterns in the South through the 1970s. But they also generated an offsetting effect. The integration of the South into the Republican Party gave
it a far more conservative cast, especially on social and moral issues. Battles over these issues, and the evangelical overtones they often assumed,
led many voters to reassess their partisan allegiances—particularly blacks,
women, and professionals in the Northeast (Manza and Brooks 1999).
The effect of these reevaluations precipitated a set of wholly secular Democratic shifts that became particularly pronounced after 1964. These secular trends were, in all likelihood, reinforced by the emergence of global
economic pressures that began to be felt in the United States in the 1970s
and 1980s, and took off in the 1990s. In many locales the Democratic
Party's stance on social safety net issues generated a series of incremental
additions to their electoral base due to the economic dislocations produced by globalization.

### THE SPATIAL ORDER ANALYSIS

The results of the spatial order analysis are reported in figure 7–2. These
results, like those for the temporal order analysis, are strongly supportive
of the patterned change thesis.[4] They document that the era-specific data
on enduring electoral change are well ordered spatially. All of the global

---

[4] I am deeply indebted to my research assistant, David Darmofal, for his efforts in conducting the spatial autocorrelation analyses. Without his expertise and industriousness I
could not have conducted these analyses in a timely manner.

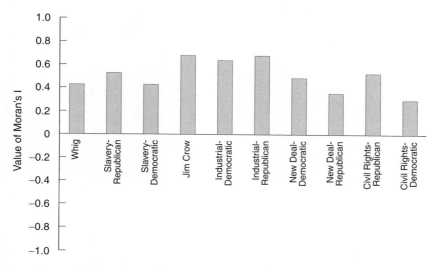

Figure 7–2. Results of the Spatial Order Analysis, by Realignment

Moran's I's are positive and significant beyond the .0001 level. The Moran's I's range from .30 (Civil Rights–Democratic Era) to .68 (Jim Crow Era, Industrial-Republican Era), with an average of .51. Table 7–1 and map 7–1 through map 7–6 produce additional insights into the spatial order of these partisan realignments. The maps report the geographic distributions of the realignments for each era. Table 7–1 provides data on the incidence of realigning change by section. It reports the weighted proportion of the section's electoral units that experienced some form of enduring electoral change (weight = TOTAL VOTES). The data in table 7–1 are valuable because the maps do not take into account the population density of the affected locales.

As is evident in both map 7–1 and table 7–1, the Whig changes that defined the Jacksonian Era were concentrated in the South and what was then the Western frontier. The Republican shifts in the Slavery Era (see map 7–2) were heavily concentrated in the Northern tier of states, particularly in New England.[5] Two Border States (Missouri and West Virginia),

---

[5] The sectional figures reported in table 7–1 are somewhat misleading. For example, several New England States (New Hampshire, Vermont, Maine, and Massachusetts) strongly embraced the Republicans, while others (Delaware, Rhode Island, and Connecticut) were hardly involved in the Republican surge. New York and Pennsylvania were the Middle Atlantic States that provided the Republicans with the largest boost. The Midwest varied significantly in its response to the Republican's message. Iowa and Michigan, followed by Illinois were the most receptive. On the other hand, the Republicans did not generate widespread shifts in Wisconsin, Ohio, or Indiana.

TABLE 7.1
Proportion of Electoral Units Experiencing Enduring Electoral Change, by Section and Era

| | Whig Change Jacksonian Era (1836–1844)* | Republican Change in Slavery Era (1856–1864) | Democratic Change in Slavery Era (1856–1864) | Democratic Change in Jim Crow Era (1872–1912) | Democratic Change in Industrial Era (1884–1896) | Republican Change in Industrial Era (1896–1912) | Democratic Change in New Deal Era (1932) | Republican Change in New Deal Era (1932–1944) | Republican Change in Civil Rights Era (1952–1960) | Democratic Change in Civil Rights Era (1952–1984) |
|---|---|---|---|---|---|---|---|---|---|---|
| New England States | .08 | .75 | .12 | .00 | .00 | .93 | .98 | .01 | .04 | .79 |
| Middle Atlantic States | .45 | .40 | .16 | .00 | .00 | .98 | .79 | .14 | .01 | .88 |
| Southern States | .59 | .00 | .00 | .69 | .00 | .00 | .34 | .48 | .51 | .15 |
| Border States | .18 | .13 | .34 | .26 | .00 | .34 | .64 | .29 | .13 | .52 |
| Midwestern States | .47 | .39 | .22 | .00 | .02 | .90 | .75 | .21 | .02 | .79 |
| Plains States | .47 | .54 | .06 | .00 | .31 | .60 | .74 | .21 | .14 | .67 |
| Mountain States | — | — | — | .00 | .41 | .53 | .92 | .07 | .14 | .53 |
| West Coast States | — | .40 | .13 | .00 | .00 | .95 | 1.00 | .00 | .02 | .82 |

* Dates in parentheses indicate critical election and/or start dates for periods of secular change

along with California, were the only other states to manifest noticeable Republican shifts. The Democratic shifts in the Slavery Era are slightly more diffuse, as is evident in figure 7–2. The Democratic shifts are most pronounced in the Border States but also were evident in some Midwestern and Middle Atlantic States. These spatial distributions undoubtedly reflect ethnocultural effects that are not evident by merely examining spatial and tabular distributions.[6]

There are no Southern States that register enduring Democratic shifts in the Slavery Era because of the disruption of Southern voting patterns by the Civil War and Reconstruction. The electoral reaction to the reemergence of the slavery issue in the South does not manifest itself until the Jim Crow Era. Democratic shifts in this era were heavily concentrated in the South and the Border States, as seen in map 7–3.[7] Like the electoral changes that occurred in the Jim Crow Era, those that unfolded in the Industrial Era had a clear spatial structure (see map 7–4 and table 7–1). Most of the Northern tier of the United States outside the Plains and Mountain States manifested some Republican shifts in this era. The Democratic gains resulting from the Populist Movement were highly concentrated in Kansas, Nebraska, and Colorado.

Map 7–3 and map 7–4, when viewed together, suggest that the electoral landscape that emerged at the end of the Civil War was fundamentally rearranged by the turn of the century. Only isolated locales were unaffected by the sweeping electoral currents that occurred in the last quarter of the nineteenth century. These results are somewhat surprising because this era is widely recognized as the height of the "party period" in American politics, a time in which partisan attachments should have been highly durable. The impact of the Great Depression had a similarly broad effect on electoral patterns. But its impact was manifested much more quickly. The Democratic shifts that occurred beginning in 1932 are well known; their prominence is clear in figure 7–1 and map 7–5. The New Deal re-

---

[6] Next to Kentucky, Wisconsin evidenced the most widespread Democratic shifts in the Slavery Era. This was almost certainly due to the reaction of German Catholics to the nativist wing of the Republican coalition (Gienapp 1987). Also surprising is the fact that several New England States (Connecticut, Delaware, Rhode Island, Massachusetts) registered Democratic shifts as marked as states such as Tennessee and Maryland. The same can be said for Middle Atlantic States such as New Jersey and New York, and Midwestern States such as Ohio, Illinois, and Indiana. These can be attributed to such factors as migration patterns that led native Southerners to states such as Illinois and Indiana as well as the distribution of immigrant populations, especially Catholics.

[7] It should be stressed that some of the highly concentrated Democratic shifts in the Jim Crow Era evidenced in map 7–3 are artifactual. There were some Democratic gains in the North during this time frame, but they were the result of the post–Civil War recession in the 1870s and were correctly not included in the Jim Crow Era. Also, there was a set of Democratic shifts in the West that had their roots in the Populist Movement. They are treated separately.

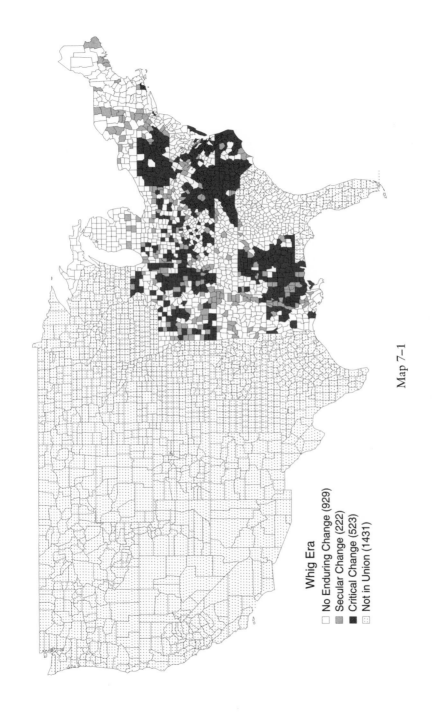

Whig Era
☐ No Enduring Change (929)
▨ Secular Change (222)
■ Critical Change (523)
⊡ Not in Union (1431)

Map 7–1

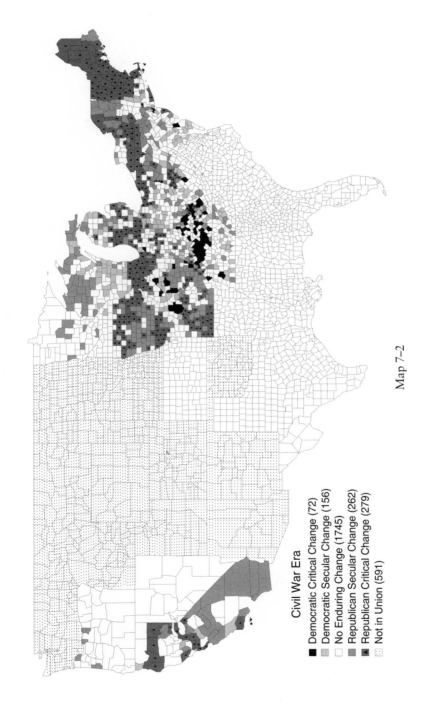

Civil War Era

■ Democratic Critical Change (72)
■ Democratic Secular Change (156)
□ No Enduring Change (1745)
■ Republican Secular Change (262)
◢ Republican Critical Change (279)
▨ Not in Union (591)

Map 7-2

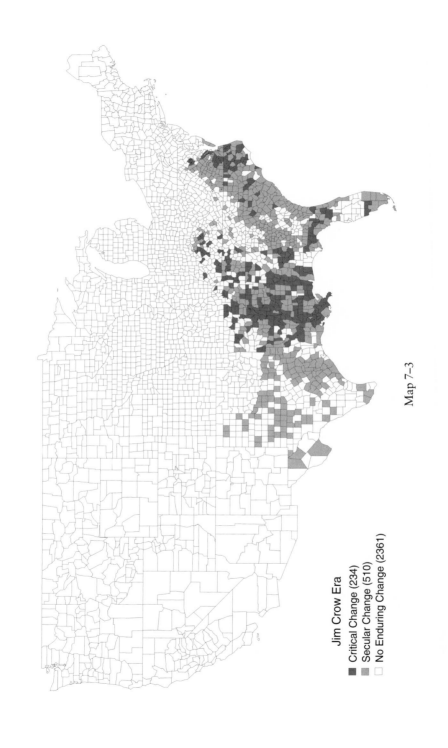

Jim Crow Era

■ Critical Change (234)

■ Secular Change (510)

□ No Enduring Change (2361)

Map 7-3

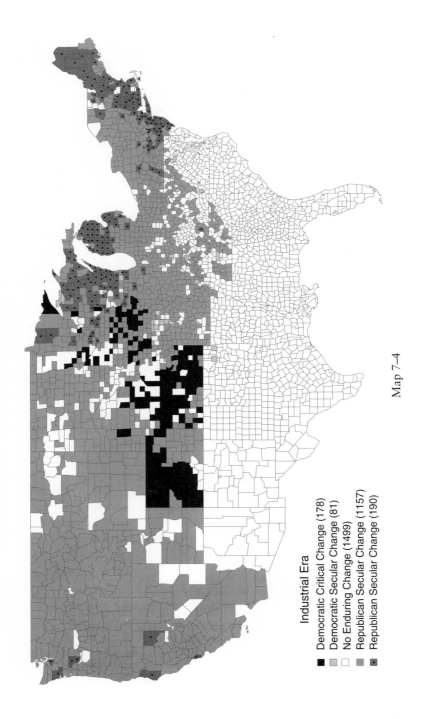

Industrial Era

Democratic Critical Change (178)

Democratic Secular Change (81)

No Enduring Change (1499)

Republican Secular Change (1157)

Republican Secular Change (190)

Map 7-4

alignment affected nearly all local electorates in New England, the Mountain States, and the West Coast States—as well as most of those in the Middle Atlantic States, the Midwest, and the Plains States.

While the Democratic shifts generated by the Great Depression are undoubtedly the most important electoral changes produced in the New Deal Era, they are not the only ones. Two discernible "bands" of enduring Republican gains are evident in map 7–5. One band is composed of a large group of counties in the Southern and Border States. Republican secular change unfolded in nearly half of the electoral units in the South and nearly one-third of those in the Border States. The second band of Republican gains runs largely thorough the rural sections of the Midwest and the Plains States.

The last period examined here is the Civil Rights Era. As map 7–6 and table 7–1 make clear, most of these critical shifts occurred in the South. However, while the 1952 critical elections were concentrated in the South, they were not confined to it. Isolated pockets of change also exist in states such as Vermont, Iowa, Utah, and New Mexico. Map 7–6 and table 7–1 show that the Democratic secular changes in the Civil Rights Era were located largely in the Northeast and in the heavily urban areas of the West Coast.

### THE IMPACT OF ENDURING ELECTORAL SHIFTS ON NORMAL VOTING PATTERNS

As the temporal and spatial order analyses demonstrate that the data on enduring electoral change are highly structured, the patterned change thesis cannot be refuted. *These data are distributed in a manner that is consistent with the assertion that they are electoral reactions to a series of related and reinforcing critical events rooted in more fundamental societal developments.* Thus, these data are distributed in a manner that is consistent with the transformation model presented in chapter 3.

This notwithstanding, before inferences about popular efficacy can be drawn from these findings, it must be demonstrated that these patterned changes are likely to have played a role in the political education of elites. To shed light on whether these enduring electoral shifts were sufficient to create an image of citizens as efficacious political actors, I examine their impact on normal voting patterns. To gauge this impact, I examine both the magnitude and duration of these electoral shifts. I begin by briefly describing the procedure used to measure magnitude and duration; then I present the results of the impact analysis for each of the realignment eras introduced earlier.

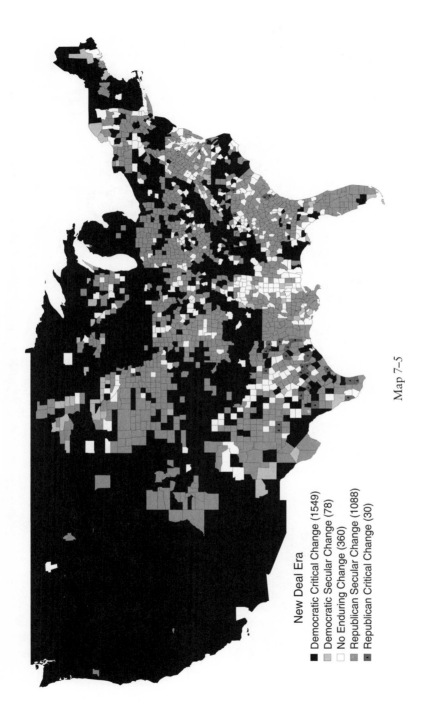

New Deal Era

- ■ Democratic Critical Change (1549)
- ▨ Democratic Secular Change (78)
- □ No Enduring Change (360)
- ▨ Republican Secular Change (1088)
- ▨ Republican Critical Change (30)

Map 7–5

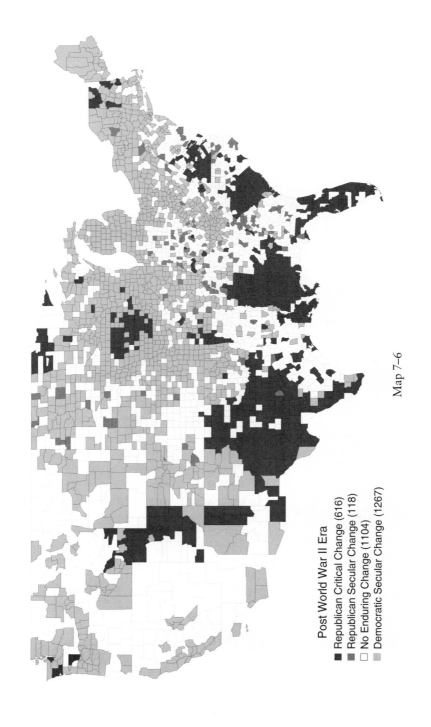

Post World War II Era

■ Republican Critical Change (616)
▨ Republican Secular Change (118)
☐ No Enduring Change (1104)
▨ Democratic Secular Change (1267)

Map 7–6

## Measuring the Magnitude and
## Duration of Enduring Electoral Change

To gauge the impact of enduring electoral change on normal voting patterns, I use two sets of era-specific measures, one at the subnational level and one at the national level. The procedures used to derive these variables are tedious to report so the details are contained in appendix IV (Gauging the Impact of Partisan Realignments on Normal Voting Patterns, available at *http://www.pol.uiuc.edu/nardulliresearch.html*). Despite the tediousness of describing the procedures in detail, the ideas involved them are straightforward and can be illustrated with a simple example.

Consider a hypothetical realignment era involving one hundred local electorates, each of which experienced a critical realignment in 1800 and again in 1828. Under the procedure developed here the two electoral impact variables, SUBNATIONAL IMPACT$_{HYPO}$ and NATIONAL IMPACT$_{HYPO}$, are defined for the seven elections from 1800 to 1824. For the hypothetical 100 local electorates used in this example, the weighted average of NORMAL PARTISAN BALANCE is 0 in 1796; 1796 is used as the base for gauging the impact of the electoral changes.

An unsettling and related series of critical events emerge early in 1800, giving rise to a set of critical changes in normal voting patterns for the 100 local electorates. These changes first manifest themselves in the Election of 1800, which is considered a critical election. Because of these enduring changes, the weighted average of NORMAL PARTISAN BALANCE for these 100 electorates jumps to .40 in 1800. After the Election of 1800 some voters have second thoughts, giving rise to some modest secular regressions. Because of these secular regressions the weighted average of NORMAL PARTISAN BALANCE declines by .02 for each election from 1804 to 1824. This yields a value of .40 for the SUBNATIONAL IMPACT$_{HYPO}$ variable in 1800, .38 in 1804, .36 in 1808, and so forth. By 1824 the value of SUBNATIONAL IMPACT$_{HYPO}$ is .28. In 1828 the value of SUBNATIONAL IMPACT$_{HYPO}$ is undefined because all 100 of the local electorates experience a subsequent realignment. Because these 100 realigning electorates constitute exactly half the actual vote in the nation for each of the elections from 1800 to 1824, the value of NATIONAL IMPACT$_{HYPO}$ is exactly half the value of SUBNATIONAL IMPACT$_{HYPO}$ (.20 in 1800; .19 in 1804, and so on).

## Partisan Realignments and Normal Voting Patterns

Figures 7–4 through 7–8 display the subnational and national impact measures for each realignment era. Because the data archive used here

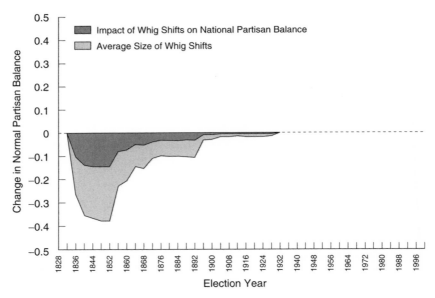

Figure 7–3. Impact of Enduring Electoral Changes on Normal Partisan Balance, Jacksonian Era *

begins in 1828, the data reported in figure 7–3 capture only the reaction to Jacksonian policies that led to the emergence of the Whig Party.[8] Figure 7–3 makes it clear that the popular reaction to those policies cut deeply into the Democrats' electoral support. The Whig realignments began at the local level in 1836 but they did not peak until 1848 (the value of the SUBNATIONAL IMPACT$_{WHIG}$ variable was –.26 in 1836 and rose to –.38 in 1848). The peak impact of the Whig realignments on national normal voting patterns was between 10 and 14 points (the NATIONAL IMPACT$_{WHIG}$ variable was –.10 in 1836; it peaked at –.14 in 1840 and remained at that level until 1856). In 1856 the slavery issue generated a fundamental reshuffling of parties and allegiances. The value of the SUBNATIONAL

---

[8] The inability to chart the electoral shifts that occurred in 1828 leaves open the possibility the Whig Realignments are simply a reversion to prior voting patterns. This would mean that Jackson's elections were simply short-term deviations, not the beginnings of a new, mass-based partisan realignment. While this is impossible to refute with the data available, it does not seem likely. The Whig Realignments were heavily concentrated in the South and West—North Carolina, Mississippi, Alabama, Virginia, Illinois, Indiana, Missouri, and Ohio (see map 7–1 and table 7–1). This suggests that the shifts depicted in figure 7–1 reflect a reaction to the policies and practices of the Jacksonians rather than the reemergence of long dormant Federalist ghosts. There simply were not many Federalist descendants in these sections of the United States at that time.

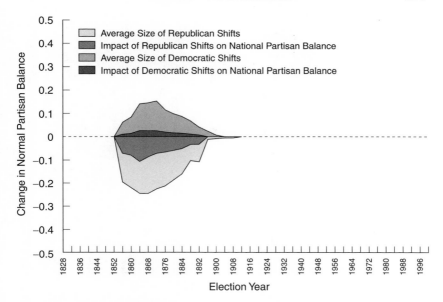

Figure 7–4. Impact of Enduring Electoral Changes on Normal Partisan Balance, Slavery Era *

IMPACT$_{\text{WHIG}}$ variable drops to −.23 in 1856 and it continues to drop throughout the nineteenth century. By 1860 the value of the NATIONAL IMPACT$_{\text{WHIG}}$ variable was at half its peak value, −.07.

The electoral impact of the ferment of the 1850s can be seen in figure 7–4. Like the electoral shifts of the 1830s and 1840s, it took several elections for the exogenous shocks of the mid-1850s to become fully realized. The initial Republican shifts were smaller than the Whig realignments (the value of the SUBNATIONAL IMPACT$_{\text{SLAVERY\_REP}}$ variable is −.20 for 1856, peaks at −.25 in 1868, and then begins to decline; in 1892 it is −.11). The Democratic shifts in the Slavery Era are even smaller (the SUBNATIONAL IMPACT$_{\text{SLAVERY\_DEM}}$ variable has a value of only .06 for 1856; it reaches its height in 1872, at .15). The impact of the Republican gains at the national level were also somewhat smaller than the Whig effects (NATIONAL IMPACT$_{\text{SLAVERY\_REP}}$ variable is −.07 in 1856 and it peaks at −.11 in 1868). The national impact of the Democratic shifts in the Slavery Era is never great (NATIONAL IMPACT$_{\text{SLAVERY\_DEM}}$ is .01 in 1856, peaking at .03 in 1868), but its effects must be interpreted in conjunction with the Democratic gains registered in the Jim Crow Era.

The Democratic gains rooted in the Jim Crow Era began to be registered just as those generated by the Democratic movements in the Slavery Era began to fade. It took the Jim Crow realignment several decades to

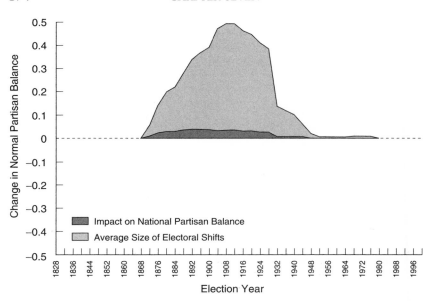

Figure 7–5. Impact of Enduring Electoral Changes on Normal Partisan Balance, Jim Crow Era *

unfold, as figure 7–5 makes clear. However, the Democratic gains generated in the Jim Crow Era had a major impact in the South. This movement gained momentum throughout the last quarter of the nineteenth century (SUBNATIONAL IMPACT$_{\text{JIM CROW}}$ has a value of .04 in 1872, .24 in 1884, .36 in 1900, and it peaks at .46 in 1908). It began to lose steam after the Wilson victories in 1912 and 1916 and was essentially depleted by the New Deal realignment. While the national impact of the Jim Crow realignment was never great (NATIONAL IMPACT$_{\text{JIM CROW}}$ varies from .01 to .04), this movement resulted in the creation of the "solid South." This bloc of "safe" votes had a marked effect on the quest for Electoral College votes.

Enhancing the national impact of the Jim Crow shifts were the Democratic gains made in some Western states as a result of the Populist Movement, which is an integral component of what I have termed the Industrial Era. The effects of the Populist revolt began to be felt as early as 1884, as can be seen in figure 7–6. The early effects of this movement were minimal at the subnational level and nonexistent at the national level. The turbulence of the 1880s and 1890s is manifested most clearly in the critical elections of 1896, after the 1893 depression. The electoral effects of the Populist Revolt peak in 1896 (when the SUBNATIONAL IMPACT$_{\text{INDUSTRIAL\_DEM}}$ is .31) and then decline precipitously. By 1932 its sub-

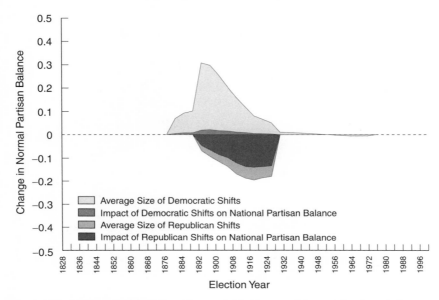

Figure 7–6. Impact of Enduring Electoral Changes on Normal Partisan Balance, Industrial Era *

national impact all but disappears. Because the Populist Movement's enduring electoral effects were concentrated in the rural sections of the West, it never had much of a national impact (NATIONAL IMPACT$_{\text{INDUSTRIAL\_DEM}}$ ranges from .01 to .02 between 1896 and 1916).

The contours of the Republican gains that began in 1896 are quite different. The initial size of the Republican gains is not even a quarter of that realized by the Democrats in 1896 (SUBNATIONAL IMPACT$_{\text{INDUSTRIAL\_REP}}$ is −.07, compared to .31 for SUBNATIONAL IMPACT$_{\text{INDUSTRIAL\_DEM}}$). But the Republican gains built momentum throughout the first quarter of the twentieth century, with their subnational effects peaking at −.20 in 1920. Moreover, the fact that these gains were in the densely populated regions of the nation translated into marked Republican gains at the national level (NATIONAL IMPACT$_{\text{INDUSTRIAL\_REP}}$ went from −.05 in 1896 to −.14 in 1916).

While Roosevelt's New Deal program generated a backlash that ultimately benefited the Republicans, its magnitude produced large and immediate electoral benefits for the Democrats. This is clear in figure 7–7, which shows an average sub-national effect of 40 points in 1932 (i.e., SUBNATIONAL IMPACT$_{\text{NEW DEAL\_DEM}}$ is .40 in 1932). While this is somewhat smaller than the peak effect of the Jim Crow realignments (.46 in 1908), it is slightly larger than the peak effects of the Whig and Populist realignments (−.38 and .31, respectively); it is 60 percent larger than the peak

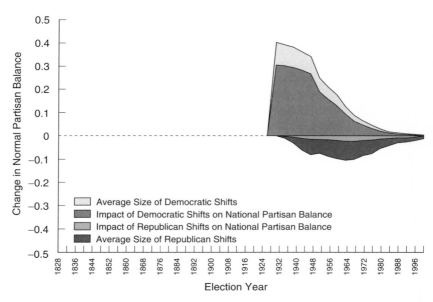

Figure 7–7. Impact of Enduring Electoral Changes on Normal Partisan Balance, New Deal Era *

effects of Republican realignments in the Civil War Era (–.25). While the impact of the New Deal realignments on local normal voting patterns begins to deteriorate almost immediately, the rate of decline is slight until 1952; the value of SUBNATIONAL IMPACT$_{\text{NEW DEAL\_DEM}}$ is still .34 in 1948.

Where the New Deal Democratic realignment stands out with respect to other realignments is in its national impact. Because its reach was so broad its impact on the national normal vote was the greatest in U.S. electoral history: about 30 points at its peak (the value of NATIONAL IMPACT$_{\text{NEW DEAL\_DEM}}$ was .30 in 1932 and was still .27 in 1948). In contrast, the peak national effects of the Whig realignments and the Republican shifts in the Industrial Era were only 14 points. The only other national impact that exceeds 10 points was generated by the Republican realignments in the Slavery Era (–.11 in 1864, when the South was not in the Union).

By 1940 an electoral reaction to the New Deal becomes discernible, composed largely of Republican secular shifts. It built slowly, peaking in 1960 (SUBNATIONAL IMPACT$_{\text{NEW DEAL\_REP}}$ is –.10 in 1960). This backlash never had much of a national impact; NATIONAL IMPACT$_{\text{NEW DEAL\_REP}}$ varies between –.01 and –.02. However, when combined with the deterioration of Democratic gains rooted in the critical elections of 1932, the Republi-

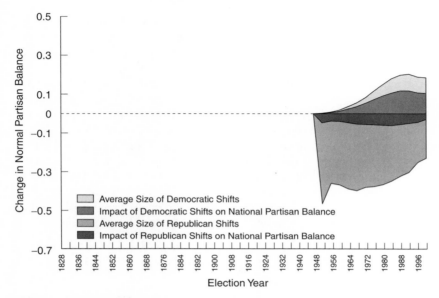

Figure 7–8. Impact of Enduring Electoral Changes on Normal Partisan Balance, Civil Rights Era *

can gains in the New Deal Era played a consequential role in reshaping presidential vote patterns by 1948.

Far more important in reshaping the national electoral setting, however, were the Republican critical shifts that occurred in 1952. These critical elections completed the demise of the "solid South," a steady decline that began in 1912 and continued throughout the New Deal Era. The importance of these Republican gains can be seen in figure 7–8. The average size of these Republican shifts is comparable to the New Deal Democratic shifts (the value of SUBNATIONAL IMPACT$_{\text{CIVIL RIGHTS\_REP}}$ is −.47 in 1952 but hovers around −.38 between 1956 and 1976). After 1976 the subnational effect of these Republican gains begins to decline somewhat, declining to 23 points by 2000. However, because these Republican realignments were fairly concentrated in the sparsely populated South, their impact on the national normal vote never exceeded 6 points. On the other hand, their impact on the Electoral College was significant.

The demise of the "solid South" has been chronicled for some time; especially after the Republican gains first registered in presidential contests were reflected in congressional and state-level races. However, far less attention has been devoted to the Democratic countermovement that the defection of the South to the Republicans produced. This is because the Democratic reaction was slow to materialize, being composed solely of secular changes in Democratic support. These Democratic gains do not become discernible at the national level until 1976, when their national effect begins to exceed the deteriorating Republicans gains rooted in 1952.

The average size of the secular Democratic gains realized in the Civil Rights Era reached 20 points in 1992, receding slightly after that. However, because this movement was so broadly based, its peak national impact is 12 points (NATIONAL IMPACT $_{CIVIL RIGHTS\_DEM}$ is .12 in 1988 and 1992). This is greater than the largest national impact of the Republican realignments in the Slavery Era (11 points), three times the largest national impact of the Democratic shifts in the Jim Crow Era, and six times as large as the national impact of the Populist revolt. Moreover, it compares favorably with the peak Whig national impact in the Jacksonian Era (14 points) and the largest Republican impact in the Industrial Era (14 points).

## Summary

The inertial effects of habitual behavior and the centripetal pulls of partisan attachments are powerful forces within the electoral arena, as chapter 4 argues and figure 5–3 demonstrates. But the data presented in chapter 6 show that partisan influences on voting are rooted in social groups and interests, suggesting that political parties may provide a sensible heuristic for voting during periods of political normalcy. The results presented in chapter 7 contribute further to our understanding of popular efficacy. They show that, at key points in time, United States citizens have evidenced the capacity to make major changes their normal voting routines.

The results reported in figure 7–1 and figure 7–2; map 7–1 through map 7–6; and table 7–1 demonstrate that the data on the incidence of enduring electoral change are highly structured. The episodic, but spatially ordered, manner in which enduring breaks occur is consistent with the conception of mass-elite linkages driving this reassessment of popular efficacy. Thus, the patterned change thesis could not be rejected; the data on enduring electoral change are consistent with the assertion that they are popular responses to a series of related and reinforcing critical events.

Reinforcing the theoretical implications of these patterned changes are those reported in the magnitude analysis. The contours of the enduring electoral changes depicted in figure 7–4 though figure 7–8 are consistent with the transformational model presented in chapter 3: simple step models of change are not manifested in any of the major realignment eras in American presidential politics. Moreover, the data on magnitude and duration of enduring changes suggest that these electoral shifts are politically consequential happenings that are likely to figure heavily in the education of political elites about democratic politics. The analyses presented in chapter 9 reinforce this conclusion.

## REFERENCES

Gienapp, W. E. 1987. *The Origins of the Republican Party, 1852–1856*. New York, NY, Oxford University Press.

Manza, J., and C. Brooks. 1999. *Social Cleavages and Political Change: Voter Alignments and U.S. Party Coalitions*. Oxford, Oxford University Press.

Moran, P. 1950a. "Notes on Continuous Stochastic Phenomena." *Biometrika* 37: 17–23.

———. 1950b. "A Test for Serial Independence of Residuals." *Biometrika* 37: 178–181.

# CHAPTER EIGHT

# Electoral Perturbations and Electoral Independence: Stewardship, Partisanship, and Accountability

The hullabaloo of a presidential campaign so commands our attention that we ascribe to campaigns great power to sway the multitude. Campaigning does change votes and it does bestir people to vote. Yet other influences doubtless outweigh the campaign in the determination of the vote. . . .The impact of events from the inauguration of an Administration to the onset of the next presidential campaign may affect far more voters than the fireworks of the campaign itself. Governments must act or not act, and action or inaction may convert supporters into opponents or opponents into supporters. Events, over which government may, or more likely may not, have control, shape the attitudes of voters to the advantage or disadvantage of the party in power.

   —V. O. KEY, *The Responsible Electorate*

Since the creation of political parties, the resilient strength of mass partisan loyalties has been one of the most important and persistent aspects of American politics. . . . [In the antebellum period] [n]ew crises, different issues, and fresh political faces normally had little impact on most voters' partisan loyalties. . . . Men were held together in parties "by the force of association and organization," the *Cincinnati Commercial* declared, and thus "under ordinary circumstances . . . mere habit is sufficient to control their acts and to supply the place of opinions which they have not time nor inclination to form." . . . Individuals viewed events, facts, and observations through the prism of party identity. Senator James A. Bayard of Delaware maintained that "the spirit of party operates unconsciously on the minds of even moderate partisans and reflecting men, and warps and perverts their judgment. With the mass of partisans its sway is overwhelming."

   —WILLIAM E. GIENAPP, *The Origins of the Republican Party, 1852–1856*

THIS CHAPTER presents the second component of the electoral independence analysis. Its concern is with deviations from normal voting patterns and their implications for popular efficacy. Scholars such as V. O. Key

view these electoral perturbations as referendums on political stewardship. To these scholars, the capacity of democratic electorates to generate
short-term electoral jolts based on performance of incumbents is a central
component of electoral accountability. To others, whose views are aptly
summarized by Gienapp, the combined effects of partisanship, inattentiveness, and inertial tendencies make meaningful electoral accountability
a fanciful notion. In their view, most citizens lack the interest and commitment to translate public failings rooted in governmental mismanagement,
ineptitude, or malfeasance into meaningful political statements. To them,
electoral perturbations are little more than uninterpretable, and ultimately inconsequential, blips in voting patterns.

To assess these competing perspectives on popular efficacy, I examine
the data on electoral perturbations in light of the transformational model
depicted in figure 3–2. The focuses of the empirical analyses are on assessing the electoral impact of variations in (1) the realization of a key
subset of core political desires and (2) partisan efforts to influence voters.
This dual focus is motivated by the desire to provide empirical insights
into (1) the conception of voters as discriminating consumers of public
goods, and (2) the relative effectiveness of performance and partisan strategies in furthering elite interests.[1] Thus, chapter 8 is of central importance
to the objectives of this work.

Meaningful correlations between the realization of core desires and
electoral perturbations—in the face of ongoing elite efforts to obscure
accountability and evade responsibility—would provide the empirical
basis for two key theoretical inferences. These correlations would suggest
a level of political discernment and electoral independence consistent with
the view of citizens as efficacious political actors. They would also support the assertion that strategic elites have been educated to realize it is
in their interest to be responsive to popular concerns.

However, if political resources can be deployed in ways that distract
and dull the evaluative capacities of citizens, then it would suggest that
elites need not be attentive to popular concerns. Consequently, this analysis can provide unique insights into the relative force of exogenous and
endogenous influences throughout the democratic era in United States
politics.

The next section outlines the methodological approach used in the empirical analysis. Then I describe the technique used to assess the theoreti-

---

[1] As defined in chapter 3, "Performance strategies are rooted in ideals epitomized by
Progressive conceptions of politics; they deploy both political leadership and tools of public
policy to protect and enhance citizens' realization of their core political desires. Partisan
strategies are rooted in Machiavellian conceptions of politics; they deploy mostly political
resources to obfuscate accountability and dull the evaluative capacities of citizens by distracting and misleading them."

cal significance of the empirical results. The fourth section reports, illustrates, and evaluates those results, while the summary develops their implications for popular efficacy.

## POLITICAL STEWARDSHIP, POLITICAL PARTIES, AND SHORT-TERM ELECTORAL EFFECTS

Generating empirical insights into the relative effectiveness of performance and partisan strategies in furthering the core political interests of political stewards requires: (1) identifying a set of performance indicators that capture variations in the realization of core political desires; (2) identifying a set of partisan indicators that capture variations in partisan activities designed to influence stewardship evaluations and vote choices; and (3) dealing with the methodological challenges involved in gauging the impact of these variables over time. This section outlines the approach used to address these matters, beginning with a discussion of the empirical strategy employed in the analysis and the methodological issues involved in implementing it. The following two subsections introduce the two sets of independent variables to be used in the empirical analyses.

### Examining the Electoral Impact of Performance and Partisan Indicators

To assess the impact of the performance and partisan indicators on electoral perturbations, I used multivariate regression analysis on a set of data pooled from state electorates across all presidential elections held between 1836 and 2000, with the exception of 1864 and 1932.[2] The state election-year is the unit of analysis here, rather than the local election-year, for both methodological and substantive reasons.[3] Methodologically, the state is the more appropriate unit of analysis because all of the indepen-

[2] The elections were excluded because preliminary analyses demonstrated that the extreme values of selected performance indicators for those years exerted undue influence on the regression coefficients. The Election of 1864 was conducted in the midst of the Civil War; the Election of 1932 was held at the depths of the Great Depression.

[3] Operating at the state level required aggregating the local normal vote data, which was done by weighting the local data by the number of votes cast in each election. In this aggregation, data from all local electorates for a given election were used, with one exception. The one exclusion was data from elections in which a local electorate experienced a critical realignment (see map 7–1 to map 7–6). The reason for excluding realigning elections is that at least some of the realignments documented in chapter 7 were generated by societal developments reflected in the performance indicators used in the regression analyses. This poses an analytic problem of some concern: for cases in which the unit realigned, the moving average process used to generate normal vote estimates eliminated most of the electoral

dent variables are measured at either the state or national level. Substantively, the state is the preferable unit of analysis because a key concern here is with assessing the impact of variations in electoral perturbations on the contest for Electoral College votes. Because this battle is waged in state-level elections, it is best to gauge the relative impact of performance and partisan indicators using state-level analyses.

Using a pooled data set was both necessary and beneficial.[4] It was necessary because many of the variables to be introduced in the next section are measured at the national level; pooling was needed to generate variance in them. But pooling also enhances the strengths of the research design employed here. It maximizes the observable variance in the independent variables measured at the state level, some of which have only limited variance in a given election. Despite the value of pooling the data, several concerns rooted in the primary objectives of this research placed limits on the extent to which it could be employed. Two are particularly important to note.

The first concerns the capacity of citizens to hold stewards accountable for their performance in office. Within conventional approaches to electoral accountability, the party that holds the presidency at the time of an election is viewed as being responsible for the state of the nation, irrespective of whether the incumbent president is running for reelection. Thus, separate analysis pools had to be created for each of the major parties. Creating party-specific pools led to a second constraint on the pooling procedure. This constraint is rooted in the fact that, over time, the identities and constituencies of the major parties change. These changes had marked effects on some regression coefficients that were large enough to be substantively meaningful. Extensive preliminary analyses indicated that the most important changes took place after 1932. Thus, elections held before 1932 were pooled separately from those held after 1932.

Addressing these two concerns required the use of four different analysis pools. These different pools, along with their corresponding acronyms are: (1) all states for elections held between 1836 and 1928 with Democratic incumbents (D1); (2) all states for elections held between 1836 and 1928 with Whig or Republican incumbents (R1); (3) all states for elections held between 1936 and 2000 with Democratic incumbents (D2); (4) all states for elections held between 1936 and 1928 with Republican incumbents (R2).

---

effects generated by those exogenous factors. Including these cases in the regression analyses could generate misleading regression coefficients for the variables.

[4] Pooling the state data required that the regression analysis had to be weighted by the number of votes cast in a state. However, the number of voters in a state varied substantially across locales and over time. Thus, conducting regression analyses on these pooled data

Using four party-specific analysis pools necessitated a modest change in the dependent variable. In chapter 5, NORMAL PARTISAN BALANCE$_{DEV}$ is used to introduce and illustrate the concept of an electoral perturbation; here I employ INCUMBENT$_{DEV}$. INCUMBENT$_{DEV}$ is simply a recoded version of NORMAL PARTISAN BALANCE$_{DEV}$. It is recoded so that positive scores indicate election-specific gains for the incumbent party and negative scores indicate election-specific losses for the incumbent party. Making this modification simplifies comparisons of the regression results across analysis pools: the sign of the coefficients will have identical meanings across equations.

While the substantive concerns with stewardship and accountability dictated the use of four analysis pools, their use also produced methodological benefits. The availability of four data pools containing comparable data made it possible to examine how voters respond to different parties and to observe temporal changes in electoral behavior. It also provided insights into the meaning of unexpected results and the opportunity to confirm them in independent settings. Despite these benefits, the use of four analysis pools also created some methodological problems. The number of variables measured at the national level (see tables 8–1 and 8–2) led to some unavoidable multicollinearity. Dealing with this multicollinearity required the use of two-stage least squares regression analysis.[5]

## Performance Indicators and Core Political Desires

To examine the electoral effects of variations in the realization of core political desires, I employ performance indicators in three domains: economic prosperity, war and peace, and personal security. I focus on these domains because prosperity, peace, and personal security are among the most basic and widely shared core political desires, as noted in table 2–1. Variations in the realization of these performance indicators over time and across space should affect stewardship evaluations and vote choices within the approach to mass-elite linkages offered here. Information on the specific performance indicators used is reported in table 8–1, along with their hypothesized effect. Each of these variables is employed in the first stage of the regression analysis.

In generating the hypotheses listed in table 8–1, I relied on both assumption A1 and the traditional reward/punishment conception of electoral accountability perhaps best illustrated in the work of V.O. Key (1966). I use this conception because it provides (1) the most straightforward set of expectations and (2) the minimal standard against which the behavior

required weighting each observation according to its contribution to the total votes cast for each election.

[5] I would like to thank Professor Brian Gaines of the University of Illinois for his advice on handling the multicollinearity problems posed by this analysis.

TABLE 8.1
Summary of Political Stewardship Variables

| Variable | Description | Level of Measurement | Data Availability | Regression Stage | Hypothesized Impact | | | |
|---|---|---|---|---|---|---|---|---|
| *Macroeconomic Performance Variables* | | | | | | | | |
| $\Delta$ RGDP | Percentage Change in Per Capita Real Gross Domestic Product for Election-year | National | 1828–2000 | First | + | + | + | + |
| $\Delta$ RGDP$_{LAG1}$ | One Year lag of RGDP | National | 1828–2000 | First | + | + | + | + |
| DEFLATION RATE$_0$ | Magnitude of Drop in Price Level for Election Year National | National | 1828–2000 | First | + | + | * | * |
| INFLATION RATE$_0$ | Magnitude of Increase in Price Level for Election Year National | National | 1828–2000 | First | – | – | – | – |
| INFLATION RATE$_{LAG1}$ | One Year Lag of INFLATION RATE | National | 1828–2000 | First | – | – | – | – |
| *War and Peace Variables* | | | | | | | | |
| WAR DEATHS | Number of War Related Deaths in the Election Year National | National | 1932–2000 | First | * | * | – | – |
| UNPOPULAR WAR | Dummy Variable Depicting Existence of an Unpopular War (Coded '1' for elections during the Korean and Vietnam conflicts; '0' for all other elections) | National | 1828–2000 | First | * | * | – | – |
| YEARS OF PEACE | Number of Years Since the Termination of the Last Major Military Conflict (Coded '0' if a War Was On-going during Election Year) | National | 1828–2000 | First | + | + | + | + |
| PEACE AND PROSPERITY | Interaction Term: YEARS OF PEACE * $\Delta$ RGDP | National | 1828–2000 | First | + | + | + | + |
| *Crime Variables* | | | | | | | | |
| UCR INDEX | Discrete Version of FBI's Uniform Crime Index | State | 1932–2000 | First | # | # | # | – |
| UCR INDEX$^2$ | Discrete Version of FBI's Uniform Crime Index Squared | State | 1932–2000 | First | # | # | # | – |
| $\Delta$ UCR INDEX | Discrete Version of One-Year Change in FBI's Uniform Crime Index | State | 1932–2000 | First | # | # | # | – |
| UCR INDEX * $\Delta$ UCR INDEX | Interaction term | State | 1932–2000 | First | # | # | # | – |

* = Not Relevant;
# = Unavailable

of citizens can be evaluated. If incumbents are not rewarded or punished for their record in office, then it is difficult to argue that voters are discriminating consumers of public goods. Despite my use of this traditional criterion, like other scholars (Chappell and Keech 1985; Fiorina 1981: 6; MacKuen, Erikson, and Stimson 1992), I recognize that more demanding standards exist. These standards involve citizens understanding the intractability and cyclical nature of some public problems, differentiating among governments in a federal system, knowing the reputation of different parties on various issues, being able to incorporate prospective conditions into their evaluation, and the like.

While each of these standards requires more sophisticated cognitive capacities than the simple reward/punishment standard, the level of sophistication they entail is not needed to unravel the paradox of elected officials. This notwithstanding, while I begin with the more traditional reward/punishment standard, I consider these more demanding standards when interpreting the regression results. Incorporating these other standards is facilitated by the use of (1) party-specific analysis pools, (2) performance indicators culled from domains in which the parties have different records, reputations and commitments, and (3) lagged terms for key measures of macroeconomic performance.

### MACROECONOMIC PERFORMANCE

With respect to prosperity, I use standard measures of macroeconomic performance—indicators of economic growth and price levels.[6] The basic indicator I use for economic growth is $\Delta$ RGDP, which measures the change in per capita real gross domestic product during the election year. To gauge the electorate's capacity to incorporate prospective economic conditions into their electoral evaluations, I use $\Delta$ RGDP$_{LAG1}$ (i.e., $\Delta$ RGDP for the year following the election). Positive effects are posited for both of these variables.

Everyone benefits from economic growth, and $\Delta$ RGDP and $\Delta$ RGDP$_{LAG1}$ should adequately capture its electoral impact. Capturing the electoral impact of changes in price levels was more challenging. Changes in price levels affect various groups (debtors, creditors, retirees, etc.) differently. Moreover, while few politicians have ever opposed growth, different parties have traditionally taken different positions on monetary policy (paper money advocates, gold bugs, silverites, etc.). Finally, before the onset of World War Two, deflation was as important a concern to many voters

---

[6] The data on real per capita gross domestic product and price levels come from Louis Johnston and Samuel H. Williamson, "The Annual Real and Nominal GDP for the United States, 1789–Present." Economic History Services, April 2002, URL http://www.eh.net/hmit.

as inflation. Thus, as seen in table 8–1, I created two variables based on price levels, DEFLATION RATE$_0$ and INFLATION RATE$_0$.[7]

Separating changes in price levels into two variables adds an additional national level variable to the pre-1932 analyses; there was only no incidence of a price drop in an election year after 1932. However, the use of two variables makes it possible to differentiate between the electoral effects of different monetary policies. Negative effects are posited for both because few voters favor high rates of inflation or deflation. To examine the effect of prospective trends in price levels I employ INFLATION RATE$_{LAG1}$, which is simply a lagged measure of the changes in price levels (increases or decreases) for the year after the election. Preliminary analyses indicated that a single variable adequately captured the electoral effects of these prospective trends. A negative effect is posited.

### WAR AND PEACE

Capturing the electoral effects of war and peace proved to be challenging even with the temporally encompassing research design employed here. One of the challenges is that very few wars overlap with presidential elections: the Civil War (1864), World War Two (1944), Korea (1952), and Vietnam (1968). Another problem is that the electoral effects of war are often realized in its aftermath, which makes them difficult to incorporate in a regression analysis. These problems notwithstanding, three variables are available to capture the electoral effects of war and peace: WAR DEATHS, UNPOPULAR WAR, and YEARS OF PEACE.

WAR DEATHS captures the number of war-related deaths in an election year.[8] It is expected to have a negative electoral effect. UNPOPULAR WAR is a dummy variable that differentiates the Korea and Vietnam conflicts from World War Two. While wars are seldom "popular," it would be myopic to ignore the differences in public support between these three conflicts, all of which are in D2. Obviously, a negative effect is posited for UNPOPULAR WAR. YEARS OF PEACE measures the number of years since the last major military conflict.[9] Periods of peace are expected to provide incum-

---

[7] Where prices were higher during an election year than the year before, DEFLATION RATE$_0$ was set to 0; where prices were lower during an election year than the year before, INFLATION RATE$_0$ was set to 0.

[8] Data on this variable were collected from various sources. The National Archives has data on war deaths by month and state from 1951 to the present. They can be accessed on line at: http://www.archives.gov/research_room/research_topics/korea_and_vietnam_casualties.html. World War Two deaths were collected by reviewing year-end summaries in the *New York Times*. While these are unofficial data, they are likely to be adequate for the study of their electoral impact, as these are the figures to which the electorate was responding.

[9] I am indebted to Professor Scott Gartner for providing the data necessary to construct the YEARS OF PEACE variable. He provided me with a Correlates of War data set that lists the beginning and ending of all major military conflicts in U.S. history.

bents with electoral benefits, benefits that are expected to be more generous during periods of economic prosperity. Consequentially, in addition
to positing a positive effect for YEARS OF PEACE, I posit a positive interactive effect for PEACE AND PROSPERITY, an interaction term involving
YEARS OF PEACE and Δ RGDP.

PERSONAL SECURITY

To gauge governmental performance affecting personal security, I employ
the FBI's Uniform Crime Reports. I use an aggregated measure of all seven
index crimes. Three points are important to note about UCR data used
in this analysis. First, because UCR data are not available earlier than the
1930s, these data are used only in the D2 and R2 analyses. Second, I
differentiate between "state" and "change" variables, using one measure
to capture the level of crime during an election year (UCR INDEX) and a
second to capture changes in crime levels during that year Δ UCR INDEX).
Third, I employ discrete versions of both variables.[10]

High levels of crime during an election year should hurt the incumbent
party. However, while a negative effect is posited for UCR INDEX, it is not
expected to be a linear effect. Crime did not become a national political
issue until the 1960s, when crime levels were much higher than in the
1940s and 1950s. Moreover, crime rates varied considerably across states
throughout this time period. As only high levels of crime are expected to
generate episodes of intensive information processing, I do not expect UCR
INDEX to have a linear relationship with INCUMBENT$_{DEV}$. Consequently,
table 8–1 posits a negative effect for UCR INDEX$^2$. Increases in crime during
an election year should hurt the incumbent party. Here again, however, a
simple linear effect is not posited. The electoral effect of election-year
crime increases should be most noticeable where existing crime rates are
relatively high. Hence, a negative interactive effect is posited for Δ UCR
INDEX* UCR INDEX.

## Partisan Indicators and Campaign Strategies

As the raison d'être of political parties is to win elective office, their success depends on the development and implementation of effective strategies to influence voting decisions. Consequently, party elites invest a great
deal of effort in the development and nurturing of enduring partisan at-

---

[10] I created discrete versions of these variable for two reasons. First, the raw crime data
are not "clean" enough to merit more finely honed distinctions, especially for the time frame
analyzed here. Second, it is unlikely that the electorate is sensitive to small changes in these
data. Thus, creating discrete versions of these variables better captures real changes in crime
at little cost to the analysis. UCR INDEX varies from 1 to 7 and Δ UCR INDEX varies from 1
to 10.

tachments. Equally important, however, are efforts to use campaign-specific tactics to generate short-term electoral gains. These gains can be realized by activating committed partisans, reassuring wavering loyalists, mobilizing sympathetic nonvoters, and attracting swing voters as well as disaffected members of the opposition party.

To achieve these gains, party elites have developed an array of tactics. Over the course of American political history these tactics have included outright bribes, political favors, voter mobilization efforts, geographically targeted visits by party nominees, and media buys. Nominating candidates who appeal to core groups or have established voter appeal in key states is another time-tested electoral tactic. Also important are the strategic allocation of pork barrel projects, the endorsement, introduction, and enactment of legislation, the invocation of symbols, smear campaigns and "dirty tricks," and the manufacturing of political issues or crises. Key to implementing many of these tactics is the existence and wise deployment of partisan resources, including strong grass-roots organizations, rich campaign chests, astute campaign staff, and the powers of incumbency and/or unified governments.

Capturing the impact of partisan activities on electoral perturbations is a methodologically challenging task. Indeed, given the scope and reach of this analysis, it is virtually impossible to capture all of the partisan tactics mentioned above. Thus, I focused most of my effort on developing two sets of variables that could be measured with some precision for all of the elections and units examined here. These include (1) variables that capture candidate-selection strategies and (2) a set of partisan "control of elective office" variables. Information on these variables is reported in table 8–2, along with their hypothesized effect. The hypotheses were generated in light of assumption A2 and using a conception of parties derived from the "machine model" described in chapter 5; it posits that parties will make decisions, devise strategies, and deploy resources so as to maximize their chance of electoral victory.

CANDIDATE VARIABLES

One of the tactics parties use to generate short-term electoral gains is the nomination of candidates with specific traits. Candidates can be chosen to placate important components of the party's electoral base, distract attention from suboptimal stewardship, or appeal to important groups outside its electoral base. While the capacity of party elites to control the nomination process has been greatly diminished by the advent of the presidential primary, these primaries affect only a small portion of the elections analyzed here.

One of the most venerable candidate nomination strategies is to nominate individuals who hail from key states. The expectation, of course, is that these candidates would generate a favorable electoral pulse within the state. Thus, two dummy variables (HOME STATE$_{DEM PRES}$, HOME STATE$_{REP PRES}$) are used here to capture the short-term electoral effect of home state nominees. As seen in table 8–2, HOME STATE$_{DEM PRES}$ is expected to have positive effects in D1 and D2 while HOME STATE$_{REP PRES}$ is expected to have negative effects. The opposite effects are posited for R1 and R2. Another nomination strategy, used particularly in the nineteenth century, is the nomination of high-profile war heroes. I created two dummy variables depicting the nomination of a war hero: WAR HERO$_{DEM}$, WAR HERO$_{REP}$. WAR HERO$_{DEM}$ is expected to have a positive effect in D1 and D2 while WAR HERO$_{REP}$ is expected to have a negative effect. The opposite set of effects is posited for R1 and R2.

The final candidate variable used here is a dummy variable depicting whether an incumbent president is running for reelection. INCUMBENT is really a hybrid variable; it is similar in effect to the partisan control of office variables. Net of stewardship, a sitting president can help his reelection effort in a variety of ways. Pork can be strategically allocated to electorally important states, targeted benefits can be provided to important constituencies, patronage jobs can be given to key political operatives, campaign issues can be influenced, campaign contributions can be more easily raised, and so forth. INCUMBENT is posited to have a positive impact, as seen in table 8–2.

PARTISAN CONTROL OF ELECTIVE OFFICES

At the state level, I developed two sets of partisan control variables that focused on state political regimes. A state political regime is defined here as control of the executive and legislative branches by the same party. Each set includes a measure of (1) the existence of a state political regime at the time of a presidential election, (2) the duration of the regime, and (3) the strength of the regime. The duration variable is defined in terms of years of unified partisan control at the time of the presidential election; the strength variable is defined in terms of the proportion of all state legislators who belonged to the monopolist party at the time of the election. One set of these variables measures these concepts for the incumbent president's party (STATE REGIME$_{INC PTY}$, REGIME DURATION$_{INC PTY}$, REGIME STRENGTH$_{INC PTY}$); the second set measures them for the "out" party (STATE REGIME$_{OUT PTY}$, REGIME DURATION$_{OUT PTY}$, REGIME STRENGTH$_{OUT PTY}$).[11]

These partisan control variables are theoretically important because the control of state elective offices represents important resources that can be mobilized to generate short-term electoral gains. It has long been a staple

---

[11] The data used to measure these variables are listed in table I-6 in appendix I, which is available at http://www.pol.uiuc.edu/nardulliresearch.html.

of American politics that the control of state political offices can affect the allocation of Electoral College votes in competitive states. Thus, as seen in table 8–2, the existence of a state regime of the incumbent's party is expected to generate electoral gains for the incumbent party. The longer the party has controlled state government, and the stronger its control, the larger the short-term gains. Just the opposite is posited for states whose governments are dominated by the out party.

I constructed a parallel set of regime variables at the national level. However, because these were measured at the national level, there was insufficient variation in most of the analysis pools to provide for a rigorous analysis of the duration and strength dimensions. Thus, while I was able to examine the impact of a national political regime for all analysis pools but R2 (where there were none), I was able to analyze the impact of all three variables only in R1—in the second stage regression analysis.[12] The expected impact of the national regime variables is specified in table 8–2.

## Normal Votes, Electoral Thresholds, and Model Predictions: Presenting and Assessing the Regression Results

Tables 8–1 and 8–2 specify the hypothesized theoretical effect of the various independent variables on electoral perturbations. But generating inferences about the relative effectiveness of performance and partisan strategies on the core political interests of elites requires some basis for gauging the impact of these sets of variables on electoral outcomes. Discerning and succinctly conveying the implications of the regression results for both of these concerns requires a two-pronged approach. The first prong entails the use of graphic displays to illustrate the *form of the relationship* between the independent variables and INCUMBENT$_{DEV}$; the second prong entails a focus on their *predicted effect* on electoral outcomes. The graphic displays are important because they yield insights into the evaluative capacities of the electorate; the focus on electoral outcomes relates the regression results to the core interests of political elites.

To assess the predicted effect of the regression results on electoral outcomes, I derived a set of electoral thresholds that defined the political sig-

---

[12] National partisan regimes existed for (1) two elections in the Democratic analysis pool for the 1836–1928 period (1840, 1916), (2) six elections in the Whig/Republican analysis pool for the 1836–1928 period (1868, 1872, 1900, 1904, 1908, 1924), and (3) seven elections in the Democratic analysis pool for the 1932–2000 period (1936–1952, 1964, 1968, 1980). Despite the existence of seven cases in D2, there was little variance in either strength or duration. No national Republican regime existed at the time of a presidential election for the 1932–2000 period.

TABLE 8.2
Summary of Partisan Activity Variables

| | | | | | Hypothesized Impact * | | | |
|---|---|---|---|---|---|---|---|---|
| | | | | | | *Whig/* | | |
| | | | | | *Democratic* | *Republican* | *Democratic* | *Republican* |
| | | | | | *Pool,* | *Pool,* | *Pool,* | *Pool,* |
| *Variable* | *Description* | *Level of Measurement* | *Data Availability* | *Regression Stage* | *1836–1928* | *1836–1928* | *1932–2000* | *1932–2000* |
| *Candidate Variables* | | | | | | | | |
| HOME STATE_DEM PRES | Home state of the Democratic presidential candidate | State | 1828–2000 | First | + | – | + | – |
| HOME STATE_REP PRES | Home state of the Whig/Republican presidential candidate | State | 1828–2000 | First | – | + | – | + |
| WAR HERO_DEM | Did the Democrats nominate a war hero for president? | National | 1828–2000 | Second | + | – | + | – |
| WAR HERO_REP | Did the Whigs/Republicans nominate a war hero for president? | National | 1828–2000 | Second | – | + | – | + |
| INCUMBENT | Is an incumbent president running for re-election? | National | 1828–2000 | Second | + | + | + | + |
| *Partisan Control Variables* | | | | | | | | |
| STATE REGIME_INC PTY | Did the incumbent president's party control both the executive and legislative branches of the state government? | State | 1836–2000 | First | + | + | + | + |
| REGIME DURATION_INC PTY | Number of years the incumbent president's party has controlled both the executive and legislative branches of the state government | State | 1836–2000 | First | + | + | + | + |
| REGIME STRENGTH_INC PTY | Proportion of all state legislators who belong to the incumbent president's party | State | 1836–2000 | First | + | + | + | + |

* = Not Relevant

TABLE 8.2 (*cont'd*)
Summary of Partisan Activity Varables

| Variable | Description | Level of Measurement | Data Availability | Regression Stage | Democratic Pool, 1836–1928 | Whig/ Republican Pool, 1836–1928 | Democratic Pool, 1932–2000 | Republican Pool, 1932–2000 |
|---|---|---|---|---|---|---|---|---|
| | | | | | | Hypothesized Impact | | |
| *Partisan Control Variables* | | | | | | | | |
| STATE REGIME$_{OUT\,PTY}$ | Did the opposition party control both the executive and legislative branches of the state government? | State | 1836–2000 | First | − | − | − | − |
| REGIME DURATION$_{OUT\,PTY}$ | Number of years the opposition party has controlled both the executive and legislative branches of the state government | State | 1836–2000 | First | − | − | − | − |
| REGIME STRENGTH$_{OUT\,PTY}$ | Proportion of all state legislators who belong to the opposition's party | State | 1836–2000 | First | − | − | − | − |
| NATIONAL REGIME$_{DEM}$ | Did the Democrats control both the executive and legislative branches of the national government? | National | 1828–2000 | First | + | N.A. | + | N.A. |
| NATIONAL REGIME$_{REP}$ | Did the Republicans control both the executive and legislative branches of the national government? | National | 1828–2000 | Second | N.A. | + | N.A. | N.A. |
| NATIONAL REGIME DURATION$_{REP}$ | Number of years the Republicans controlled both the executive and legislative branches of the national government | National | 1828–2000 | Second | N.A. | + | N.A. | N.A. |
| NATIONAL REGIME STRENGTH$_{REP}$ | Proportion of all national legislators who were Republicans | National | 1828–2000 | Second | N.A. | + | N.A. | N.A. |

* = Not Relevant

nificance of perturbations at both the state and national level. To determine the political significance of the regression results, I compare the predicted impact of an independent variable or set of independent variables with the relevant threshold. The next two sections introduce (1) the procedure used to derive electoral thresholds at the state and national level, and (2) the technique used to generate predictions for the independent variables.

### Electoral Thresholds

Normal voting patterns in a state were used to derive state-level electoral thresholds. For party elites, the difference between the value of STATE NOR-MAL PARTISAN BALANCE and 0 is what determines the significance of an electoral perturbation. For the "majority party" in a state (i.e., the party that enjoys an electoral advantage derived from normal voting patterns), this threshold defines their "comfort margin." They can absorb a short-term electoral loss and still win the state, as long as that loss is smaller than their comfort margin. For the "minority party" in a state, the difference between the value of STATE NORMAL PARTISAN BALANCE and 0 is their "normal vote deficit." In order for them to win a state, they need an electoral perturbation that is larger than this deficit.

Deriving national-level electoral thresholds is more involved than deriving state-level thresholds, but it is still based on state normal voting patterns. Complications emerge at the national level because Electoral College votes must be joined with state normal voting patterns to derive a measure of majority party vulnerability. To gauge the vulnerability of the majority party, which defines national electoral thresholds, required a two-step procedure.

The first step involved determining majority and minority party status for each election. I did this by examining the values of the STATE NORMAL PARTISAN BALANCE variable in conjunction with their Electoral College votes. The Electoral College votes of states with positive values on STATE NORMAL PARTISAN BALANCE were assigned to the electoral base of the Democrats; those with negative values were assigned to that of the Republicans (or Whigs). States with a 0 value on the STATE NORMAL PARTI-SAN BALANCE variable were unassigned. For every election since 1836 this procedure resulted in the identification of a majority party and a minority party.

The second step involved using the information on majority/minority party status to determine the number of states the minority party had to win, with the smallest set of deviations from normal voting patterns, in order to gain a majority of Electoral College votes. These states are defined as "must-win" states. To identify these "must-win" states, I arrayed STATE NORMAL PARTISAN BALANCE from high to low for each election (see

TABLE 8.3
Array of STATE NORMAL PARTISAN BALANCE and Electoral College Votes for 1940

| State | STATE NORMAL PARTISAN BALANCE | *Electoral College Votes* | State | STATE NORMAL PARTISAN BALANCE | *Electoral College Votes* |
|---|---|---|---|---|---|
| VT | −0.18 | 3 | WV | 0.11 | 8 |
| NE | −0.17 | 7 | MD | 0.12 | 8 |
| ND | −0.1 | 4 | MN | 0.12 | 11 |
| KS | −0.09 | 9 | OR | 0.12 | 5 |
| ME | −0.09 | 5 | KY | 0.13 | 11 |
| SD | −0.04 | 4 | MO | 0.13 | 15 |
| IN | −0.02 | 14 | CA | 0.15 | 22 |
| WI | −0.02 | 12 | NV | 0.15 | 3 |
| NH | −0.01 | 4 | UT | 0.16 | 4 |
| IA | 0.01 | 11 | MT | 0.17 | 4 |
| CO | 0.03 | 6 | WA | 0.18 | 8 |
| MI | 0.03 | 19 | OK | 0.21 | 11 |
| NJ | 0.03 | 16 | AZ | 0.23 | 3 |
| PA | 0.03 | 36 | TN | 0.26 | 11 |
| CT | 0.04 | 8 | VA | 0.3 | 11 |
| OH | 0.04 | 26 | NC | 0.38 | 13 |
| DE | 0.05 | 3 | FL | 0.5 | 7 |
| IL | 0.05 | 29 | AR | 0.51 | 9 |
| WY | 0.05 | 3 | TX | 0.58 | 23 |
| MA | 0.06 | 17 | GA | 0.62 | 12 |
| NY | 0.07 | 47 | LA | 0.62 | 10 |
| | | | AL | 0.7 | 11 |
| ID | 0.09 | 4 | SC | 0.8 | 8 |
| NM | 0.09 | 3 | MS | 0.87 | 9 |
| RI | 0.11 | 4 | | | |

The rows IA through NY (left column) are bracketed and labeled "Must Win" States.

table 8–3). I then examined that array to determine which states the minority party had to win in order to capture a majority of Electoral College votes—while overcoming the smallest set of normal vote deficits. That subset of states defined the "must-win" states for that election. The *largest* normal vote deficit needed to win *all* the "must-win" states, along with the number of states needed for victory, defines the national-level electoral thresholds to be used in determining the electoral significance of the regression results (see table 8–4).

To illustrate this procedure consider the Election of 1940. In 1940 there were 531 votes in the Electoral College, with 266 votes needed to capture the presidency. table 8–3 displays STATE NORMAL PARTISAN BALANCE and the Electoral College vote allocations for 1940. The Democratic Party is considered the majority party: STATE NORMAL PARTISAN BALANCE reveals

TABLE 8.4
Perturbations Required to Generate a Minority Party Victory, by Election

| Election Year | Electoral College Votes Needed for Minority Party Victory | Number of Battleground States | Largest Perturbation Needed among Battleground States | Election Year | Electoral College Votes Needed for Minority Party Victory | Number of Battleground States | Largest Perturbation Needed among Battleground States |
|---|---|---|---|---|---|---|---|
| 1836 | 17 | 1 | 0.01 | 1920 | 117 | 15 | 0.19 |
| 1840 | 17 | 1 | 0.01 | 1924 | 127 | 13 | 0.19 |
| 1844 | 30 | 2 | 0.001 | 1928 | 127 | 11 | 0.17 |
| 1848 | 39 | 2 | 0.001 | 1932 | 224 | 15 | 0.10 |
| 1852 | 32 | 2 | 0.01 | 1936 | 212 | 13 | 0.09 |
| 1856 | 27 | 1 | 0.03 | 1940 | 204 | 12 | 0.07 |
| 1860 | 46 | 2 | 0.03 | 1944 | 191 | 11 | 0.06 |
| 1864 | 74 | 6 | 0.05 | 1948 | 61 | 4 | 0.02 |
| 1868 | 56 | 4 | 0.03 | 1952 | 66 | 5 | 0.01 |
| 1872 | 47 | 2 | 0.02 | 1956 | 147 | 11 | 0.04 |
| 1876 | 48 | 2 | 0.02 | 1960 | 147 | 11 | 0.04 |
| 1880 | 38 | 2 | 0.01 | 1964 | 188 | 12 | 0.04 |
| 1884 | 39 | 2 | 0.02 | 1968 | 191 | 11 | 0.05 |
| 1888 | 39 | 2 | 0.03 | 1972 | 193 | 13 | 0.06 |
| 1892 | 48 | 4 | 0.05 | 1976 | 219 | 16 | 0.06 |
| 1896 | 79 | 8 | 0.09 | 1980 | 219 | 17 | 0.06 |
| 1900 | 75 | 6 | 0.09 | 1984 | 184 | 15 | 0.05 |
| 1904 | 83 | 5 | 0.12 | 1988 | 141 | 11 | 0.03 |
| 1908 | 79 | 9 | 0.14 | 1992 | 31 | 2 | 0.01 |
| 1912 | 93 | 13 | 0.15 | 1996 | 30 | 4 | 0.02 |
| 1916 | 117 | 15 | 0.17 | 2000 | 30 | 4 | 0.04 |

that thirty-nine states (with a total of 469 Electoral College votes) had positive values. The Republican Party is the minority party because the distribution of STATE NORMAL PARTISAN BALANCE revealed that only nine states with a total of 62 Electoral College votes had negative values. A 469 to 62 edge in Electoral College votes suggests a significant Democratic electoral advantage. However, analyzing table 8–3 from the perspective of Republican strategists provides some insights into the vulnerability of the Democrats.

Crucial to any winning Republican strategy in 1940 is that they "hold their own" in states where they have some electoral advantage. *Thus, the procedure developed to define electoral thresholds rests on the assumption that the short-term electoral forces favor the minority party.*[13] The

[13] Data to be reported in figure 9–3 suggest that this is not an unrealistic assumption. Those data make it very clear that there are a number of elections in which the preponder-

challenge facing the Republicans in 1940, in addition to "holding their own," was to win at least 204 Electoral College votes in states where they had the smallest normal vote deficits. To do this the Republicans would have to capture twelve "must-win" states: Colorado, New Jersey, Ohio, Connecticut, Iowa, Michigan, Pennsylvania, Illinois, Delaware, Wyoming, Massachusetts, and New York (see the blocked portion of table 9–5). The largest normal vote deficit among the "must-win" states is .07.

The data on majority party vulnerability for each election from 1836 to 2000 are reported in table 8–4; they provide important insights into electoral accountability. For the period from 1836 to 1928 the minority party could have won half of all presidential elections (12 of 24) by generating a 3-point deviation from normal voting patterns in no more than two states. These elections include all those before 1892 with the exception of those affected by the Civil War, 1864, and 1868. A 5-point shift in just six states would have generated a minority party victory in almost two-thirds (15/24) of these elections: all those before the critical elections of 1896. After the Election of 1896, the Democrats needed, on average, a 15-point shift in ten states. For the 1932–2000 time frame a 6-point national shift in favor of the minority party would have won 15 of 18 elections, all those held after 1940. The range of variation in "must win" states varies considerably after 1928, ranging from 2 to 17. But a 6-point perturbation is electorally significant for this period, in contrast to the 5-point perturbation for the 1836–1928 period.

## Predicted Electoral Impacts

To predict the electoral impact of most of the variables employed here, I assign all variables in the regression model their pool mean and then adjust the intercept so that the model predicts a value of 0. I then let the variable of interest take on its full range of values and use that variance to generate a set of predictions. This approach was not applicable to the macroeconomic performance variables because multicollinearity problems made it suspect. Thus, for these variables I estimate an overall effect, as well as some selected independent effects, using a slightly different approach. To estimate the overall electoral effect of macroeconomic performance, I assign *all* of the economic performance indicators their actual values and then generate a set of election-specific predictions. I determine the independent effect of prospective economic conditions, and the peace and prosperity interaction, by estimating the regression equation and gen-

ance of short-term effects favored one party or the other. This is particularly true after the turn of the twentieth century.

erating predictions with and without these variables. More will be said of this technique below.

## POLITICAL STEWARDSHIP, POLITICAL PARTIES, AND ELECTORAL PERTURBATIONS

The results of the four regression analyses are presented in table 8–5. The adjusted $R^2$'s are as follows: D1, .45; R1, .53; D2, .69; R2, .74.[14] Given the

[14] In addition to the variables listed in tables 8–1 and 8–2, I used two year-specific dummy variables in the regression analyses. They had to be employed to capture accurately the underlying relationships that existed in the main body of the respective analysis pools. Without these dummy variables these underlying relationships are obscured by a few outlier years. ELECTION OF 1856 was employed in the D1 analysis (where the slavery issue trumped other factors) and DEPRESSION ERA (this variable captures both 1936 and 1940, when the lingering depression affected voting decisions in unique ways) was employed in D2. While neither of these variables is of any theoretical import and I do not discuss their effects in the text, a few comments are in order concerning their inclusion in the regression analysis.

First, to demonstrate that the final regressions simply reflect underlying relationships in the main body of the analysis pools, I recalculated the regressions without the elections affected by the dummy variables. Consider first D1. The first equation reported below is for the regression with 1856 excluded; the second is the reported equation.

D1: INCUMBENT$_{DEV}$ = −.12** − .02*$\Delta$ RGDP + .01*$\Delta$ RGDP$_{LAG1}$*** + .01*YEARS OF PEACE** + .002*PEACE AND PROSPERITY*** + .05*STATE REGIME$_{INC\,PTY}$ − .003* DURATION OF STATE REGIME$_{INC\,PTY}$** −.06*STATE REGIME$_{OPP\,PTY}$** + .003*DURATION OF STATE REGIME$_{OPP\,PTY}$**; Adj. $R^2$ = .49.

D1: INCUMBENT$_{DEV}$ = −.13* + .20*ELECTION OF 1856*** − .02*$\Delta$ RGDP + .01*$\Delta$ RGDP$_{LAG1}$*** + .01*YEARS OF PEACE** + .002* PEACE AND PROSPERITY*** + .07* STATE REGIME$_{INC\,PTY}$* −.003*DURATION OF STATE REGIME$_{INC\,PTY}$* − .06* STATE REGIME$_{OPP\,PTY}$** + .003*DURATION OF STATE REGIME$_{OPP\,PTY}$**; Adj. $R^2$=. 45.

The $R^2$ is somewhat larger when 1856 is excluded but the B-coefficients are virtually identical, as are the significance levels. The next two equations are for D2. The first equation reports the results with the two depression elections excluded; the second is the equation reported in the text. The main difference in the two equations is that without 1936 and 1940 in the equation, the war-related variables lose their statistical significance, as does INFLATION RATE$_{LAG1}$. Thus, the inclusion of 1936 and 1940, the elections preceding the United States' entry into World War Two are crucial in capturing the relationship between the war and peace variables and voting. It should also be noted that the coefficient for STRENGTH OF STATE REGIME$_{INC\,PTY}$ term is significantly larger in the first equation, though still negative. When 1936 and 1940 are excluded, much more explanatory power is attributed to economic variables, particularly *$\Delta$ RGDP, as well as STATE REGIME$_{INC\,PTY}$.

D2: INCUMBENT$_{DEV}$ = −.57*** + .12*$\Delta$ RGDP* + .05*$\Delta$ RGDP$_{LAG1}$* + .04*INFLATION RATE$_0$*** − .02*INFLATION RATE$_{LAG1}$ + .02*UNPOPULAR WAR + .04*YEARS OF PEACE − .01*PEACE AND PROSPERITY + .14*STATE REGIME$_{INC\,PTY}$*** − .24*STRENGTH OF STATE REGIME$_{INC\,PTY}$*** − .06*HOME STATE REGIME$_{REP\,P}$***; Adj. $R^2$ = .70.

scope and reach of the analysis, the explanatory strength of the regression models is reassuring.[15] The next two sections develop the implications of specific results reported in table 8–5. Before these specifics are detailed, however, two more general observations can be made that will provide succinct insights into the theoretical import and utility of the regression results.

The first is that the regression analyses strongly support the theoretical observations made in chapter 3 about the superiority of performance strategies over partisan strategies. In all but one analysis pool (R1) the performance indicators are, by far, the most important determinants of state-level electoral perturbations. To demonstrate this point I estimated two "reduced" regression models, using only subsets of the variables used to generate the results reported in table 8–5. One reduced model included only the performance indicators; the other included only the partisan activity variables. The adjusted $R^2$'s for the performance model are as fol-

---

D2: INCUMBENT$_{DEV}$ = $-.33^{***}$ $- 1.48^*$DEPRESSION ERA$^{***}$ + $.06^*\Delta$ RGDP$^*$ + $.04^*\Delta$ RGDP$_{LAG1}^*$ + $.03^*$INFLATION RATE$_0^*$ + $-.09^*$UNPOPULAR WAR$^{***}$ $-.015^*$YEARS OF PEACE$^{**}$ + $.006^*$ PEACE AND PROSPERITY$^{**}$ + $.05^*$STATE REGIME$_{INC PTY}$ $-.10^*$STRENGTH OF STATE REGIME$_{INC PTY}^*$ $- .05^*$HOME STATE REGIME$_{REPP}^{***}$; Adj. $R^2$ = .69.

I also employed an $F$-test for structural change that examines the Residual Sum of Squares from regressions for (1) all cases, (2) all cases except those in question (1856, 1936, and 1940 in this case) and (3) just questionable cases. The F-statistic for D1 is 9.45 and 24.9 for D2. Both F-statistics are statistically significant well beyond the 0.001 level, giving evidence that these elections differed substantially and should be distinguished in the regression analyses. I wish to thank Wendy Cho for her advice in dealing with this issue, as well as in her assistance in conducting the F-test analyses.

[15] Because so many of the most powerful variables in the regression analyses were national-level variables, I reconducted the analyses at the national level, using only the national-level variables. The coefficients for these variables are very similar to those produced by the state-level analyses, although all are not statistically significant because of the small n's. Only two coefficients had different signs (YEARS OF PEACE in R1 and $\Delta$ RGDP in R2). One of the variables with a different sign ($\Delta$ RGDP in R2) is of less concern because it is part of an interaction term, PEACE AND PROSPERITY.

D1: INCUMBENT$_{DEV}$ = .11 + $.29^*$ELECTION OF 1856$^{***}$ $- .02^*\Delta$ RGDP$^*$ + $.01^*\Delta$ RGDP$_{LAG1}^{**}$ + $.007^*$YEARS OF PEACE$^*$ + $.002^*$ PEACE AND PROSPERITY$^{**}$; $R^2$ = .99.

R1: INCUMBENT$_{DEV}$ = .06 + $.01^*\Delta$ RGDP + $.07^*$DEFLATION RATE$_0$ $- .08^*$INFLATION RATE$_0^*$ $-- .03^*$INFLATION RATE$_{LAG1}$ $- .001^*$YEARS OF PEACE $- .08^*$INCUMBENT $\pm .09^*$ NATIONAL REGIME$_{REP}$; $R^2$ = .64.

D2: INCUMBENT$_{DEV}$ = $-.30$ $- 1.44^*$DEPRESSION ERA$^*$ + $.05^*\Delta$ RGDP$^*$ + $.04^*$ $\Delta$ RGDP$_{LAG1}^*$ + $.03^*$INFLATION RATE$_0^*$ + $.01^*$INFLATION RATE$_{LAG1}$ $- .09^*$UNPOPULAR WAR $- .01^*$YEARS OF PEACE + $.01^*$ PEACE AND PROSPERITY$^*$; $R^2$ = .99.

R2: INCUMBENT$_{DEV}$ = .13 + $.01^*\Delta$ RGDP $- .14^*$INFLATION RATE$_0$ + $.07^*$INFLATION RATE$_{LAG1}$ $- .01^*$YEARS OF PEACE + $.01^*$ PEACE AND PROSPERITY; $R^2$ = .87.

TABLE 8.5
Summary of Regression Results for the Electoral Perturbations Analysis

| ANALYSIS POOL | Democratic Pool, 1836–1928 (D1) | Whig/Republican Pool, 1836–1928 (R1) | Democratic Pool, 1932–2000 (D2) | Republican Pool, 1932–2000 (R2) |
|---|---|---|---|---|
| INTERCEPT | −0.13* | 0.030 | −0.33*** | 0.12*** |
| DEPRESSION ERA | | | −1.48*** | |
| ELECTION OF 1856 | 0.20*** | | | |
| Δ RGDP | −0.02 | 0.001 | 0.06*** | −0.01* |
| Δ RGDP$_{LAG1}$ | 0.01*** | | 0.04*** | |
| DEFLATION RATE$_0$ | | 0.06*** | | |
| INFLATION RATE$_0$ | | −0.08*** | 0.03*** | −0.12*** |
| INFLATION RATE$_{LAG1}$ | | −0.03*** | 0.01*** | 0.08*** |
| WAR DEATHS | | | | |
| UNPOPULAR WAR | | | −0.09*** | |
| YEARS OF PEACE | 0.01** | −0.001 | −0.015** | −0.02*** |
| PEACE AND PROSPERITY | 0.002*** | 0.001* | 0.006*** | 0.01*** |
| UCR INDEX | | | | −0.04*** |
| UCR INDEX$^2$ | | | | 0.004*** |
| Δ UCR INDEX | | | | 0.01** |
| UCR INDEX * Δ UCR INDEX | | | | −0.002** |
| STATE REGIME$_{INC PTY}$ | 0.07* | | 0.05 | 0.21* |
| DURATION OF STATE REGIME$_{INC PTY}$ | −0.003* | | | |
| STRENGTH OF STATE REGIME$_{INC PTY}$ | | | −0.10* | −0.34** |
| STATE REGIME$_{OPP PTY}$ | −0.06** | −0.04** | | 0.03*** |
| DURATION OF STATE REGIME$_{OPP PTY}$ | 0.003** | 0.003*** | | |
| STRENGTH OF STATE REGIME$_{OPP PTY}$ | | | | |
| HOME STATE$_{DEM P}$ | | −0.03* | | −0.06* |
| HOME STATE$_{REP P}$ | | | −0.05*** | |
| INCUMBENT | | −0.11*** | | |
| NATIONAL REGIME$_{DEM}$ | | | | |
| NATIONAL REGIME$_{REP}$ | | 0.13*** | | |
| N of Cases | 323 | 562 | 472 | 328 |
| Adjusted $R^2$ | 0.45 | 0.53 | 0.69 | 0.74 |

| SECOND STAGE RESULTS | | | | |
|---|---|---|---|---|
| INTERCEPT | 0.002 | | | |
| WAR HERO$_{DEM}$ | 0.05** | | | |
| WAR HERO$_{REP}$ | −0.06*** | | | |
| NATIONAL REGIME DURATION$_{REP}$ | −0.01** | | | |
| NATIONAL REGIME STRENGTH$_{REP}$ | 0.08** | | | |
| N of Cases | 562 | | | |
| Adjusted $R^2$ | 0.06 | | | |

\* = Statistically Significant at the .05 level
\** = Statistically Significant at the .01 level
\*** = Statistically Significant at the .001 level

lows: D1, .42; R1, .38; D2, .67; R2, .73. The adjusted $R^2$'s for the partisan activity model are: D1, .08; R1, .31; D2, .04; R2, .02.

These regression results make it clear that, with the exception of R1, the performance indicators are vastly more powerful in explaining electoral perturbations than the partisan activity variables. In terms of its implications for our understanding of popular efficacy, this is a conservative estimate of the relative importance of performance and partisan influences on perturbations, for two reasons. First, many of the partisan activity variables have unanticipated effects that call into question their ability to translate political power into electoral advantage. Second, several of the performance indicators have unanticipated effects that are suggestive of evaluative capacities that far exceed the reward/punishment standard used to specify the hypotheses embodied in table 8–1.

A second general point here is that, while the adjusted $R^2$'s reported in table 8–5 above are quite respectable, they understate the utility of the regression models for one of the key aims of this analysis: assessing the impact of the independent variables on electoral outcomes. This is particularly true for the economic variables. While levels of economic activity vary significantly at the subnational level, economic data are available only at the national level for the time frame used here. The national level indicators fail to reflect this subnational variation, which is reflected in higher levels of unexplained variance state-level analyses. At the national level these errors should be offset, generating better model predictions and providing a better basis for assessing predicted effects on electoral outcomes.

To demonstrate this point, I analyzed a set of model predictions across levels of analysis. I created the PREDICTED DEVIATION$_{STATE}$ variable by using the coefficients for each of the four regression models reported in Table 8–5 in conjunction with the data used to estimate the relevant models. This generated a value of PREDICTED DEVIATION$_{STATE}$ for every state and election analyzed. I aggregated these state-level predictions to the national level to produce PREDICTED DEVIATION$_{NAT}$. The correlation between ACTUAL DEVIATION$_{STATE}$ and PREDICTED DEVIATION$_{STATE}$ is .65, while the correlation between ACTUAL DEVIATION$_{NAT}$ and PREDICTED DEVIATION$_{NAT}$ is .94. This, of course, suggests that the state-level prediction errors are, indeed, offset at the national level.

Examining figure 8–1 produces more insights into the predictive capacities of the regression analyses. It displays the values for both ACTUAL DEVIATION$_{NAT}$ and PREDICTED DEVIATION$_{NAT}$ for each election. Figure 8–1 demonstrates a remarkable level of correspondence between these two variables, particularly for the D2 and R2 predictions. The sign of PREDICTED DEVIATION$_{NAT}$ is the same as the sign of ACTUAL DEVIATION$_{NAT}$ in all but two elections (1868 and 1908). The mean absolute value of the

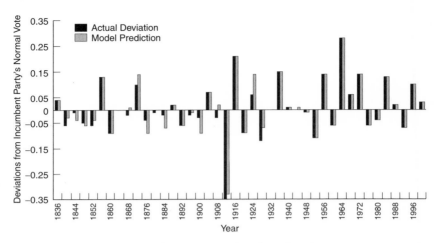

Figure 8–1. Correspondence between Actual and Predicted Deviations

prediction error (PREDICTED DEVIATION$_{NAT}$ – ACTUAL DEVIATION$_{NAT}$) is .02 for all forty elections. Most of the large prediction errors come in the period between 1868 and 1908 (mean = .03); the mean absolute value of the prediction errors is .00 for the seventeen elections held after 1932. These results provide a firm basis for using projections from the regression models to provide insights into the impact of the independent variables on both electoral perturbations and outcomes, generating important insights into popular efficacy.

## Core Political Desires, Stewardship, and Electoral Accountability

The empirical findings related to the performance indicators pertaining to prosperity, war and peace, and personal security are presented in the next three subsections. The first deals with macroeconomic performance (Δ RGDP, Δ RGDP$_{LAG1}$, DEFLATION RATE$_0$, INFLATION RATE$_0$ and, INFLATION RATE$_{LAG1}$). The second section examines the impact of the war and peace variables (WAR DEATHS, UNPOPULAR WAR, and YEARS OF PEACE) as well as the interaction between economic growth and periods of peace (PEACE AND PROSPERITY). The third section addresses stewardship in the personal security domain and presents the results for UCR INDEX and Δ UCR INDEX.

### MACROECONOMIC PERFORMANCE

Table 8–5 demonstrates that most of the hypotheses for the economic variables specified could not be rejected. Of the eight coefficients for Δ RGDP and Δ RGDP$_{LAG1}$, six were statistically significant and all were posi-

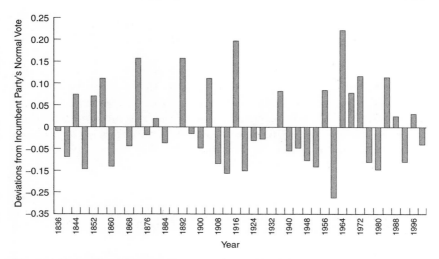

Figure 8–2. Predicted Electoral Impact of Incumbent's Economic Performance

tive, as hypothesized. The only two null findings were for $\Delta$ RGDP$_{LAG1}$ in R1 and R2. The price level variables were statistically significant in seven of ten tests, the only exceptions being in D1, where none were significant. There were three statistically significant effects that were unanticipated: INFLATION RATE$_{LAG1}$ had positive effects in both R2 and D2, and INFLATION RATE$_0$ had a positive effect in D2.

Most of the null and unanticipated results are consistent with Hibbs's party cleavage model of political economy (1987). Moreover, the findings reported here suggest that partisan preferences for different economic outcomes embodied in Hibbs's model are rooted in nineteenth-century electoral lessons provided by the parties' respective electoral bases. While price levels had no apparent effect on Democratic incumbents before 1932, they were the strongest determinant of short-term electoral gains for the opposition. After 1932 inflation, on balance, helps Democratic incumbents, while it hurts Republican incumbents; controlling for other factors, inflationary trends evident on Election Day are helpful to both parties. While stable prices are important for Republican stewards, the Democrats are rewarded for policies that generate economic growth. Overall, economic growth is the most important determinant of short-term electoral gains for Democratic stewards.

Figure 8–2 displays the predicted electoral impact of macroeconomic performance and demonstrates that economic stewardship has significant electoral effects. Indeed, the impact of economic factors far exceeds that of any other set of independent variables analyzed. The mean of the absolute values for all of the electoral effects depicted in figure 8–2 is .08. For the elections held before 1900, the mean effect is .06; for those from 1900 to 2000, it is .09. While the quality of the economic data undoubtedly contributes to these differences, social and political factors contribute as well. The Industrial Revolution certainly decreased the isolation of what was a largely rural society. This, of course, made economic fluctuations more relevant to the lives of more voters. Also important is the fact that after the Great Depression citizens began to change their expectations about the role of government in managing the economy and providing for social welfare.

The magnitude of the predicted effects in figure 8–2 is impressive because they are national effects. Being national effects, an assessment of their political significance is straightforward. In the nineteenth century, the *average* predicted effect of economic stewardship is larger than the electoral thresholds reported in table 8–4 for all elections but one, the Election of 1896. The *average* impact in the twentieth century is larger than the electoral thresholds in all but eight elections held from 1900 to 2000; all eight were held before 1936. This suggests that for 75 percent of the presidential elections since 1836, all other factors held constant, the *average* effect of macroeconomic performance is large enough to have affected the outcome of the election. Effects of this magnitude provide political elites with powerful lessons about the importance of economic stewardship to their core political interests. These lessons were reinforced by the role of economic factors in the partisan realignments of 1836, 1896 and 1932, as seen in chapter 7.

Comparing the economic effects displayed in figure 8–2 with the electoral thresholds reported in table 8–4, by election, provides a more direct assessment of the electoral importance of economic stewardship. This comparison shows that the independent electoral effect of macroeconomic performance has been sufficient to eliminate the incumbent party's comfort margin (or normal vote deficit) in nearly one-third of all elections held since 1836 (eleven of forty). Two categories of elections are important to consider.

The first category includes elections in which the incumbent majority party's economic performance was poor enough to eliminate its comfort margin. There are nine elections in this category: 1836, 1840, 1848, 1876, 1884, 1948, 1960, 1976, and 1992. The incumbent majority party lost six of these nine elections: 1840, 1848, 1884, 1960, 1976, and 1992. The second category involves incumbent minority party administrations whose macroeconomic performance was strong enough to overcome their normal vote deficit. There are four elections in this category: 1844, 1852,

1964, and 1968. Despite their strong economic performances, the incumbent party won only one of these elections (1964).

In the remaining twenty-seven elections the predicted electoral effect of the incumbent's economic performance is smaller than the relevant electoral threshold. That is not to say, however, that economic performances in these elections had no electoral significance. Weak economic performances by majority party incumbents eroded their comfort margins considerably in 1868, 1912, and 1940, resulting in one loss (1912) and two narrow victories. Strong performances offset other problems in 1872 and 1944, and led to overwhelming Republican victories in 1956, 1972, and 1984. The Democrats' strong economic performance in 1916 was not sufficient to overcome their normal vote deficit, but it was almost certainly the most important factor in their victory.

While this analysis demonstrates the importance of economic stewardship, it also illustrates that economics is seldom determinative of electoral outcomes. Other factors matter. Before proceeding to an analysis of these other factors, however, it is important to consider the electoral effects of prospective economic conditions. Knowing whether prospective economic conditions play an important electoral role can provide important insights into the level of political discernment within the American electorate.

THE ELECTORAL IMPACT OF PROSPECTIVE ECONOMIC CONDITIONS

The regression analyses demonstrate that the lagged economic indicators had a statistically significant effect in each of the four analysis pools, suggesting that prospective economic conditions have long been a part of electoral calculations. This observation is particularly noteworthy for the D1 and R1 analysis pools. They gauge electoral behavior before the availability of more sophisticated economic reports and the widely disseminated releases of highly anticipated "leading economic indicators." Thus, the regression analyses for D1 and R1 are arguably capturing the electoral effects of "felt" economic experiences.

To provide some empirically grounded sense of the electoral significance of prospective economic conditions, I employed a two-step procedure. First, I reestimated the regression models without the lagged economic terms ($\Delta$ RGDP$_{LAG1}$ and INFLATION RATE$_{LAG1}$). I used predictions from this reduced model as estimates of the impact of election-year economic conditions. I then subtracted these retrospective effects from the predicted economic effects reported in figure 8–2. I attribute the difference between the two sets of predictions as the effect of prospective economic conditions.

Figure 8–3 displays both sets of predictions and demonstrates that the electoral effects of prospective economic conditions are sizable. There

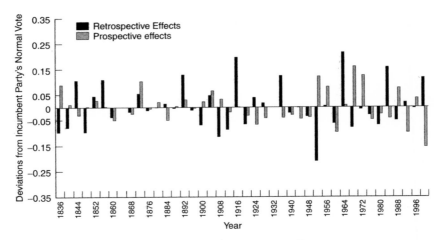

Figure 8–3. Retrospective and Prospective Economic Effects

were only five elections in which prospective effects were nonexistent (1848, 1856, 1888, 1896, and 1916) and, in the aggregate, the electoral impact of prospective economic conditions is similar to that of election-year economic conditions. The mean of the absolute value of the election-year effects reported in figure 8–3 is .07; the mean for the prospective effects is .05. Thus, to ignore the electoral impact of prospective economic conditions is to miss almost half of the electoral impact of economic stewardship. A related point is that ignoring the effect of prospective economic conditions can lead to misleading assessments of the electoral effects of economic stewardship. If the lagged variables had not been included in the regression analyses, the predicted economic effects reported in figure 8–2 would have had a differently signed prediction in ten out of forty elections, *six of which occurred after 1960*. These elections are as follows: 1884, 1924, 1928, 1944, 1968, 1972, 1988, 1992, 1996, and 2000.

One final point is that prospective economic conditions frequently have a consequential electoral impact. Of the thirty-five elections in which prospective economic conditions had a nonzero electoral impact (i.e., all but 1848, 1856, 1888, 1896, and 1916), they had consequential effects in more than one-third (fourteen of thirty-five). In one set of elections (1968, 1972, and 1988), the positive effects of prospective economic conditions more than offset the negative effects of election-year conditions. In two of these elections (1972 and 1968) the *net* effect of prospective economic conditions was larger than the relevant electoral threshold. The incumbent party won one of those elections (1972).

In a second set of elections (1884, 1924, 1928, 1944, 1992, and 2000), the negative effects of prospective economic conditions offset the positive effects of election-year conditions. The incumbent party lost three of those elections (1884, 1992, 2000). In a third set of elections negative prospective effects joined with negative retrospective effects to generate a negative effect that exceeded the relevant electoral threshold (1860, 1868, 1876, 1948). This notwithstanding, the majority party won each of these elections. In one other election (1996), a positive prospective effect joined with a 0 election-year effect to provide the crucial margin for victory for the incumbent Democrats.

WAR, PEACE, AND PROSPERITY

While WAR DEATHS did not have a statistically significant effect in D2, the hypotheses for UNPOPULAR WAR, YEARS OF PEACE, and PEACE AND PROSPERITY could not be rejected. The next two sections discuss the regression results, beginning with war. The theoretical significance of war, and the difficulty of capturing its electoral effects in regression equations, leads me to look beyond these equations to examine war's electoral aftershocks. The second section discusses the electoral effects of peace and prosperity.

WARS AND THEIR ELECTORAL AFTERSHOCKS

The only variable in the regression analyses that provides insights into the electoral effect of war is a dummy variable, UNPOPULAR WAR. The coefficient for UNPOPULAR WAR is −.09, which suggests that the incumbents suffered a 9-point loss in 1952 and 1968.[16] The Democrats' dismal economic performance, in conjunction with Southern discontent over their civil rights policies, would have been enough to produce a Republican victory in 1952. However, the electoral effect of the Korean War contributed to the Democrats' most dismal presidential returns since 1924. The analysis of Vietnam leads to a different conclusion for 1968: its predicted electoral effect affected the election's outcome. The 9-point boost the Democrats received from the economy's performance was enough to offset their normal vote deficit of .05. However, the electoral effect of the war was decisive in a very narrow defeat.

The regression analyses yield few insights into the electoral effects of either the Civil War or World War Two, both of which were ongoing on Election Day. However, a perusal of the normal vote data for 1864 and 1944, at the national level, provides some insights into the electoral effect of wars that are not as demonstrably unpopular as the Korean and Viet-

[16] Technically the Vietnam conflict also overlapped with the Election of 1964 and the Election of 1972. But the war was hardly on the radar screen of voters in 1964. By November of 1972 the draft had ended and Nixon's "Vietnamization" process was well under way; a truce was signed in 1973.

nam conflicts. In both cases the incumbents received about 3 points more than their normal party vote. This suggests that even in wars that are being waged for arguably noble causes, the images, realities, and lingering effects of war's human tragedies, economic dislocations, and social costs largely offset any "rally" effects that may benefit the incumbent party. There were minimal electoral dividends for saving the Union and freeing the slaves or protecting the world from fascists. Indeed, both Lincoln's and Roosevelt's actual margin of victory in 1864 and 1944, respectively, was smaller than in the preceding election.

This conclusion is reinforced by the fact that in 1868 the Republican Party received no more than their normal party vote, despite the fact that most of the South was still not voting. And the Republican nominee was a popular military hero. It is also telling that the relative size of the Republicans' electoral base continued to drop for almost a decade after the end of the Civil War (see figure 7–5). The Republicans' comfort margin at the national level peaks in 1864 at 8 points, drops to 5 points in 1868, 3 points in 1872, and then levels off at 1 point until the Election of 1896. Thus, rather than receiving long-term electoral dividends as a reward for victory in the Civil War, disillusionment with the Republicans' stewardship virtually eliminated any electoral advantage they enjoyed by 1876. Moreover, while the Republicans controlled the presidency for much of the period between the end of Reconstruction and the Election of 1896, the Democrats outpolled the Republicans in 1876, 1884, 1888, and 1892—and only fell 2,000 votes short in 1880 (out of 9.21 million votes cast). Truman did relatively better in 1948 than Grant did in 1868 (a 3-point perturbation compared to none at all), but the Democrats suffered a long-term electoral decline thereafter.

An examination of the electoral wake of other wars reinforces the conclusions drawn from the analyses of the normal vote data for the Civil War and World War Two. The first war in the post-1836 era was the Mexican-American War. It ended months before the Election of 1848, and the incumbent Democrats received 4 points less than their national vote, losing the election. It was only the second election the Democrats lost to the Whigs; the other was the Election of 1840, which was the first presidential election held after the economic depression of the late 1830s. To put the 1848 victory in perspective, it must be noted that the Whigs were so weak that, despite a strong economic performance, they lost the Election of 1852 and evaporated as a political power after the Election of 1856.

The Spanish-American War, completed shortly before the Election of 1900, is consistent with the assertion that there is no electoral "war dividend" for the incumbent party: the Republicans received 1 point less than their normal vote at the national level. World War I presents a different picture of the relationship between war and electoral performance. Despite the presence of an overwhelming Republican comfort margin (see table 8–4), Woodrow Wilson was able to win reelection in 1916. His victory was due to a strong economic performance (see figure 8–2) and the fact that he had kept the nation out of World War One. However, in 1917 the United States declared war against the Axis powers; by the war's end over 100,000 Americans had died. Despite a resounding military victory that made the world safe for democracy and catapulted the United States onto the world scene as a major power, the economic and social costs of the war contributed to one of the most devastating defeats in the history of U.S. presidential elections. Harding's margin of victory of 27 points in 1920 exceeded Roosevelt's margin of victory in 1932 (25 points), Johnson's margin in 1964 (23 points), and Nixon's in 1972 (21 points). The only margin of victory that compares to that in 1920 is Coolidge's margin for the Election of 1924 (also 27 points).

The Persian Gulf War clearly conforms to the dominant pattern of war's aftershocks. The "rally effect" evident in polls conducted at the end of the war had little staying power, and the incumbent Republicans suffered adverse electoral consequences. The electorate quickly refocused its attention on a set of pressing domestic concerns, and the Republicans suffered only their second presidential defeat since the end of the Vietnam War.

THE PEACE AND PROSPERITY ELECTORAL DIVIDEND

Figure 8–4 reports the predicted electoral effects of PEACE AND PROSPERITY, which were calculated using the same technique employed to estimate the effects of prospective economic conditions. An examination of these predictions demonstrates two points. The first is that the peace and prosperity dividend is a double-edged sword. INCUMBENTS are expected to produce economic growth during periods of peace. When they do, they receive an electoral dividend; when they do not, they fare worse than their economic growth rate would suggest. The second point is that these variables do not begin to manifest large effects until the United States became established as a military power, one that was increasingly drawn into international conflicts.

Because war was less of a concern to voters before the nation emerged as a military power, the effects of peace and prosperity are relatively small before 1932. But this does not mean that they were electorally inconsequential. In 1836, 1848, and 1860, the predicted negative effects of PEACE AND PROSPERITY were large enough to have eliminated the incumbent Democrat's comfort margin. While other factors were certainly influential, the Democrats lost in both 1848 and 1860. The only other nineteenth-century election in which PEACE AND PROSPERITY comes into play

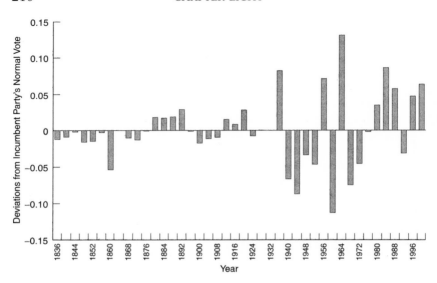

Figure 8–4. Predicted Electoral Impact of Peace and Prosperity

is the Election of 1884. A weak economic performance by the Republicans was large enough to eliminate their comfort margin, but the peace and prosperity effect was large enough to offset it. While the Republicans lost the election, the peace dividend contributed to an extremely tight race.

The predicted peace and prosperity effects for the post 1932 period were large enough to have affected a number of presidential elections. The negative effects for 1940, 1944, and 1952 were sufficient to eliminate the Democrats' comfort margins, even though the Democrats lost only in 1952. Negative peace and prosperity effects were also large enough to have decided the 1960 and 1992 elections. Negative peace and prosperity effects in both these elections aggravated the effects of a poor Republican economic performance, and they lost both elections.

The positive peace and prosperity effect for the Election of 1964 was large enough to have offset the Democrat's normal vote deficit; it combined with an impressive economic performance to generate one of the most sweeping victories in the history of U.S. presidential elections. The positive peace dividend that the Republicans enjoyed in 1984 was not essential to their victory but, as in 1964, it contributed to an electoral landslide. In contrast, the positive peace and prosperity effects in 1996 and 2000 were large enough to have insured victory for the Democrats. While the 2000 effect was large enough to offset a negative economic effect and produce an electoral plurality for the Democrats, they lost the election due to the distribution of Electoral College votes.

## CRIME RATES AND PERSONAL SECURITY

The regression results for the crime variables (UCR INDEX$^2$, UCR INDEX, $\Delta$ UCR INDEX and UCR INDEX$^*\Delta$ UCR INDEX) are very different from those posited in table 8–1. The reason for these differences can be attributed to the electoral effects of party reputations, policy positions, and issue ownership (i.e., the strong appeal of the Republicans "get tough" policies on crime). While these effects were not incorporated into the theoretical expectations outlined in table 8–1, they are very clear in the results within the personal security domain.

The most straightforward findings are those from the D2 analysis: none of the crime variables affected the electoral prospects of Democratic incumbents. These null results are almost certainly due to crosscutting pressures on the behavior of important components of the national electorate. When threats to personal security were salient, the Republicans' "get tough" policies on crime undoubtedly appealed to some components of the electorate. To other components, however, Republican analyses of the causes of crime, and their prescriptions for addressing them, seemed less persuasive than Democratic analyses and prescriptions. This led at least some components of the electorate to endorse the Democrats' focus on the social roots of crime and cast doubt on the efficaciousness of the Republicans' assertions about deterrence.

The findings generated by the R2 analysis were complicated because of the Republicans' "ownership" of the crime issue. In contrast to what was posited in table 8–1, the Republican's position on crime generated electoral benefits even when the Republicans were the incumbent party and crime rates were high or rising. This can be seen in the positive coefficients for the UCR INDEX$^2$ and $\Delta$ UCR INDEX variables in the R2 analysis, both of which are inconsistent with what was hypothesized. A compelling explanation for this seeming anomaly is that, in comparing party positions on the crime issue, many voters apparently concluded they would not be better off by supporting the Democrats.

Despite the results for UCR INDEX$^2$ and $\Delta$ UCR INDEX, the Republicans' ownership of the crime issue does not mean that they were not electorally accountable for their record on crime. Rather, as was the case with price stability and economic growth, while party reputations can generate electoral gains, they are held accountable for their policy positions and assertions. This can be demonstrated by examining the *joint impact* of the two crime-level variables, UCR INDEX and UCR INDEX$^2$. On average, the Republican incumbents are advantaged most when crime is low. When UCR INDEX is at its lowest value (1), the predicted value for INCUM-BENT$_{DEV}$ in R2 is .09. However, the higher the level of crime, the less the Republicans' electoral advantage. When the value of UCR INDEX is at its highest value (7), the predicted value for INCUMBENT$_{DEV}$ drops to −.03, a 12-point swing.

These findings suggest that when Republican incumbents perform poorly with respect to crime, they squander the electoral benefits of issue ownership. This point is vividly illustrated by the interaction between UCR INDEX and Δ UCR INDEX in R2. The model predictions for this interaction are displayed in figure 8–5. These data demonstrate quite clearly that the impact of Δ UCR INDEX varies dramatically with UCR INDEX. At lower crime levels, greater increases in crime produce significant short-term gains for the Republican candidate. For example, at the lowest level of UCR INDEX (1), election year *increases* in crime levels can generate as much as a 5-point electoral bonus for the Republicans. As the level of crime increases, the Republicans' electoral advantage declines. At the highest level of UCR INDEX (7), election year increases in crime can generate as much as a 4-point *loss*.

Examining the impact of the crime variables on state-level contests for Electoral College votes produces additional insights. While the predicted electoral effects of these variables vary from −.13 to .04, 92 percent are *negative*. Despite this, only a handful of *positive* predictions were larger than the relevant electoral thresholds. Only 5 out of 336 elections were affected, about 1.5 percent of all R2 state contests. These results suggest that while the crime issue is seldom large enough to affect electoral outcomes, its electoral effect varies with the Republicans' stewardship.

## POLITICAL PARTIES, ELECTION CAMPAIGNS, AND SHORT-TERM GAINS

The next two subsections present the findings with respect to the partisan activity variables, some of which come from the second-stage regression analysis in R1. The first subsection deals with the electoral effects of candidate traits; the second discusses the impact of state- and national-level partisan regimes.

### Candidate Traits

Table 8–6 presents data on the electoral effects of home state candidates, war heroes, and incumbents. The analysis makes it clear that home state electoral advantages exist only for the "out" party's candidate, and that no home state effects at all were found in D1. The home state advantages that did exist ranged between 3 and 6 points. Bonuses of this magnitude are sizable when compared to the electoral thresholds in "must-win" states. However, the electoral impact of these bonuses is limited by the fact that they affect only one state and frequently it is not a "must-win"

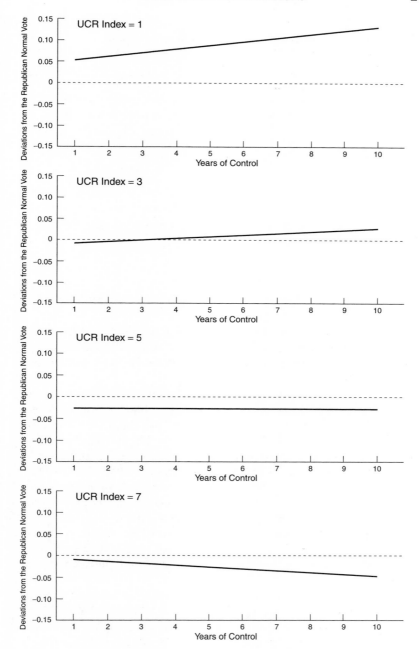

Figure 8–5. Interactive Effect of Crime Levels and Crime Rate Increases

TABLE 8.6
Electoral Effects of Candidate Traits

| Candidate Effect | Analysis Pool | | | |
|---|---|---|---|---|
| | Democrats, 1836–1928 (D1) | Republicans, 1836–1928 (R1) | Democrats, 1932–2000 (d2) | Republicans, 1932–2000 (R2) |
| Home State | | | | |
| Democratic Nominee | — | −0.03 | — | −0.06 |
| Whig/Republican Nominee | — | — | −0.05 | — |
| War Hero | | | | |
| Democratic Nominee | — | 0.05 | N.A. | N.A. |
| Whig/Republican Nominee | — | −0.06 | — | — |
| Incumbency | | | | |
| Incumbent President | — | −0.11 | — | — |

state. Consequently, the predicted impact was 0 in over 98 percent of all state contests. The independent electoral effect of home state advantage was large enough to affect the outcome of state elections in only one instance (NY, 1892).

Nominating a war hero for president was largely a nineteenth-century electoral tactic used mostly by Whigs and Republicans. Indeed, every presidential candidate the Whigs/Republicans put forth from the Election of 1836 to the Election of 1872, except for Henry Clay and Abraham Lincoln, had a military background. Since 1836 the Democrats have nominated only two: George B. McClellan (1864) and Winfield S. Hancock (1880). Dwight D. Eisenhower is the only war hero to be nominated for president by one of the major parties since Hancock. Another characteristic of this electoral tactic is that it has been used largely by the "out" party. Excluding the second terms of Grant and Eisenhower, only two of the nine nominations of war heroes have been made by a party that controlled the presidency: Winfield Scott in 1852 and Ulysses S. Grant in 1868.

The origins of this electoral tactic could well be in the electoral successes of early military figures such as George Washington, Andrew Jackson, and William Henry Harrison. This notwithstanding, the regression analyses demonstrate that it has not proven to be effective. The war hero dummy variables were not significant in three of the four second-stage analyses, as seen in table 8–5. Moreover, in the one analysis pool where statistically significant effects were found (R1), the war hero variables had unanticipated effects. All other factors considered, Democratic war heroes helped the opposition party and Whig/Republican war heroes hurt their party. Moreover, the coefficients for both variables (–.06 for WAR HERO$_{REP}$ and .05 for WAR HERO$_{DEM}$) were large enough to offset all of the national electoral thresholds before 1896.

Given the powers of the presidency, and the stake that incumbents have in a reelection campaign, positive effects were posited for the INCUMBENT variable in table 8–2. Table 8–6 makes it clear that these expectations were not realized. INCUMBENT was significant only in R1, where it had a sizable *negative* effect, –.11. This effect was large enough to have affected about eleven state outcomes in each of five elections in R1: 1872, 1892, 1900, 1904, and 1912. However, in gauging its real electoral impact, this coefficient must be interpreted in light of the strong positive effect of NA-TIONAL REGIME$_{REP}$ (.13). There were only two instances in which an incumbent Republican president sought reelection when his party was not in control of the national government (1892, 1912). Thus, for the most part, the effect of an incumbent president running for reelection was to drastically reduce the partisan edge the party received from controlling the national government. But even when NATIONAL REGIME$_{REP}$ is removed from the R1 regression analysis, the B-coefficient for INCUMBENT is –.08. Thus, it is not a surprise that the Republicans lost two of the four elections (1872, 1892, 1904, 1912) in which an incumbent president was running; both occurred when they did not control the national government: 1892 and 1912.

*Partisan Regimes*

The existence, duration, and strength of partisan regimes at both the state and national level were hypothesized to generate short-term electoral dividends for the monopolist party's candidates. The regression analyses show that these dividends were rarely realized. Rather, they suggest that highly concentrated political power, or monopolistic power that endured for long periods of time, was likely to generate electoral deficits.

The results concerning the electoral effect of state partisan regimes are graphically displayed in figure 8–6 (duration) and figure 8–7 (strength). The intercepts in these figures depict the electoral impact of a situation in which a state regime has existed for one year at the time of the presidential election, and enjoys the allegiance of just 51 percent of all state legislators. Examining these intercepts makes it clear that the electoral effects of state partisan regimes have varied over time and across parties; statistically significant effects for the dummy state regime variables emerged in just

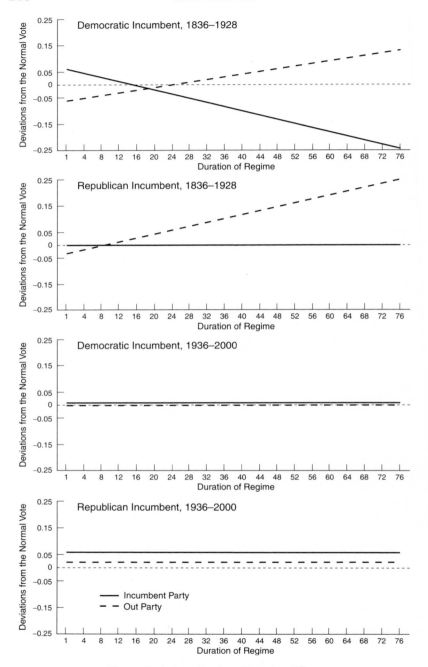

Figure 8–6. State Regime Duration Effect

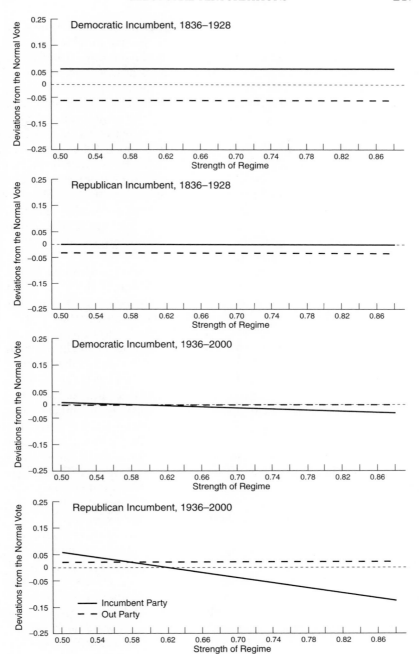

Figure 8–7. State Regime Strength Effect

three of the six analyses. The sign of the coefficients for each of the state regime variables was consistent with what was posited in table 8–2.

In D1 and R1 the results for the state regime dummy variables are straightforward. Compared to electoral contexts in which no party controls the state, political domination provides the incumbent Democrats with a 7-point gain in D1. If the opposition party controls the state government, the Democrats lose 6 points. In R1, the incumbent party, on average, gains no electoral advantage from the existence of a state regime. However, if the out-party Democrats control the state in R1 elections, the incumbent party gains 4 points. In D2 and R2 the results with respect to incumbent parties are almost a mirror image of the D1/R1 results. The existence of a state regime provides the Republicans with a 6-point dividend, while the Democrats receive none at all. State political domination by the "out" party provides incumbent parties with very little electoral advantage after 1932. In R2 the out-party Democrats are able to gain about a 1-point advantage if they control a state.

Only one-third of the twelve regime duration and strength effects that were posited in table 8–2 were statistically significant. Moreover, all of the significant findings had unanticipated effects, effects that suggest voter fatigue with and electoral backlashes against monopolist parties. Fatigue effects are evident in the pre-1932 era and backlash effects are evident in the post-1932 era. Examining the slope of the predicted regression lines in figure 8–7 and figure 8–8 for each analysis pool demonstrates these points.

In D1 and R1 a clear fatigue effect emerges in three of the four analyses. Rather than generating short-term electoral gains, regime duration produces electoral deficits. The opposite happens when an incumbent party competes for votes in a state dominated by the opposition party: the longer the "out" party has dominated the state government, the greater the short-term electoral gains for the incumbent president's party. While these fatigue effects do not exist in the post-1932 era, backlash effects emerge when an incumbent president's party controls state government: the larger the monopolist party's majority in the state legislature, the larger the electoral deficit. This effect is particularly strong in R2.

The predicted electoral effects of the state political regime variables range from −.17 to .19. However, in 95 percent of all cases these predictions ranged from −.05 to .05, with the predicted impact being 0 in 64 percent of all cases. Consequently, these predicted effects were large enough to affect the outcome of the election in only about 1 percent of all state elections. While it was more difficult to gauge the electoral effects of national political regimes, what evidence exists presents a fairly similar picture, with one exception. National political regimes existed in only three of the four analysis pools: D1, R1 and D2. But the existence of national political regime produced electoral benefits for the monopolist

(a) Regime Duration

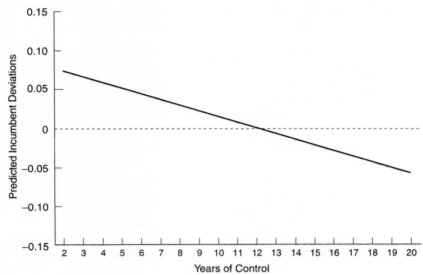

(b) Regime Strength

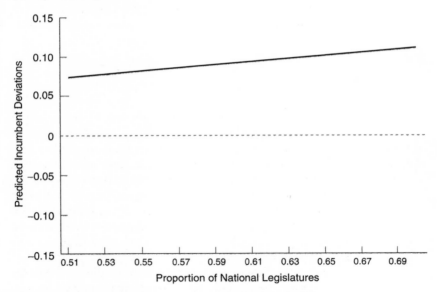

Figure 8–8. The Electoral Effects of National Political Regimes

party only in R1—an 8-point dividend. There was sufficient variation to gauge the electoral effects of the duration and strength of national regimes in R1 because they dominated the national scene for six of fourteen elections.

Figure 8–8 presents the predicted effects for both duration and strength in R1, and the results are mixed. Fatigue effects are clear in figure 8–8 (a), as they were in analyses of state political regimes for the pre-1932 era. After two presidential terms the electoral benefits of a national Republican regime is cut in half; after three terms it begins to generate negative effects. Figure 8–8 (b) demonstrates that the Republicans were quite effective in translating national legislative strength into electoral gains during this era.

The predicted effect of the three national regime variables ranges from −.12 to .19. For the seven elections held when a national Republican regime existed, negative effects are predicted for two: 1892 (−.12) and 1912 (−.12). While this negative effect was sufficient, by itself, to eliminate the Republicans' comfort margin only in 1892, it joined with negative economic effects in 1912 to produce electoral upsets in both years. Electoral dividends were produced in the other six elections in which the Republicans enjoyed a national political regime: 1868, 1872, 1900, 1904, 1908, and 1924. These dividends were instrumental in overcoming poor stewardship in 1868, but they did not play an important role in the other elections, all of which were won handily by the majority party Republicans.

## Summary

The results presented in this chapter make important contributions to our understanding of mass-elite linkages. First and foremost, these results provide strong empirical support for the assertion that citizens have the capacity to be discriminating consumers of public goods. Variations in the realization of core political desires have a strong impact on deviations from normal voting patterns, consistent with the transformational model presented in chapter 3. These results also provide strong support for the theoretical observations made in chapter 3 about the relative effectiveness of performance strategies over partisan strategies in furthering the core political interests of political stewards.

Figure 8–9 graphically illustrates the importance of the performance indicators in affecting election-specific deviations from normal voting patterns. Figure 8–9 is analogous to figure 8–1 in that it displays the correspondence between ACTUAL DEVIATION$_{NAT}$ and PREDICTED DEVIATION$_{NAT}$ for each election. However, the PREDICTED DEVIATION$_{NAT}$ variable dis-

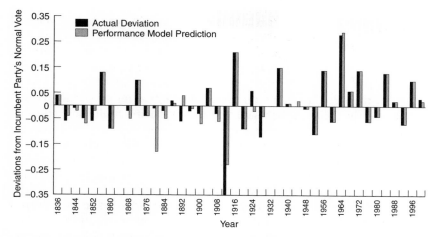

Figure 8–9. Correspondence between Actual Deviations and Performance Model Predictions

played in figure 8–9 was generated using only the performance indicators. Figure 8–9 demonstrates a remarkable level of correspondence between the model predictions and the actual data at the national level, particularly for the D2 and R2 predictions. The sign of PREDICTED DEVIATION$_{NAT}$ is the same as the sign of ACTUAL DEVIATION$_{NAT}$ in all but two elections (1892 and 1924). The mean absolute value of the prediction error (PREDICTED DEVIATION$_{NAT}$ − ACTUAL DEVIATION$_{NAT}$) is .02 for all forty elections. Most of the large prediction errors occur in the period between 1880 and 1912 (mean = .04), when partisan activities had a more discernible impact on electoral perturbations. The mean absolute value of the prediction errors is .002 for the seventeen elections held after 1932.

*The implications of figure 8–9 for elite strategies to further their core political interests are clear: preserve, protect, and enhance citizens' realization of their core political desires.* Work to ensure that citizens are "better off today than they were four years ago." Reinforcing the implications of figure 8–9 for elite strategies are the regression results for the partisan indicators. These results parallel the findings reported in chapter 6 and demonstrate that the capacity of political parties to "manage" electoral behavior is quite limited. Few of the candidate-selection strategies that have been used over the past two centuries have had much of an electoral impact. Indeed, some tactics, such as the nomination of war heroes, have likely had unanticipated consequences. The same can be said for the partisan regime variables. The mixed results for the partisan regime variables are arguably rooted in the long-standing American concern with concentrated power. While the evidence for voter fatigue and electoral backlash effects was uneven, this should not obscure the real import of the regression results. *Scant empirical support is generated for the proposition that parties can transform their control of institutional resources into meaningful electoral gains that can be used to perpetuate political power.*

At least a partial explanation for the difficulty political parties have in managing the electoral behavior of citizens can be found in two more subtle implications of the regression results reported here. One deals with the level of political discernment within the electorate; the other deals with the experiential base of at least some evaluations of stewardship.

With respect to the level of political discernment within the electorate, the regression analyses suggest that the electorate's evaluative capacities far exceed the traditional reward/punishment standard. This was clearest in the electoral effects of prospective economic conditions and the reputation of political parties. This unexpectedly high level of political discernment could be due to the contextual effects noted in chapter 3. But whatever the mechanism is that provides for it, this level of discernment is important because it speaks to the capacity of citizens to exact electoral accountability. The regression results demonstrate that voters reward incumbents if the state of the nation is improving and that they will not desert incumbents if the opposition offers little hope for improvement. On the other hand, the data demonstrate that incumbents are held accountable both for their record of achievements and the policy stances and assertions of their party.

Evidence that stewardship evaluations are, at least in part, experientially based stems from the temporal reach of the regression analyses. The existence of fairly sophisticated evaluations of political stewardship dating to the second quarter of the nineteenth century suggests that not all politics is "out of reach, out of sight, out of mind." In domains that affect their core political desires, voters do not need detailed government reports to inform them that all is not well. And, when all was not well, citizens have proven themselves capable of demonstrating their displeasure within the electoral arena—even at the height of the party period. Indeed, citizens seem quite capable of reexamining and recalibrating their political heuristics without "high-tech" priming from interest groups, political parties, or media puppet masters. The existence of sophisticated political evaluations of political stewardship before the pervasiveness of mass media should provide pause to those who tend to stress the primacy of elite priming and framing on electoral evaluations in the modern era.

The overarching substantive implications of the regression results for our understanding of mass-elite linkages are clear when the findings for the partisan activities variables and the performance indicators are viewed jointly; they speak directly to the caricature of voters as "manageable fools." The ability of voters to incorporate important exogenous events into their voting behavior in a fairly sophisticated manner makes them seem anything but foolish. The inability of political parties to devise effective campaign tactics and routinely translate institutional resources into electoral gains makes them look anything but magisterial.

## REFERENCES

Chappell, Henry W., and William R. Keech. 1985. "A New View of Political Accountability for Economic Performance." *American Political Science Review* 79 (March):10–27.

Fiorina, Morris P. 1981. *Retrospective Voting in American National Elections.* New Haven, Yale University Press.

Hibbs, Douglas A. 1987. *The American Political Economy.* Cambridge, Harvard University Press.

Key, V. O. 1966. *The Responsible Electorate: Rationality in Presidential Voting, 1936–1960.* Cambridge, Harvard University Press.

MacKuen, Michael B., Robert S. Erikson, and James A. Stimson. 1992. "Peasants or Bankers? The American Electorate and the U.S. Economy." *American Political Science Review* 86:598–611.

# CHAPTER NINE

# The Electoral Impact of Departures from Normal Voting Patterns: Electoral Jolts and the Aspirations of Political Elites

Let us step back for a moment and consider a deceptively simple question. What is an election? In principle, two or more groups of like-minded people put forth alternative visions of future societies. After carefully weighing the alternatives, the citizenry entrusts one of the competing parties with the mantle of leadership. In practice, however, an incumbent party attempts to convince an appropriate proportion of the electorate that it lives in the best of all possible worlds, while an opposition rails at the incumbents and advances a collection of unrealistic promises.

Citizens are not fools. Having observed political equivocation, if not outright lying, should they listen carefully to campaign promises? . . . But are the citizens' choices actually so unclear? After all, they typically have one comparatively hard bit of data: they know what life has been during the incumbent's administration.
—MORRIS P. FIORINA, *Retrospective Voting in American National Elections*

[The] story of unmotivated, ill-informed, and inattentive voters is as old as the first examinations of individual voters, and it is confirmed anew by every subsequent voting study. Looked upon as individuals, most Americans care little about politics and possess a level of knowledge of the details of public life that is consistent with not caring. . . . All these facts, insofar as they lead us to believe that the electorate acts without purpose, lead us astray.
—ROBERT S. ERIKSON, MICHAEL B. MACKUEN, AND JAMES A. STIMSON, *The Macro Polity*

THE ANALYSES presented in chapter 7 and chapter 8 focused primarily on electoral independence and document that citizens have regularly demonstrated their capacity to overcome the inertial and centripetal forces that dominate the electoral arena. Some of the empirical analyses in these chapters have had implications for the impact of the electorate's independence on the education of political elites and the strategies they should use in securing electoral success. But there is some ambiguity about what the fickleness of the American electorate has taught political elites; the electoral independence analyses have not directly examined the impact of electoral jolts on the electoral aspirations of political elites. This chapter addresses this ambiguity by examining the effects of departures from normal voting patterns on electoral settings and outcomes, matters that directly affect political elites' desire for electoral success.

The first part of this chapter is concerned with electoral settings and realigning elections. It operationalizes these concepts and presents data on their incidence. I then join these data to generate additional insights into the impact of enduring electoral shifts on the core interests of political elites. The second part of this chapter is concerned with disequilibrating electoral outcomes defined by deviations from normal voting patterns: deviating and endorsement elections. After operationalizing these concepts, I present data on their incidence. To garner additional insights into the education of political elites, I integrate data on the incidence of competitive electoral settings and disequilibrating electoral outcomes and develop their implications for mass-elite linkages.

## ELECTORAL SETTINGS AND REALIGNING ELECTIONS

Electoral settings are defined by the relative size of the electoral bases of the major parties. In chapter 5 the relative size of a party's electoral base is discussed in terms of comfort margins and normal vote deficits. As demonstrated in chapter 8, the size of these electoral thresholds is of vital concern to party elites. Large comfort margins can insulate the majority party from routine electoral perturbations; large normal vote deficits can make victory seem unattainable to the minority party. In some cases, however, these electoral thresholds are so small when compared to garden variety fluctuations that neither party can be said to have an *ex ante* electoral advantage. Thus, competitive electoral contests are defined as those instances in which no party enters an election campaign with an electoral edge derived from the relative size of its electoral base. Competitive electoral contests make party elites electorally vulnerable and more attentive to the concerns of the electorate; gauging their incidence is central to the study of democratic responsiveness.

Realigning elections are defined as critical elections that trigger enduring electoral shifts large enough to either create a new majority party or eliminate the electoral advantage of the *ex ante* majority party (i.e., create a competitive electoral setting). Because realigning elections are devastating electoral jolts that underscore the centrality of the electorate in democratic politics, gauging their incidence is important to our understanding of popular efficacy. Because it is not possible to define a realigning election without information on electoral settings, the next section outlines the procedure used to differentiate among electoral settings (competitive, secure or safe). The following two sections report data on the distribution of electoral settings and the incidence of realigning elections. Next, I join these data to generate a unique perspective on the tenuousness of electoral advantage, a tenuousness that has important implications for elite perceptions of the electorate and for our understanding of mass-elite linkages.

### Electoral Thresholds and Electoral Settings

In order to differentiate among electoral settings, it was necessary to clarify the relationship between electoral thresholds and electoral outcomes. To do this, I examined the impact of thresholds on the probability of an electoral upset at both the local and the state level.[1] To illustrate this analysis, I outline the procedure used at the local level. Then I report how the results were used to differentiate among electoral settings.

To examine the relationship between electoral thresholds and electoral outcomes at the local level, I created a dummy variable depicting an electoral upset. I constructed ELECTORAL UPSET by comparing the normal vote data with the data on electoral outcomes on an election-by-election basis. Consider, for example, those electoral units with a normal Democratic majority at a particular point in time (i.e., electorates with a positive value on the NORMAL PARTISAN BALANCE variable for a given election). In elections where these "Democratic" electorates gave a plurality of their votes to the Democratic candidate for president, the ELECTORAL UPSET variable was given a score of 0. When these "Democratic" electorates provided the Whig or Republican candidate with a plurality of their votes, the ELECTORAL UPSET variable was given a score of 1. The same procedure was used with respect to locales with normal Whig/Republican majorities. Next, I derived a nonpartisan measure of electoral thresholds by taking the absolute value of NORMAL PARTISAN BALANCE (ABS [NORMAL PARTISAN BALANCE]). Finally, I examined the relationship between ABS (NORMAL PARTISAN BALANCE) and ELECTORAL UPSET, using all of the local election outcomes in the data archive.

---

[1] It made no sense to do this at the national level both because of the small number of cases and the compounding effects of the Electoral College. It will be possible, however, to define competitive electoral contests at the national level by examining the competitiveness of state electoral settings in conjunction with the distribution of Electoral College votes.

TABLE 9.1
Probability of an Electoral Upset for Different "Comfort" Levels

| Comfort Margin | Proportion of Electoral Upsets | Categorization of Electoral Setting | Number of Cases |
|---|---|---|---|
| Local Electorates | | | |
| .00–.029* | 0.44 | Competitive | 8,055 |
| .03–.100 | 0.28 | Secure | 23,607 |
| .101–1.00 | 0.08 | Safe | 80,152 |
| State Electorates | | | |
| .00–.029* | 0.42 | Competitive | 250 |
| .03–.100 | 0.2 | Secure | 695 |
| .101–1.00 | 0.09 | Safe | 907 |

* An electoral upset is undefined for perfectly competitive electoral setting (i.e, NORMAL PARTISAN BALANCE = 0) so the probability is defined as .5.

To determine how thresholds relate to electoral outcomes, I examined the proportion of electoral upsets across the values of ABS (NORMAL PARTISAN BALANCE). Clear breakpoints emerged, and the results were fairly similar at both the local and state level. These results, which are reported in table 9–1, provide an empirically validated basis for differentiating among three types of electoral settings: competitive, secure, and safe.

When a party's electoral threshold is less than 3 points, the electoral outcome is a virtual toss-up: at the local level 44 percent of these outcomes were categorized as upsets; at the state level 42 percent were categorized as upsets. The incidence of upsets is so great in these situations that neither party has a reasonable expectation of victory. Hence, these are considered to be "competitive" electoral settings. When a party's electoral threshold is between 3 and 10 points, there is about one chance in four of an electoral upset at the local level; there is one chance in five at the state level. Because the majority party clearly has a reasonable expectation of electoral success under these conditions, these settings are categorized as "secure." If a party has an electoral threshold that exceeds 10 points, there is less than one chance in ten of an electoral upset at both the state and local level. These electoral settings are considered to be "safe," as most campaign strategists would consider the dominant party's prospects for victory as being excellent.

These results were used to create two sets of dummy variables that capture the electoral setting at the local and state level. The state level categorizations were then used in conjunction with data on the allocation of Electoral College votes to create a set of national-level electoral setting variables. Examining electoral settings over time provides insights into

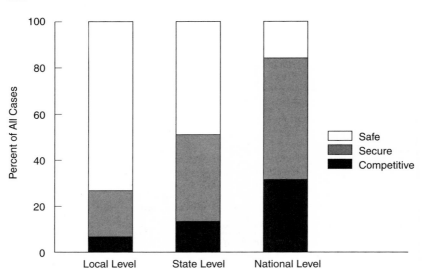

Figure 9–1. Electoral Settings, by Level

how mass-elite linkages have varied over the course of U.S. electoral history; examining these settings across levels of analysis (local, state, and national) provides valuable insights into electoral accountability.

## The Incidence and Distribution of Electoral Settings

At the local level, 7 percent of all weighted unit-elections (weight = Total Votes) since 1828 were conducted in competitive electoral settings, 20 percent were conducted in secure electoral settings, and 73 percent were conducted in safe electoral settings. These data suggest that competitive electoral contests are a rarity at the local level. A more competitive picture emerges at the state level. Overall, 13 percent of all state contests were conducted in competitive settings, as compared to 38 percent in secure and 49 percent in safe electoral settings. The national level data on electoral settings yield a radically different view of competitiveness. These national level data show that 32 percent of all presidential elections were held in competitive electoral settings while only 16 percent were held in safe electoral settings. The cross-level differences are summarized in figure 9–1. It shows that the ratio of safe to competitive settings drops from 10:1 at the local level, to .5:1 at the national level.

The national picture reflects the fact that larger states tend to be electorally more diverse and, hence, more competitive. As such, the data reported in figure 9–1 provide the basis for a corollary to Madison's observations about the virtues of an "extended Republic." The existence of a wide array of diverse local electorates enhances electoral competitiveness at the national level: nearly one-third of all presidential elections since the emergence of the Whig Party in 1836 have been conducted in competitive electoral settings. In contrast, less than one-sixth of all elections held since 1836 have been conducted in electoral settings in which a majority of Electoral College votes were in states that could be considered "safe" for one of the major political parties. All of these elections were conducted in the period from 1904 to 1928.

More historical insights can be gained by examining table 9–2, which reports data on electoral settings by level and year. The local level entries show that the distribution of electoral settings ebbs and flows over time, but within a fairly narrow range. The state level entries, in contrast, demonstrate a good deal of variability over time. Competitive state contests were relatively more common in the pre–Civil War era. Electoral competitiveness declines dramatically at the state level after the Civil War and does not begin to increase until 1944. The national level entries show that competitiveness was a defining characteristic of nineteenth-century presidential politics at the dawn of the democratic era in American politics.[2] Between 1832 and 1884 the parties were spared the rigors of competition only during the Civil War period. The national electoral setting becomes less competitive only after 1884. The existence of sequential competitive electoral contests occurs only twice after 1884: 1948–52 and 1992–96.

### The Incidence and Distribution of Realigning Elections

Realigning elections are defined as critical elections that trigger enduring electoral shifts large enough to either create a new majority party or eliminate the electoral advantage of the ex ante majority party (i.e., create a competitive electoral setting).[3] Thus, for a realigning election to occur two

---

[2] The national-level data in table 9–2 reflect the following situations. Safe electoral settings are those elections in which a majority of Electoral College votes are in states in which one of the parties enjoys a safe electoral setting. Secure electoral settings are those elections in which a majority of Electoral College votes are in states in which one of the parties enjoys a "safe" or "secure" electoral setting. Competitive electoral settings are those elections in which neither of the major parties has a majority of Electoral College votes in states considered "safe" or "secure."

[3] The normal vote analyses described in appendix II defined critical elections only at the local level. Thus, state and national level versions of this variable had to be derived. To create the state version of this variable, the local critical election dummy variable (CRITICAL ELECTON) was aggregated to the state level (weight = TOTAL VOTES). The state level variable was coded 1 only if the weighted state mean of CRITICAL ELECTON variable was greater than .50 for a given election in a given state. All other valid cases were coded 0. To define the national version of this variable, the data from the temporal order analysis reported in figure 6–1 was used. Only those five elections that stood out in figure 6–1 (1836, 1856, 1896, 1932, and 1952) were defined as critical elections at the national level.

TABLE 9.2
Distribution of Safe and Competitive Electoral Contests, by Year and Level

| Election Year | Local Level | | State Level | | National Level | |
|---|---|---|---|---|---|---|
| | Safe Electoral Contests | Competitive Electoral Contests | Safe Electoral Contests | Competitive Electoral Contests | Safe Electoral Contests | Competitive Electoral Contests |
| 1828 | 0.66 | 0.08 | 0.65 | 0.14 | 0 | 0 |
| 1832 | 0.65 | 0.09 | 0.57 | 0.17 | 0 | 1 |
| 1836 | 0.56 | 0.12 | 0.30 | 0.19 | 0 | 1 |
| 1840 | 0.54 | 0.13 | 0.33 | 0.27 | 0 | 1 |
| 1844 | 0.52 | 0.12 | 0.30 | 0.27 | 0 | 1 |
| 1848 | 0.50 | 0.12 | 0.37 | 0.28 | 0 | 1 |
| 1852 | 0.50 | 0.14 | 0.35 | 0.27 | 0 | 1 |
| 1856 | 0.62 | 0.10 | 0.41 | 0.23 | 0 | 0 |
| 1860 | 0.60 | 0.10 | 0.38 | 0.12 | 0 | 0 |
| 1864 | 0.58 | 0.10 | 0.35 | 0.09 | 0 | 0 |
| 1868 | 0.59 | 0.09 | 0.38 | 0.03 | 0 | 0 |
| 1872 | 0.62 | 0.09 | 0.37 | 0.11 | 0 | 1 |
| 1876 | 0.61 | 0.10 | 0.47 | 0.14 | 0 | 1 |
| 1880 | 0.61 | 0.10 | 0.49 | 0.13 | 0 | 1 |
| 1884 | 0.58 | 0.10 | 0.46 | 0.11 | 0 | 1 |
| 1888 | 0.57 | 0.09 | 0.49 | 0.11 | 0 | 0 |
| 1892 | 0.57 | 0.08 | 0.51 | 0.16 | 0 | 0 |
| 1896 | 0.66 | 0.08 | 0.61 | 0.11 | 0 | 0 |
| 1900 | 0.66 | 0.08 | 0.61 | 0.09 | 0 | 0 |
| 1904 | 0.68 | 0.06 | 0.67 | 0.04 | 1 | 0 |
| 1908 | 0.71 | 0.09 | 0.74 | 0.02 | 1 | 0 |
| 1912 | 0.76 | 0.09 | 0.78 | 0.06 | 1 | 0 |

conditions must be met: (1) a critical election must occur, and (2) the resulting critical shift must effect a change in electoral settings. Using information on electoral settings from table 9–1 in conjunction with data on critical elections, realigning elections were identified at the local, state, and national level.[4]

---

[4] In defining realigning elections at the national level, this second criterion had to be modified somewhat to reflect the impact of the Electoral College scheme embodied in the U.S. Constitution. Because of this complication, the impact of the critical election had to be measured in terms of shifts in Electoral College votes across state-level electoral settings.

TABLE 9.2 (cont'd)
Distribution of Safe and Competitive Electoral Contests, by Year and Level

| | Local Level | | State Level | | National Level | |
|---|---|---|---|---|---|---|
| Election Year | Safe Electoral Contests | Competitive Electoral Contests | Safe Electoral Contests | Competitive Electoral Contests | Safe Electoral Contests | Competitive Electoral Contests |
| 1916 | 0.80 | 0.04 | 0.80 | 0.06 | 1 | 0 |
| 1920 | 0.80 | 0.04 | 0.80 | 0.04 | 1 | 0 |
| 1924 | 0.81 | 0.04 | 0.84 | 0.04 | 1 | 0 |
| 1928 | 0.82 | 0.04 | 0.86 | 0.02 | 1 | 0 |
| 1932 | 0.69 | 0.08 | 0.59 | 0.08 | 0 | 0 |
| 1936 | 0.69 | 0.09 | 0.57 | 0.08 | 0 | 0 |
| 1940 | 0.68 | 0.09 | 0.57 | 0.08 | 0 | 0 |
| 1944 | 0.66 | 0.12 | 0.41 | 0.17 | 0 | 0 |
| 1948 | 0.65 | 0.11 | 0.35 | 0.19 | 0 | 1 |
| 1952 | 0.60 | 0.12 | 0.29 | 0.31 | 0 | 1 |
| 1956 | 0.60 | 0.10 | 0.29 | 0.23 | 0 | 0 |
| 1960 | 0.63 | 0.08 | 0.37 | 0.22 | 0 | 0 |
| 1964 | 0.62 | 0.09 | 0.38 | 0.22 | 0 | 0 |
| 1968 | 0.62 | 0.08 | 0.42 | 0.18 | 0 | 0 |
| 1972 | 0.63 | 0.07 | 0.38 | 0.14 | 0 | 0 |
| 1976 | 0.64 | 0.08 | 0.38 | 0.18 | 0 | 0 |
| 1980 | 0.62 | 0.09 | 0.38 | 0.08 | 0 | 0 |
| 1984 | 0.60 | 0.09 | 0.38 | 0.1 | 0 | 0 |
| 1988 | 0.60 | 0.09 | 0.41 | 0.25 | 0 | 0 |
| 1992 | 0.57 | 0.12 | 0.35 | 0.18 | 0 | 1 |
| 1996 | 0.55 | 0.12 | 0.39 | 0.08 | 0 | 1 |
| 2000 | 0.53 | 0.12 | 0.37 | 0.08 | 0 | 0 |

Table 9–3 reports data on the incidence of realigning elections by level and year. Realigning elections at the local level account for 10 percent or more of the national electorate in only three of forty-four elections: 1836, 1856, and 1932. The only other elections with an appreciable number of realigning elections are 1896 and 1952. At the local level 77

Thus, for a critical election to qualify as a realigning election at the national level, a majority of the Electoral College votes would have to shift from (a) Republican states to competitive or Democratic states, (b) Democratic states to competitive or Republican states, or (c) from competitive to Democratic or Republican states.

TABLE 9.3
Distribution of Realigning Elections, by Year and Level

| Election Year | Local Level | State Level | National Level | Election Year | Local Level | State Level | National Level |
|---|---|---|---|---|---|---|---|
| 1828 | 0.00 | 0.00 | 0 | 1916 | 0.00 | 0.00 | 0 |
| 1832 | 0.00 | 0.00 | 0 | 1920 | 0.00 | 0.00 | 0 |
| 1836 | **0.10** | **0.07** | 0 | 1924 | 0.00 | 0.00 | 0 |
| 1840 | 0.01 | 0.00 | 0 | 1928 | 0.00 | 0.00 | 0 |
| 1844 | 0.00 | 0.00 | 0 | 1932 | **0.54** | **0.65** | 1 |
| 1848 | 0.00 | 0.00 | 0 | 1936 | 0.00 | 0.00 | 0 |
| 1852 | 0.00 | 0.00 | 0 | 1940 | 0.00 | 0.00 | 0 |
| 1856 | **0.15** | **0.13** | 1 | 1944 | 0.00 | 0.00 | 0 |
| 1860 | 0.01 | 0.00 | 0 | 1948 | 0.00 | 0.00 | 0 |
| 1864 | 0.01 | 0.00 | 0 | 1952 | **0.06** | **0.06** | 0 |
| 1868 | 0.00 | 0.00 | 0 | 1956 | 0.00 | 0.00 | 0 |
| 1872 | 0.02 | 0.00 | 0 | 1960 | 0.00 | 0.00 | 0 |
| 1876 | 0.00 | 0.00 | 0 | 1964 | 0.00 | 0.00 | 0 |
| 1880 | 0.00 | 0.00 | 0 | 1968 | 0.00 | 0.00 | 0 |
| 1884 | 0.00 | 0.00 | 0 | 1972 | 0.00 | 0.00 | 0 |
| 1888 | 0.00 | 0.00 | 0 | 1976 | 0.00 | 0.00 | 0 |
| 1892 | 0.00 | 0.00 | 0 | 1980 | 0.00 | 0.00 | 0 |
| 1896 | **0.07** | **0.03** | 0 | 1984 | 0.00 | 0.00 | 0 |
| 1900 | 0.00 | 0.00 | 0 | 1988 | 0.00 | 0.00 | 0 |
| 1904 | 0.00 | 0.00 | 0 | 1992 | 0.00 | 0.00 | 0 |
| 1908 | 0.00 | 0.00 | 0 | 1996 | 0.00 | 0.00 | 0 |
| 1912 | 0.00 | 0.00 | 0 | 2000 | 0.00 | 0.00 | 0 |

percent of all *critical elections* qualified as *realigning elections*. Only 50 percent of the critical elections at the state level qualified as realigning elections; they were concentrated in five elections: 1836, 1856, 1896, 1932, and 1952. Of the five elections in which some states experienced realigning elections, only two (40 percent) qualify as realigning elections at the national level: 1856 and 1932. The elections of 1836, 1896, and 1952 do not qualify as realigning elections because they did not produce a change in the electoral setting.

### Enduring Electoral Changes, Electoral Settings, and Electoral Aspirations

While the data in table 9–3 document that realigning elections are rare electoral events, they produce a misleading impression of the impact that enduring partisan shifts have on the electoral aspirations of political elites. To present a more telling picture, I combine the data on enduring

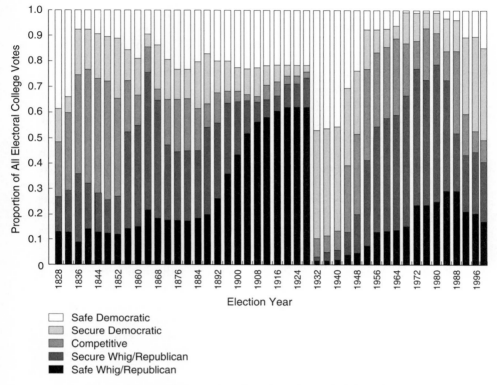

Figure 9–2. Proportion of Electoral College Votes by Probability of Upset*

electoral change with the data on competitiveness of state electoral settings, taking into account the Electoral College scheme embedded in the
U.S. Constitution. These data are presented in figure 9–2. It reports, for
each election between 1828 and 2000, the proportion of Electoral College votes across partisan electoral settings (i.e., the proportion in safe
Democratic states, secure Democratic states, competitive states, etc.). Integrating the data on electoral settings with the data on enduring electoral changes underscores the ebb and flow of partisanship and the tenuousness of electoral advantage.

   Consider first the impact of the Election of 1836 on the competition
for Electoral College votes. While eight states manifest critical changes in
their normal voting patterns, North Carolina and Pennsylvania were the
only states that experienced realigning elections in 1836. While these critical elections did not produce a change in the national electoral setting,
they did create a marked shift in the electoral balance. The electoral setting in 1832 was competitive, but the Democrats enjoyed normal vote

advantages in states that controlled 40 percent of all Electoral College votes. After the 1836 Whig critical elections, the Democrats had normal vote advantages in states that controlled only 25 percent of the Electoral College, compared to 36 percent for the Whigs. The competitive electoral setting that began in 1832 continued until 1856. The realigning elections that occurred in 1856 transformed the national electoral setting to one in which the newly created Republican Party became the majority party.

The electoral advantage of the Republicans grew until the Election of 1872, when the last of the seceding Southern states began to participate in presidential elections. These additions, plus the receding strength of the Republicans in both the North and the South, transformed the national electoral setting into a highly competitive one. This newly competitive national setting persisted for the next four elections. While individual states became increasingly uncompetitive in the post–Civil War period, the booming populations of the industrializing North provided the Republicans with a slight electoral advantage at the national level by 1888. The fact that the Republicans were already the majority party is why the Election of 1896 does not qualify as a realigning election at the national level. It simply reinforced the existing electoral edge of the Republicans.

The Republican's edge in Electoral College votes continued to increase after 1888. After the critical elections in 1896 the Republicans enjoyed normal vote advantages in states with nearly two-thirds of all Electoral College votes; by 1928 nearly three-quarters of the Electoral College votes were in states in which the Republicans held an electoral advantage. This highly advantageous situation, however, was transformed by the largest electoral jolt in United States electoral history: the Election of 1932. This realigning election created a situation in which the Democrats held an electoral advantage in states with almost 90 percent of the Electoral College votes, as seen in figure 9–2. However, by 1940 the Democrat's electoral advantage was reduced by a third, to 60 percent; by 1948 they lost their position as the majority party.

The 1952 critical elections, which occurred mainly in the South and favored the Republicans, led to the Republicans' emergence as the majority party in 1956, when they enjoyed comfort margins in states with almost 55 percent of all Electoral College votes. Ongoing Republican secular gains contributed to the Republican's electoral edge. By 1980 they enjoyed an electoral advantage in states that comprised nearly 79 percent of all Electoral College votes, exceeding previous peaks they enjoyed in 1864 and 1928. After 1980, however, the effects of the Democratic secular changes depicted in figure 7–8 began to be felt in the battle for Electoral College votes. These secular shifts initially generated a bulge in the number of competitive states. By 1992 a competitive electoral setting emerged for the first time in forty years, with the Republicans losing their majority party status, just as the Democrats did in 1948. By the Election of 2000 the Democrats emerged as the majority party by the most tenuous of margins. While the Democrats had comfort margins in states that controlled 50.7 percent of all Electoral College votes, the Republican shared dropped to 40.8 percent. Competitive states accounted for the remaining 8.5% of Electoral College votes. Thus, the Republican secular losses between 1980 and 2000 nearly match the secular losses the Democrats experienced between 1932 and 1948.

The data depicted in figure 9–2 provide a unique set of insights into mass-elite linkages within American democracy. No strategically minded party stalwart could be oblivious to the electoral implications of the undulations seen in figure 9–2, which reinforce the findings reported in the examination of the patterned change thesis presented in chapter 6. The ebb and flow of a party's core electoral support introduces so much uncertainty into presidential campaigns that party strategists must constantly be concerned with tending to the party's electoral base. This message is reinforced by state-level realities that are obscured by these national data. Those realities are that even when the competitiveness of the national electoral context remains relatively constant, states drift in and out of a party's electoral base with some regularity.

Shifting electoral bases are an important component of the process by which political elites are educated about the role of the electorate in democratic politics. Dealing with these uncertainties on a quadrennial basis teaches party strategists that they are not working with an electorate that is a static entity forged by the unalterable effects of partisan "inoculations" administered early in life. The uncertainties generated by shifting electoral bases compound the problems posed by the frequency of competitive electoral contexts. The effects of these uncertainties on political elites are exacerbated further by the impact of electoral perturbations on electoral outcomes.

## Normal, Deviating, and Endorsement Elections

This section is concerned with a set of election types defined by patterns of electoral perturbations: normal, deviating, and endorsement elections. A normal election is an election in which the deviations from normal voting patterns are distributed in a manner that would be expected if partisan and inertial forces were determinative of electoral outcomes. The mean of the deviations would be 0 and they would be normally distributed around the mean. A deviating election is an election that the majority party loses. An endorsement election is an election in which the stewardship of the majority party is strongly endorsed by the electorate.

Like realigning elections, deviating and endorsement elections are disequilibrating electoral outcomes. They are highly salient, and unmistak-
able, manifestations of electoral independence. This is easy to see in the
case of deviating elections. Any time a majority party loses an election the
outcome represents an electoral jolt that adversely affects the interests of
party elites. But an endorsement election is the functional equivalent, to
the minority party, of a deviating election. A major electoral rebuke to
the minority party cannot, by definition, be a deviating election. But a set
of election returns that strongly endorses the majority party can jolt the
minority party in much the same way that a deviating election jolts the
majority party.

The next section describes how I operationalize these three election
types. Then I report data on the incidence of the various election types.
In the third section, I report these data across levels of analysis (local,
state, and national), comparing the incidence of disequilibrating elections
with that of normal elections.

### Differentiating among Normal, Deviating, and Endorsement Elections

In order to operationalize these election types it is necessary to integrate
four types of data: (1) data on election-specific means of electoral perturbations; (2) data on the distribution of perturbations across local electorates for a given election; (3) information on majority party status; and (4)
information on who won the election. Figure 9–3 illustrates one approach
to integrating these data at the national level. It reports the mean of NOR-
MAL PARTISAN BALANCE$_{DEV}$ as well as a truncated range of values for NOR-
MAL PARTISAN BALANCE$_{DEV}$ (i.e., a range with the "tails" of the distribution
eliminated). The distributions reported in figure 9–3 depict the range for
75 percent of the cases in each election.

The mean and distribution of the NORMAL PARTISAN BALANCE$_{DEV}$ variable reported in figure 9–3 for the Elections of 1880, 1884, and 1888
suggest that these are prototypical normal elections. Their mean is very
close to 0 and the distribution of perturbations is fairly even across parties
(i.e., on either side of the 0 point on the vertical axis). In other years
(1904, 1912, 1916, 1920, 1964, 1972, 1976, 1984, for example) the data
displayed in figure 9–3 suggest that these represent disequilibrating electoral outcomes. In these elections the means are very different—from 0
and 75 percent of the perturbations favor one party (i.e., they are distributed on only one side of the 0 point on the vertical axis).

To determine whether these eight disequilibrating elections are deviating elections or endorsement elections, the distributional data in figure
9–3 must be joined with the data on majority party status reported in

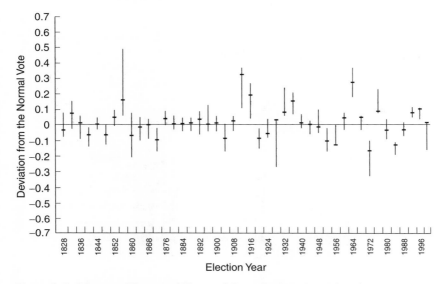

Figure 9–3. Mean and Range of Electoral Perturbations Data, by Election

figure 9–2 as well as with information on who actually won the election. Figure 9–2 shows that the Republicans were the majority party in each of these eight elections. This means that 1912, 1916, 1964, and 1976 were deviating elections. The elections of 1904, 1920, 1972, and 1984 represent sweeping victories for the Republicans, with far more than 75 percent of the electorate moving toward them. Thus, they represent endorsement elections.

To report the incidence of these election types across levels of analysis, I had to develop procedures to construct nine dummy election-type variables, one for each election type at each level of analysis. Because these procedures differed somewhat across levels of analysis, their explanation is tedious. Thus, they are presented in appendix V, available at *http:// www.pol.uiuc.edu/nardulliresearch.html.* While the details of these derivations are somewhat involved, the ideas behind the different election types are quite simple. Normal elections are those in which the distributions of deviations from normal voting patterns are small and balanced. Also, by definition, a normal election cannot occur in a year in which an electoral unit registers a critical election. Deviating elections are those elections in which 1) a majority party exists and 2) the majority party fails to win a plurality of the vote. Endorsement elections are those in which 1) a majority party exists and 2) the majority party wins an overwhelming victory, holding their own or doing better than expected in 75 percent of all electoral units.

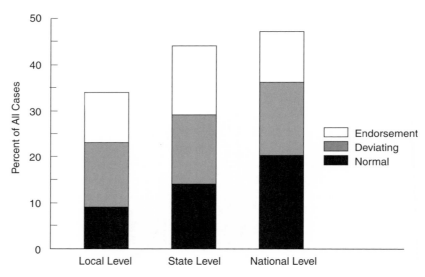

Figure 9–4. Election Types, by Level

### The Incidence and Distribution of Normal, Deviating, and Endorsement Elections

The data on the incidence of these election types are summarized in fig-ure 9–4 and are reported by year and level in table 9–4. The aggregated data summarized in figure 9–4 demonstrate that the ratio of disequili-brating to normal elections varies across levels of analysis. It also shows that the incidence of normal elections is fairly comparable to the inci-dence of disequilibrating elections at the national level, 1.3:1.[5] These distributions of election types suggest that political elites have received a fairly balanced and somewhat ambiguous set of lessons about electoral independence.

The data reported in figure 9–4 are literally true. But, for several rea-sons, an exclusive focus on these aggregated data would generate mis-leading inferences about what political elites have been taught about dem-ocratic politics. One reason is that there is a close correspondence between

---

[5] At the local level 9 percent of weighted unit-elections (weight = TOTAL VOTES) since 1828 were categorized as normal elections, 14 percent were categorized as deviating elec-tions, and 11 percent were categorized as endorsement elections. At the state level 17 percent of weighted state-elections (weight = ELECTORAL COLLEGE VOTES) since 1828 were catego-rized as normal elections, 14 percent were categorized as deviating elections, and 14 percent were categorized as endorsement elections. At the national level 20 percent of all elections meet the criteria for being a normal election; 14 percent were deviating elections; and 11 percent were endorsement elections.

normal elections at the national level and competitive electoral contexts. Indeed, three of the nine national normal elections (1844, 1880, and 1884) were also competitive electoral contests, as seen in table 9–2. A second reason is the effect of the INCUMBENT variable (introduced in chapter 8) on disequilibrating electoral outcomes. The impact of INCUMBENT on electoral outcomes is partially due to the electoral backlash effects noted in the perturbations regression analyses. Also important, however, is the fact that it is cognitively easier for voters to hold incumbents accountable for their stewardship than it is to hold their party accountable.[6] A final reason is that the aggregated data reported in figure 9–4 ignore an important historical dimension that is rooted in the electoral effects of the Progressive reforms. The electoral effect of these reforms began to manifest themselves in the twentieth century.[7]

The Progressive reforms are relevant here because they embody a set of institutional changes designed to reinvigorate American democracy.[8] These reforms, along with those extending suffrage, are among the most important democratic reforms in the United States since the adoption of the Bill of Rights. Indeed, no set of institutional reforms has been more important to the conduct of elections than those advocated by the Pro-

---

[6] Two factors, in particular, make it more difficult to evaluate stewardship when the incumbent is not seeking reelection: elections not involving incumbents involve more uncertainty and they generate more "noise." Candidates in *nonincumbent elections* will undoubtedly emphasize stewardship if, by doing so, they can secure a strategic advantage. But, without an established record as chief steward, uncertainties exist as to the contestants' future performance. Long-term partisan affiliations are likely to be very influential in resolving these uncertainties, at least for many voters. In addition to more uncertainty, there is more noise in elections not involving an incumbent president. When an incumbent is seeking reelection it is difficult for him, and his party, to evade responsibility for his stewardship. However, when there is no incumbent seeking reelection, the incumbent president's party can employ several strategies to avoid being held accountable for the immediate past. They can do this by remaking the party's image, staking out new policy positions, or nominating a starkly different candidate from the incumbent. Tactics such as these obscure the role of stewardship in nonincumbent elections and make it more difficult for voters to use elections as referenda.

[7] It is impossible to identify precisely the beginning of the Progressive Era because different states and locales adopted various reforms at different times. But by 1904 most of the relevant reforms were in place. Thus, I use the Election of 1904 as the point of demarcation between the pre– and post–Progressive Era.

[8] See Morone, James A.—1998. *The Democratic Wish: Popular Participation and the Limits of American Government, rev. ed.* New Haven, Yale University Press—for a contemporary perspective on the role of the Progressive reforms in the American democratic experience. Another recent work—Eisenach, Eldon J. 1994. *The Lost Promise of Progressivism.* Lawrence, University of Kansas Press—reconsiders the Progressive Movement from a neoinstitutionalist perspective. The Eisenach work provides a comprehensive and up-to-date bibliography on the Progressives, as does an older work, Ekirch, Arthur A. 1974. *Progressivism in America.* New York, New Viewpoints.

TABLE 9.4

Distribution of Normal, Deviating and Endorsement Elections, by Year and Level

| Election Year | Local Level | | | State Level | | | National Level | | |
|---|---|---|---|---|---|---|---|---|---|
| | Normal Elections | Deviating Elections | Endorsement Elections | Normal Elections | Deviating Elections | Endorsement Elections | Normal Elections | Deviating Elections | Endorsement Elections |
| 1828 | 0.08 | 0.14 | 0.13 | 0.05 | 0.16 | 0.24 | 0 | 0 | 0 |
| 1832 | 0.09 | 0.11 | 0.08 | 0.09 | 0.06 | 0.25 | 0 | 0 | 0 |
| 1836 | 0.00 | 0.06 | 0.10 | 0.15 | 0.14 | 0.1 | 0 | 0 | 0 |
| 1840 | 0.13 | 0.10 | 0.04 | 0.15 | 0.21 | 0.09 | 0 | 0 | 0 |
| 1844 | 0.12 | 0.04 | 0.01 | 0.23 | 0 | 0 | 0 | 0 | 0 |
| 1848 | 0.12 | 0.17 | 0.05 | 0.31 | 0.1 | 0 | 1 | 0 | 0 |
| 1852 | 0.14 | 0.14 | 0.02 | 0.27 | 0.23 | 0.14 | 0 | 0 | 0 |
| 1856 | 0.00 | 0.23 | 0.25 | 0.16 | 0.08 | 0.46 | 0 | 0 | 0 |
| 1860 | 0.10 | 0.32 | 0.10 | 0.15 | 0.03 | 0.14 | 0 | 0 | 0 |
| 1864 | 0.10 | 0.06 | 0.05 | 0.04 | 0.09 | 0.13 | 1 | 0 | 0 |
| 1868 | 0.09 | 0.05 | 0.07 | 0.03 | 0.25 | 0.16 | 1 | 0 | 0 |
| 1872 | 0.09 | 0.12 | 0.10 | 0.14 | 0.27 | 0.22 | 0 | 0 | 0 |
| 1876 | 0.10 | 0.05 | 0.04 | 0.14 | 0.09 | 0.03 | 1 | 0 | 0 |
| 1880 | 0.11 | 0.03 | 0.02 | 0.16 | 0.06 | 0 | 1 | 0 | 0 |
| 1884 | 0.10 | 0.03 | 0.01 | 0.11 | 0 | 0 | 1 | 0 | 0 |
| 1888 | 0.09 | 0.05 | 0.01 | 0.11 | 0 | 0.03 | 1 | 0 | 0 |
| 1892 | 0.08 | 0.14 | 0.07 | 0.16 | 0.14 | 0.24 | 0 | 1 | 0 |
| 1896 | 0.00 | 0.12 | 0.06 | 0.09 | 0.23 | 0.15 | 0 | 0 | 0 |
| 1900 | 0.08 | 0.04 | 0.01 | 0.07 | 0.02 | 0 | 1 | 0 | 0 |
| 1904 | 0.06 | 0.04 | 0.21 | 0.09 | 0.05 | 0.39 | 0 | 0 | 0 |
| 1908 | 0.09 | 0.05 | 0.00 | 0.07 | 0.07 | 0 | 0 | 0 | 1 |
| 1912 | 0.09 | 0.64 | 0.07 | 0.06 | 0.64 | 0.11 | 0 | 1 | 0 |

Table 9.4 (cont'd)

Distribution of Normal, Deviating and Endorsement Elections, by Year and Level

| Election Year | Local Level | | | State Level | | | National Level | | |
|---|---|---|---|---|---|---|---|---|---|
| | Normal Elections | Deviating Elections | Endorsement Elections | Normal Elections | Deviating Elections | Endorsement Elections | Normal Elections | Deviating Elections | Endorsement Elections |
| 1916 | 0.04 | 0.29 | 0.02 | 0.06 | 0.31 | 0.04 | 0 | 1 | 0 |
| 1920 | 0.04 | 0.02 | 0.17 | 0.04 | 0.04 | 0.17 | 0 | 0 | 1 |
| 1924 | 0.04 | 0.07 | 0.09 | 0.06 | 0 | 0.09 | 0 | 0 | 0 |
| 1928 | 0.04 | 0.21 | 0.10 | 0.06 | 0.17 | 0.04 | 0 | 0 | 0 |
| 1932 | 0.00 | 0.18 | 0.10 | 0 | 0.11 | 0.25 | 0 | 0 | 0 |
| 1936 | 0.09 | 0.15 | 0.26 | 0.13 | 0.07 | 0.5 | 0 | 0 | 1 |
| 1940 | 0.09 | 0.04 | 0.02 | 0.19 | 0.05 | 0.03 | 0 | 0 | 0 |
| 1944 | 0.12 | 0.02 | 0.01 | 0.19 | 0.03 | 0 | 1 | 0 | 0 |
| 1948 | 0.11 | 0.06 | 0.02 | 0.15 | 0.21 | 0.05 | 1 | 0 | 0 |
| 1952 | 0.00 | 0.12 | 0.10 | 0.3 | 0.12 | 0.32 | 0 | 0 | 0 |
| 1956 | 0.10 | 0.2 | 0.17 | 0.23 | 0.08 | 0.27 | 0 | 0 | 0 |
| 1960 | 0.08 | 0.08 | 0.02 | 0.18 | 0.21 | 0.05 | 0 | 1 | 0 |
| 1964 | 0.09 | 0.50 | 0.27 | 0.16 | 0.85 | 0.07 | 0 | 1 | 0 |
| 1968 | 0.08 | 0.15 | 0.03 | 0.1 | 0.19 | 0.02 | 0 | 0 | 0 |
| 1972 | 0.07 | 0.14 | 0.24 | 0.1 | 0.11 | 0.48 | 0 | 0 | 0 |
| 1976 | 0.08 | 0.14 | 0.04 | 0.14 | 0.24 | 0.02 | 0 | 1 | 0 |
| 1980 | 0.09 | 0.06 | 0.03 | 0.18 | 0.02 | 0.17 | 0 | 0 | 0 |
| 1984 | 0.09 | 0.09 | 0.24 | 0.14 | 0.13 | 0.73 | 0 | 0 | 1 |
| 1988 | 0.09 | 0.03 | 0.02 | 0.18 | 0.03 | 0.05 | 0 | 0 | 0 |
| 1992 | 0.12 | 0.15 | 0.01 | 0.27 | 0.19 | 0.03 | 0 | 0 | 0 |
| 1996 | 0.12 | 0.17 | 0.12 | 0.2 | 0.15 | 0.17 | 0 | 0 | 0 |
| 2000 | 0.12 | 0.08 | 0.13 | 0.16 | 0.04 | 0.14 | 0 | 1 | 0 |

gressives. Reforms such as the Australian ballot, registration systems, literacy tests and civil service reform were intended to loosen the grip of parties on voters and enhance electoral accountability. The Australian ballot provided disgruntled citizens with the "cover" to register their discontent. The use of registration systems and literacy tests limits the ability of local party machines to "recruit" disengaged voters on Election Day, thus limiting their ability to dilute the dissenting votes of disgruntled citizens. Civil service reform made it much more difficult for parties to recruit and maintain the workers they needed to make their electoral machines run efficiently.

These observations suggest that a more refined analysis of the incidence of disequilibrating elections would uncover a temporal pattern with important implications for the debate over popular efficacy. Contributing to this pattern is a multiplier effect that magnifies the impact of local and state electoral outcomes at the national level. This multiplier effect is similar to the one reported in the discussion of competitive electoral contests.[9] The role of this multiplier effect in generating a discernible temporal trend is clearest when its interaction with INCUMBENT is examined in the post–Progressive Era.

Consider, for example, the incidence of disequilibrating elections in post–Progressive Era incumbent elections. At the local level disequilibrating elections occurred in 30 percent of incumbent elections held since 1904, at the state level they occurred in 27 percent, while at the national level they occurred in 61 percent. These joint effects lead to a very different set of inferences about the political impact of electoral independence in the twentieth century than in the nineteenth century. At the national level, 44 percent of all presidential elections in the post–Progressive Era have been deviating or endorsement elections. Indeed only one deviating election (1892) occurred before 1904, and there were no endorsement elections. The ratio of disequilibrating elections to normal elections since 1904 is more than 5:1. There have been no normal elections at all in the last half of the twentieth century.

---

[9] Here the multiplier effect is produced by the temporal and spatial clustering of local electoral perturbations interacting with more competitive electoral contexts at the state and national level. A handful of local deviating elections can result in a deviating election at the state level, particularly when the majority party's comfort margin is small. The same thing can happen at the national level. The spatial concentration of local endorsement elections within a group of states for a given election can generate a higher incidence of endorsement elections at the state level. The temporal structure of local endorsement elections can affect the likelihood of a national-level endorsement election. The effect of this multiplier generates an incidence of disequilibrating elections of 25 percent at the local level, 29 percent at the state level, and 34 percent at the national level.

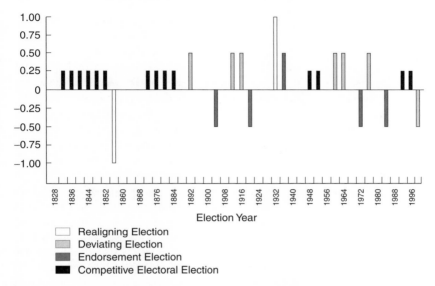

Figure 9–5. Competitive Electoral Settings and Disequilibrating Elections, by Year*

## THE ELECTORATE IN DEMOCRATIC POLITICS: A SYNOPTIC VIEW

Examining the impact of electoral independence on electoral settings and outcomes has produced important insights into popular efficacy. To realize the full theoretical import of the impact analyses, however, the data on deviating and endorsement elections must be joined with the data on competitive electoral contests and realigning elections. Figure 9–5 joins these data; it displays the incidence of competitive electoral contests and the incidence of disequilibrating elections (realigning, deviating, and endorsement) at the national level.

Since the beginnings of a two-party system in 1836, there have been thirteen competitive electoral contests: 1836, 1840, 1844, 1848, 1852, 1872, 1876, 1880, 1884, 1948, 1952, 1992, and 1996 (see table 9–2). These account for 31 percent of all elections held since 1836. In addition, there have been two realigning elections (1856 and 1932), seven deviating elections (1892, 1912, 1916, 1960, 1964, 1976, and 2000) and five endorsement elections (1904, 1920, 1936, 1972, and 1984). These disequilibrating elections account for one-third of American presidential elections since 1836. Thus, elections in which the importance of the electorate was underscored either going into a presidential campaign, or in the outcome of the election, account for almost two-thirds of all elections since the emergence of a two-party system in 1836.

The integrated findings summarized in figure 9–5 provide a solution to the paradox of elected officials. The number of elections in which a party's electoral base was insufficient to insure victory or deserted it underscores the central role the electorate must play in the calculations of strategic political elites. So do the alternating pulses depicted in figure 9–3 and the undulations in electoral advantages depicted in figure 9–2. No strategic politician could reflect on the alternating pattern of realignments, the ebb and flow of electoral bases, or the effects of short-term electoral jolts and feel secure about the support of their party's electoral base.

The importance of enduring partisan attachments in voting decisions (noted in figure 5–3) makes the job of party elites doable. But they have been taught throughout the democratic era in American politics that the electoral advantage these attachments provide is seldom significant enough to make their job comfortable. Because voters have shown themselves to be discriminating consumers of political goods, they have been anything but "silent partners" in democratic governance. Rather, through their actions within the electoral arena, voters have taught political elites that they must continually be concerned with the electorate's reaction to their stewardship.

## References

Eisenach, Eldon J. 1994. *The Lost Promise of Progressivism*. Lawrence, University of Kansas Press.

Ekirch, Arthur A. 1974. *Progressivism in America*. New York, New Viewpoints.

Morone, James A. 1998. *The Democratic Wish: Popular Participation and the Limits of American Government. Rev. ed*. New Haven, Yale University Press.

# Chapter Ten

# Popular Efficacy in the Democratic Era

> Most systems of interest to humankind—economies, political organizations, games, ecologies, the central nervous system, biological evolution, etc.—rarely, if ever, "settle down" to some repetitive or other easily described pattern. Such systems are . . . intrinsically dynamic, . . . continually adapting to new circumstances.
> —Bryan A. Jones, *Reconceiving Decision-Making in Democratic Politics*

> [T]he fundamental voter model should include a conditional component. That is to say, voters act differently under different conditions. . . . Voters' emphasis on conscious rational choice (as opposed to long-standing commitment) will be conditioned on their emotional state. Voters can, and often will, vote their "standing decisions." However, they will also rely on their internal emotional states to signal when to abandon their predispositions and begin conscious political choice.
> —George E. Marcus and Michael MacKuen, "Anxiety, Enthusiasm and the Vote"

In this book I have sought to determine whether a theoretical and empirical basis exists for challenging the conventional wisdom concerning popular efficacy, a key tenet of democratic theory. I focused my efforts on the electoral arena. It offers the best venue ordinary citizens have for exerting influence within representative democracies, where popular efficacy derives principally from mechanisms that provide for electoral accountability. Despite the vote's potential as a valuable political resource, the image of voters as "manageable fools" has been a durable one. It gives rise to grave concerns about the efficaciousness of citizens as political actors. This image is based on the accumulated empirical evidence compiled by a variety of observers employing diverse methodologies. While the prevailing conventional wisdom about voters is anchored in observations that date to the nineteenth century, the era of survey research has only reinforced it.

I chose to reexamine the conventional wisdom about popular efficacy because its close relationship to democratic responsiveness has both theoretical and practical implications of some import. The theoretical distinctiveness of democracy as a form of government, and an important source of its normative appeal, is rooted in mechanisms that provide for an exceptional level of responsiveness to broad popular concerns. Despite the uncertainty over whether democratic political orders can, in fact, "induce government to act in the interest of the people" (Przeworski, Stokes et al. 1999: 3), democracy has, in Fukuyama's terms, "proven not just durable, but resurgent." However, while democracy shows no signs of abating in the immediate future, various forms of government have ebbed and flowed throughout history. If democracy does not or cannot fulfill its promise, then its allure will surely fade—as it has before. Research on popular efficacy is valuable because it can clarify how, or if, democracy can realize its potential as a uniquely responsive form of government.

Uncertainty about popular efficacy is rooted in empirical research documenting the suspect cognitive capacities of citizens, their inattentiveness to politics, the existence of formidable political competitors within liberal democracies, and the density and complexity of policy-making institutions. Efforts to incorporate these observations into democratic theory have led some scholars to formulate restatements that downplay the role of ordinary citizens. In these process models it is the structure of democratic processes that provides for desirable outcomes, not the competence of citizens.

While process models make democracy less dependent on the well-documented frailties of ordinary citizens, many observers question their democratic *bona fides*. To these observers process models are too similar to protective forms of government in which political participation is highly limited and elites are expected to act as altruistic custodians of the common good. Reinforcing these concerns is the fact that much of the survey-based research on voting behavior raises questions about the capacity of citizens to perform even the minimal roles process models provide them. Thus, broadly conceived, the goal of this book has been to determine if it is possible to "bring the people back in" to our conceptions of democratic governance. If an efficacious popular component to democratic governance is inconceivable, or unattainable, then it is difficult to see how democracy can fulfill its promise as being uniquely responsive to popular concerns.

The next section summarizes the argument that underlies this effort. The second section summarizes and discusses the empirical evidence. Then I develop the implications of this analysis for democratic theory and American politics. Finally, I discuss some directions for future research.

## The Argument

The approach to reexamining popular efficacy offered here rests on two pillars—one theoretical, the other methodological. The theoretical pillar is a set of dynamics that flow from the conception of mass-elite linkages introduced in chapter 1. These dynamics are driven by the interactions among exogenous events, citizens' core political desires, and political elites' core political interests. This approach draws inferences about popular efficacy by examining the capacity of voters to react electorally to exogenous events whose radiated effects impinge upon their core political desires (life, liberty, prosperity, personal security, etc.). The radiated effects of these exogenous events can initiate intense episodes of information processing that lead citizens to update their political cognitions and deviate from their normal voting behavior, thereby impinging on the core political interests of elites: their desire for electoral success.

This approach rests on a synthesis presented in chapter 2 that integrates an evaluative conception of democratic citizenship with insights on decision making drawn from cognitive research. It necessarily provides a key role to heuristic devices and information shortcuts. Research in the cognitive sciences suggests that these "low-rationality" modes of information processing characterize most decision making in nonpolitical arenas. Given this, there is no reason to think that more deliberative modes of information processing would characterize routine decision making in the political arena. When viewed from a normative perspective, however, the peripheral processing of political information generates serious concerns about popular efficacy. These concerns are reinforced by the fact that many of the political heuristics citizens use to make electoral decisions are tainted by endogenous influences.

Despite these concerns, electoral accountability, and thus democratic responsiveness, is conceivable because of the energizing effects of exogenous events. When these exogenous events bear on core political desires they can evoke emotional responses that initiate episodes of intense processing of political information. During these episodes many citizens may search for new information sources and be more receptive to the information to which they are exposed. They may also reexamine their political heuristics and replace them if they are adjudged to be dysfunctional. Neither core political desires nor exogenous events are controllable by political elites, at least in the short term. Thus, the dynamics that generate these interludes of relatively intense information processing provide the theoretical basis for believing that citizens can be efficacious political actors.

These dynamics explain why the complacent, inattentive "politics of normalcy" is not always an apt characterization of democratic politics.

At some times, in some places the "politics of upheaval" is a more apt description of democratic politics, at least for some people. The politics of upheaval is characterized by uncertainty and anxiety, emotions that can induce learning and, in the words of Marcus and MacKuen, "conscious political choice." If these interludes of conscious political choice are sufficient to generate disequilibrating electoral jolts that affect elites' core political interests, then elites will learn to be attentive to citizens' core political desires. The joint learning induced by these dynamics can provide for a uniquely democratic form of governmental responsiveness. However, the path between event-induced learning, stewardship evaluations, and vote choices can be convoluted, as the transformational model presented in chapter 3 demonstrates.

The contingencies embedded in the model depicted in figure 3–2 introduce a good deal of ambiguity into the level of joint learning that will be induced by critical events and the behavioral effects of that learning. This ambiguity is compounded by the incentives competing stewards have for deploying political resources in ways that interfere with learning, thereby distracting citizens, dulling their evaluative capacities, and allowing stewards to evade responsibility for their record. The transformational model demonstrates, theoretically, the relative effectiveness of performance strategies over partisan strategies in dealing with the electoral effects of critical events. These theoretical observations suggest that stewards have incentives to both anticipate and address matters that affect citizens' core political desires. But the durability, pervasiveness, and strength of endogenous influences within democratic political orders outlined in chapter 4 casts a dark pall over these theoretical expectations.

The ambiguity introduced by the conflicting effects of exogenous and endogenous influences on political learning and behavior required working outside the survey research paradigm. Thus, the methodological pillar upon which this effort rests is a longitudinal, subnational research design. A macro-level extension of the Michigan model of voting behavior is used, in conjunction with local level electoral data, as the conceptual basis for differentiating between endogenous and exogenous influences on electoral behavior. At the core of this model is the concept of a normal vote. The procedure used to operationalize the concept of a normal vote at the local level produced valid and reliable data on normal voting patterns that were used to determine the relative importance of exogenous and endogenous influences on electoral behavior.

The availability of normal vote estimates for a large number of units over forty-four elections provided for an examination of (1) variations in normal voting patterns across locales, (2) enduring changes in voting patterns, and (3) election-specific deviations from expected votes. These analyses made it possible to gauge (1) the capacity of citizens to overcome inertial and centripetal influences on their voting behavior and (2) the impact of departures from normal voting patterns on electoral settings and outcomes. The findings from these analyses provide the empirical basis for making inferences about democratic governance that differ substantially from those drawn from evidence produced within the survey research paradigm.


## THE EVIDENCE

The analyses reported in chapter 6 through chapter 9 produce important insights into popular efficacy and electoral accountability. The results reported in these chapters provide both an empirical basis for construing citizens as discriminating consumers of public goods and an explanation for the paradox of elected officials. As such, these findings constitute the empirical foundation for a more efficacious image of democratic citizens, one that provides insights into uniquely democratic sources of governmental responsiveness to popular concerns. In conjunction with the theoretical contributions from chapter 2 and chapter 3, these empirical results provide the basis for recentering citizens in our conceptions of how democratic governance works. I provide a general summary and discussion of the key empirical findings below.

*The social and geo-political roots of normal voting patterns suggest that during times of political normalcy, partisanship may be a useful political heuristic.*

Democratic skeptics since Michels have argued that political parties are not vehicles of democracy but tools of political elites. The dominant role party identification plays in determining voting behavior is an integral part of the image of voters as manageable fools. But the fact that the relative size of local electoral bases is largely determined by demographics and geo-politics cast doubt on the elitist view of mass-elite linkages within political parties. Neither the pluralist thesis nor the patterned change thesis examined in chapter 6 could be rejected. Parties have been powerful forces within American politics since their inception, and remain so today. But, throughout the democratic era in American politics, the ability of party elites to forge local electoral coalitions has been bounded by the distribution of social groups and interests. Moreover, the examination of group-based partisan allegiances over time suggests that social groups and interests have regularly switched their partisan loyalties.

These findings have important implications for the meaning of partisan influences on voting, as well as for popular efficacy. At the very least, they suggest that the interpretation of partisanship as an endogenous influence on voting is an extremely conservative one. Viewed more generously, these findings underscore both the importance of societal interests to the electoral base of parties and the tenuousness of partisan allegiances. This more generous view suggests that party may be a low-cost, but valuable, source of information during times of political normalcy. The dynamic engagement of social group leaders provides for the periodic updating of party positions and tightens the linkage between party actions and the core desires of the party's electoral base. The electorate's capacity to generate disequilibrating electoral jolts, documented in the electoral independence analyses, provides the impetus for this updating to occur.

*The distributions of the enduring electoral change data are sufficiently structured to be consistent with the assertion that they are popular responses to the radiated effects of exogenous events; the electoral perturbations analysis reinforced the importance of exogenous influences on electoral behavior, providing strong support for the approach to understanding mass-elite linkages offered here.*

The data analyses reported in chapter 7 (the results reported in figure 7–1 and figure 7–2; map 7–1 through map 7–6; and table 7–1) demonstrate that the data on the incidence of enduring electoral change are structured both temporally and spatially. Ninety-seven percent of all critical changes and 90 percent of all secular changes fell within one of six realignment eras. In addition, it is clear that the partisan realignments captured by these various eras have been largely regional phenomena. The perturbations analysis reported in chapter 8 provided more direct empirical support for the transformational model developed in chapter 3. Variations in the realization of core political desires are important determinants of electoral perturbations, far more important than partisan activities designed to influence stewardship evaluations and vote choices. Together, these core findings demonstrate a level of electoral independence that is capable of disciplining political parties, reinforcing their value as a political heuristic.

The perturbations analysis also yields a rich set of insights into the evaluative capacities of the electorate. These insights suggest that electorate's judgments are far more sophisticated than many have presumed, which speaks to its efficaciousness as a political actor. The perturbations analysis documents that the electorate has the capacity to incorporate prospective economic conditions, as well as the reputation of political parties, into its quadrennial evaluations of presidential stewardship. Moreover, the fact that the American electorate has been making relatively sophisticated evaluations since the early-nineteenth century suggests that it has the capacity to render experientially based judgments. The ineffectiveness of many partisan electoral tactics, and the general inability of parties to transform institutional resources into electoral gains that can perpetuate political power, further enhances the view of the electorate as an efficacious component of democratic political orders.

*The magnitude of the departures from normal voting patterns, in conjunction with the incidence and distribution of competitive electoral contests and disequilibrating electoral outcomes, suggests that citizens have regularly demonstrated their capacity to affect the core interests of political elites, thereby educating them about the central role of popular concerns in American democracy.*

The inertial effects of habitual behavior and the centripetal pulls of partisan attachments are powerful forces within the electoral arena, as seen in figure 5–3. But the magnitude of critical changes in normal voting patterns reported in chapter 7 (figures 7–4 through 7–9) and the estimates of exogenously driven electoral perturbations provided in chapter 8 present a dramatically different picture. They suggest that the electorate has the capacity to wield a big stick and has regularly made its voice heard in the cacophonous milieu of democratic politics in the United States. This was confirmed in chapter 9, which showed that the American electorate has regularly demonstrated its capacity to overcome inertial and habitual forces in ways that impinge upon the core interests of political elites.

The number of elections in which a party's electoral base was insufficient to insure victory or deserted it underscores the central role the electorate must play in the calculations of political elites. No strategic party elite could reflect on the ebb and flow of electoral bases over time (figure 9–2) or the effects of short-term electoral jolts (figure 9–3) and feel secure about the support of the electoral base of his or her party. Dealing with these electoral uncertainties teaches political elites that they are not working with a static electorate forged by the unalterable effects of partisan "inoculations" administered early in life. This point is underscored by the summary data presented in figure 9–5, which generate an unconventional set of inferences about American democracy. Rather than giving rise to an image of the electorate as an inert and inattentive assemblage of fools, these data suggest an image of the electorate as a capacious eight-hundred-pound gorilla that is easily aroused by the missteps of political stewards.

Also noteworthy is the fact that the synoptic data presented in figure 9–5 show that disequilibrating electoral outcomes and competitive electoral contests have been distributed over time in such a way that few prominent American political leaders have been spared their sobering effects. Only twice since the inception of the two-party system in 1836 has a majority party enjoyed more than two consecutive elections without some disequilibrating electoral outcome: 1860–64–68 and 1940–44–48; both periods include major military conflicts. Thus, no generation of political elites in the democratic era has had the luxury of treating citizens as silent partners in democratic governance. Elite experiences with shifting electoral fortunes has been an integral part of their political education and are almost certainly part of the lore passed on from one generation of political elites to the next. Herein lies the solution to the paradox of elected officials.

## Implications of the Argument and the Evidence

### Conceptions of Democratic Governance

This work makes several contributions to democratic theory. Most important, it reinvigorates process models of democracy. The theoretical analyses provided in chapter 2 and chapter 3 anchor process models in core political desires and well-established cognitive processes. The analyses presented in chapter 6 shed new, albeit indirect, light on the pluralist model. The pattern of group-specific and section-specific partisan realignments documented there underscores the importance of social and interest group leaders for the conduct of party affairs. The data presented in chapter 7 through chapter 9 put "teeth" into the competing elites model. The electorate's capacity to deliver disequilibrating electoral jolts provides a "democratic" check on both group leaders and party professionals. Thus, the theoretical and empirical contributions made here invest process models with a more democratic hue and clearly differentiate them from protective or custodial models

The reinvigoration of process models notwithstanding, the picture of democratic governance that emerges here is not a particularly pretty one. Despite the sophisticated evaluative capacities suggested by some findings in chapter 8, the political engagement of most citizens is intermittent and most political information is processed peripherally. As noted earlier, the perspective on democratic citizens adopted here suggests that they monitor political stewards like firefighters, not police officers (McCubbins and Schwartz 1984). Most citizens do not engage in the constant surveillance of political stewards, evaluating their actions in light of well-informed policy preferences. Rather, the political engagement of most citizens is activated by fire alarms.

These fire alarms have the potential to arouse an otherwise inattentive public and generate a transformation from the politics of normalcy to the politics of upheaval. But the contingencies that envelop these arousals, as noted in the discussion of figure 3–2, suggest a messy and uncertain process. Moreover, the political effects of these periodic reawakenings depend both on the number of citizens aroused and the competitiveness of electoral settings. On the other hand, the incentives political elites have to prevent political upheavals enhance democratic responsiveness beyond what would be expected given the limited and episodic political involvement of most citizens.

The untidy image of democratic politics that emerges here is particularly stark in contrast to the elegance and symmetry of utilitarian conceptions. However, as noted earlier, utilitarian conceptions are all but unattainable by ordinary humans living in modern societies. This realization has led to a great deal of pessimism about the possibility of "real" (i.e., responsive) democratic governance. However, the analyses presented here suggest that real democracy is not as dependent as earlier empirical democratic theorists thought on the expectations, norms, and interdependencies embedded in utilitarianism (Berelson, Lazarsfeld, et al. 1954; Campbell, Converse, et al. 1960). Thus, the hopeful message of this book is that effective democratic governance, while not often pretty, is eminently attainable. The model of electoral accountability offered here merely requires that citizens use the same cognitive tactics within the political arena that they deploy in other domains of life. Moreover, political stewards need not be altruistic civic actors. They need be only strategic and purposive political actors, driven by the desire to gain elective office and capable of learning from their collective electoral experiences.

From the perspective of this research, what *is* important for effective democratic government are factors that affect the capacity of citizens to translate exogenous events into disequilibrating electoral jolts. Core democratic freedoms, institutions, and processes must be maintained, and elections must be free, fair, competitive, and regular. These assertions run counter to the utilitarian tradition, which views democracy as a fragile, highly interdependent system. The utilitarian tradition is grounded in the belief that democratic governance can offer more than process models deliver. These aspirations are laudable, and it may be that the minimalism implicit in process models of democracy is not all that is desirable or obtainable from self-government. It may also be the case that the inelegant model of democracy that emerges here is not the only one that is conceivable. But expecting more of democratic governance may be like "waiting for Godot." The pervasiveness of suboptimality in other spheres of life makes it unlikely to expect optimal arrangements in the political sphere.

While these observations are not particularly profound, they are meaningful in a diverse world continually struggling with governance issues. In advanced industrial democracies few citizens have the luxury of investing large amounts of cognitive energies in public affairs. The analysis presented here suggests that effective democratic governance is possible in such settings. The inattentiveness of largely ill-informed citizens does not mean that democracy is a fraud perpetrated by elites and dominated by meaningless, symbolic actions (Edelman 1964, 1989). In developing nations struggling to create democratic institutions, this analysis suggests that meaningful democracy is attainable. As long as basic freedoms and democratic institutions are established and maintained, it may not be so important that the indigenous populations appear ill-equipped to discharge democratic responsibilities. Citizens in such societies are not necessarily the hapless "dupes of unscrupulous demagogues," in Schlesinger's terms. Waiting for educational and economic reforms before implementing democratic reforms may be both unwarranted and self-defeating.

## Conceptions of American Politics

Some of the insights about democratic governance noted above obviously have implications for our understanding of American politics, and others could be developed. But perhaps the most important insight generated from the empirical analyses presented here bears on the image of American democracy as a staid, lumbering leviathan. The image of U.S. politics as being equilibrium-prone and averse to nonincremental change is deeply rooted in the American experience. It is the result of a confluence of factors, but the intransigence of the electorate has been an important component of this image.[1] The data presented here have undermined the image of an inert electorate paralyzed by centripetal forces. These data present an image of an American electorate that is far more dynamic than suggested by earlier empirical research. However, the potential implications of this electoral dynamism for our image of American politics cannot be fully appreciated until it is joined with the insights generated by a refreshingly innovative perspective on policy making: the comparative issue dynamics approach developed by Baumgartner and Jones (1993).

In a manner paralleling the subnational, longitudinal approach developed here, Baumgartner and Jones examine individual policy areas over

---

[1] The cumbersome design of the U.S. Constitution is one of the most important contributing factors here. This design reflected the Founders' fears of governmental tyranny; its intent was to make it difficult for the whims of either political demagogues or transient majorities to be translated into public action. At the institutional level the effectiveness of the Founders' efforts has been reflected in repeated observations about bureaucratic intransigence, the density and impenetrability of policy-making infrastructures, and the emergence of iron triangles, policy whirlpools, and subgovernments. At the mass level the ability of voters to penetrate and mobilize complex policy networks has been hampered by a variety of factors, including inattentiveness, the resources and influence of organized interests, and the centripetal pulls of partisanship within the electoral arena.

time. Their analysis focuses on policy images and institutional venues, and stresses the importance of positive feedback systems in the generation of disequilibrating policy changes. By positive feedback systems they refer to a process in which initial disturbances become reinforced and grow larger over time. Most studies of policy making emphasize the prominence of negative feedback systems, a process in which disturbances become smaller over time, thereby reinforcing the status quo ante. Positive feedback can transform policy images and lead to changes in institutional venues, both of which generate nonincremental policy changes.

As a result of their innovative conceptual framework and meticulous empirical analyses, they generate an unconventional view of policy making. The image of the policy-making process they develop differs fundamentally from the static, incrementalist perspective that has come to dominate our understanding of it. Their research is replete with fresh insights into policy making, the gist of which they summarize as follows:

> Policymaking in many areas of American politics may not always be ruled by incrementalism, decreasing marginal returns, and slow changes (although these features remain important); rather there are critical periods of mobilization of antagonists during which dramatic changes are put into effect. At any one time, there may be little change, but periods of relative stability may be punctuated by fitful bursts of mobilization that change the structure of bias for decades to come. Institutions are the legacies of short periods of attention by the public to a given issue. They remain intact until attention increases at some later date to cause more institutional change. (Baumgartner and Jones 1993: 101–2)

The broad parallels between the conclusions they draw about policy making and those drawn here about electoral behavior are striking. The fact that both sets of conclusions were produced by disaggregated, longitudinal analyses has important methodological implications. More important, however, is the intriguing potential these parallels hold for a new synthesis about American politics—one with a more dynamic, and democratic, hue. An enormous amount of theoretical development and empirical analysis needs to be done before it can be determined whether this intriguing potential can yield well-grounded qualifications to our understanding of how American politics works. In particular, much research needs to be done to enhance our understanding of the relationship between positive feedback systems at the elite level and exogenous events that impinge on core political desires at the mass level.

The primary interest of Baumgartner and Jones is with the impact of attention shifts on policy images and institutional venues; they are less concerned with the origins of these shifts or their integrative potential. But future research focusing on role of exogenous events, core political desires, disequilibrating electoral jolts, positive feedback mechanisms, and policy innovations could enhance the theoretical power of their approach. As it is, they do not devote much attention to the linkages between mass concerns, electoral processes, and nonincremental policy change. Nor, given the state of the literature on electoral behavior, would a focus on these linkages be expected. With the exception of the literature on critical realignments, there is little to warrant or guide research in this area. However, the approach to mass-elite linkages offered here, in conjunction with the data on the incidence of disequilibrating electoral jolts, provides the theoretical and empirical impetus for examining the linkages between electoral eruptions and policy innovations.

Research targeting these linkages should not proceed with simplistic notions of the relationship between popular concerns, electoral processes, and policy outputs. It would be naive to believe that all attention shifts at the elite level are rooted in popular discontents or are reflections of deeply held popular desires. Nor should it be expected that all exogenous events that impinge upon core political desires will generate electoral jolts that initiate positive feedback and produce policy innovations. Sometimes political elites, schooled in electoral politics, will anticipate the impact of exogenous events on core political desires and act proactively. Other times the costs of action will be prohibitive and elites will elect to take their electoral lumps. It will require much research to sort out these contingencies. But we are unlikely to develop a comprehensive understanding of mass-elite linkages in U.S. politics until that research is conducted.

## FUTURE RESEARCH

The analyses presented here provide support for an unconventional view of mass-elite linkages in the United States. But these analyses provide only the first step in reassessing the conventional wisdom about ordinary citizens and the role they play in democratic politics. While the mode of analysis developed here could be refined considerably and extended in a number of ways, I focus here on two potentially fruitful extensions. The first is to extend the approach developed here to other elective offices and electoral systems. This would enhance our understanding of electoral behavior in general and mass-elite linkages in particular. A second, and far more ambitious, extension involves integrating the study of exogenous events and electoral jolts with the study of policy innovations. Only when this integration takes place will we begin to generate a more theoretically encompassing, empirically based understanding of democratic governance.

*Extending the Macro-Level Normal Vote Approach*
*to Other Electoral Settings*

A natural extension of this mode of analysis would be to apply it to other elective offices in the United States, as well as cross-nationally. The application of the macro-level, normal vote approach to senatorial, congressional, and gubernatorial election returns, as well as those for state legislative races, would be a significant undertaking. But a centralized, publicly funded effort to assemble these diverse sets of electoral data, and derive normal vote estimates for them, would produce significant economies. Building on the lessons learned here, uniform resolutions to the problems encountered in deriving normal vote estimates could be implemented across electoral series. Information about temporal and/or regional anomalies could be gathered, systematized, and applied across elective offices. The adoption of a common unit of analysis, such as the county election and the city election, would facilitate the assembly of a set of independent variables that could be developed and exploited across data series. While costly, such a collective effort would consume only a fraction of the resources that have been invested in the American National Election Studies.

The development of an historical archive of normal vote data for the United States would pay handsome dividends. By enabling researchers to examine the electoral impact of a wide array of exogenous events, social settings, electoral institutions, and political actors, it would enrich our understanding of democratic processes greatly. Such an archive would make it feasible, indeed routine, to test hypotheses across election types, time frames, and locales. It would also make it possible to determine if electoral jolts are unique to particular offices or manifested across offices. The value of such an archive would be enhanced by the incentives it would provide enterprising scholars. They would be motivated to assemble innovative sets of independent variables by the payoffs that would accrue from merging them with the historical archive. The recent development and refinement of techniques for the analysis of spatially and temporally organized data further enhance the potential payoffs from such an electoral archive. For these reasons the extension of this approach to other offices would enrich our understanding of the American experience, in general, and American democracy, in particular.

An even more challenging extension of this mode of analysis would be to apply it cross-nationally. Cross-national applications could generate refreshingly new insights concerning the electoral effects of cultural factors, party systems, electoral institutions, economic turbulence, and the like. A comparative focus on the capacity of citizens to transform exogenous events into disequilibrating electoral jolts, while challenging, would be particularly rewarding. Understanding systemic differences in this capacity would add a new dimension to the study of democratization. Indeed, it would provide a new, outcome-oriented basis for evaluating the responsiveness of different democratic nations, as well as enhance our understanding of the factors that affect electoral accountability and democratic responsiveness. It could also provide important insights into the effects of globalization. An analysis of the capacity of similar exogenous events to generate disequilibrating electoral jolts, across nations and over time, would provide insights into the debate over whether democratic nations are converging or diverging in the post–Cold War era (Huntington 1996).

The extensions of the macro-level normal vote approach advocated here would revitalize electoral research. Political science as a discipline, and the subfield of American political behavior in particular, has arguably become too dependent on survey research. Survey methods are valuable tools for social scientists, and recent innovations in survey techniques have enhanced their power. But their familiarity has had an untoward effect on the questions we ask, how we examine them, and what we can say about them. A macro-level, normal vote approach would be useful in moving electoral studies away from a fixation with the correlates of individual level voting behavior and toward a focus on electoral change and democratic governance. No discipline or subdiscipline can progress without employing a wide array of tools and approaches. The insights generated here are no more than limited and early examples of the types of theoretical insights that can be generated by temporally and spatially organized aggregate electoral data. The potential dividends that could flow from the development of encompassing normal vote archives across elective offices and electoral systems are too great to ignore.

### Integrating the Study of Exogenous Events, Electoral Jolts, and Policy Innovations

An even more challenging research extension that follows from the logic and results of the analyses presented here concerns the integration of electoral behavior and policy making: relating exogenous events and electoral jolts to policy innovations. The macro-level, normal vote approach, in conjunction with Baumgartner and Jones's comparative issue dynamics approach (1993; Jones 1994), provides the basis for integrating these fields of study.

The fact that the disequilibrating electoral jolts identified here are well structured both spatially and temporally bodes well for this type of integrative analysis. It follows from most versions of democratic theory that representatives from regions experiencing the effects of exogenous events would have the most incentive to pursue ameliorative actions, either in response to an electoral eruption or to ward one off. As noted in chapter 3, many factors may enhance, negate, or obscure the translation of exogenous events into policy innovations. Their impact may vary over time and across policy areas. But integrating spatially and temporally organized data on policy activities with exogenous events and/or major electoral eruptions provides a starting point for developing a "democratic" perspective on policy innovations.

The integration of electoral analyses with policy making would be a massive undertaking that could only be begun after an enormous investment has been made in the study of electoral phenomena and a reorientation of policy studies. But it would also be an undertaking with enormous payoffs in terms of our understanding of democratic governance. The fact that this could be done historically, cross-nationally, and across policy fields makes it all the more valuable.

## References

Althaus, S., P. F. Nardulli, et al. 2001a. *The Impact of Media Buys on Presidential Voting*. Annual Meeting of the American Political Science Association, San Francisco, CA.

———. 2001b. *Patterns and Effects of Candidate Appearances in Presidential Elections, 1972–2000*. Campaign Studies 2000: Lessons Learned, Santa Barbara, CA.

Baumgartner, F. R,. and B. D. Jones. 1993. *Agendas and Instability in American Politics*. Chicago, University of Chicago Press.

Berelson, B. R., P. F. Lazarsfeld, et al. 1954. *Voting: A Study of Opinion Formation in a Presidential Campaign*. Chicago, University of Chicago Press.

Campbell, A., P. E. Converse, et al. 1960. *The American Voter*. New York, John Wiley and Sons.

Edelman, M. 1964. *The Symbolic Uses of Politics*. Urbana, University of Illinois Press.

———. 1989. *Constructing the Political Spectacle*. Chicago, University of Chicago Press.

Held, D. (1987). *Models of Democracy*. Stanford, Stanford University Press.

Huntington, S. P. 1996. *The Clash of Civilizations and the Remaking of World Order*. New York, Simon and Schuster.

Jones, B. D. 1994. *Reconceiving Decision-Making in Democratic Politics*. Chicago, University of Chicago Press.

McCubbins, M., and T. Schwartz. 1984. "Congressional Oversight Overlooked: Police Patrols versus Fire Alarms." *American Journal of Political Science* 28:165–79.

Nardulli, P. F., and D. Darmofal. 1998. *The Dynamics of Critical Realignments: Citizens, Parties and Political Accountability in the U.S., 1828–1996*. Annual Meeting of the American Political Science Association, Boston, MA.

Przeworski, A., S. C. Stokes, et al., eds. 1999. *Democracy, Accountability, and Representation*. Cambridge Studies in the Theory of Democracy. New York, Cambridge University Press.

Rosenstone, S. J., R. L. Behr, et al. 1996. *Third Parties in America*. Princeton, Princeton University Press.

# INDEX

accountability: crucial phenomena for, 10–11; empirical analysis reexamining, 11–13; popular efficacy and, 3 (*see also* popular efficacy); the Progressive reforms and, 242

Achen, C. H., 29

aggregate electoral analysis, 11n

Aldrich, John H., 85–86, 120–24, 133

American politics: conceptions of, 254–56; conceptions of citizenship relevant to, 20–21; popular efficacy and institutional factors in, 4–5

*American Voter, The,* 90–91, 101

Bartels, L. M., 90n, 98–99

Baumgartner, F. R., 254–55, 258

beliefs, political. *See* political belief systems

Bentham, Jeremy, 20n.3

Bentley, Arthur F., 126

Berent, M. K., 37

Binkley, Wilfred, 120, 122n, 126n.3

Blackstone, William, 78–79

Brody, R. A., 29–30

Burke, Edmund, 84n

candidate traits, electoral impact of, 189–90, 212, 214–15

citizens/voters: abilities of, 4–5, 10, 21–23, 25–26, 96–97, 100, 181, 220–23, 245 (*see also* cognition/cognitive science; discernment, political; electoral independence); attributes of and duration of impact of critical events, 66–68; attributes of and transforming critical events into vote choices, 50–51, 55–58, 62–63; conceptions of, 23, 252–54; as consumers (*see* consumers); core political desires of (*see* core political desires); vote choice, definition of, 50; vote choices of, exogenous events and (*see* exogenous events; transformational model); the vote as resource for, 9–10. See also democracy

Civil Rights Era, 159–60, 177. *See also* critical elections

Civil War Era, 165

cognition/cognitive science: decision-making models and popular efficacy, 22–23; democratic theory and, 23–28; reconfigurations of political phenomena and, 38–41 (*see also* exogenous events). *See also* political psychology

comparative issue dynamics perspective on policy making, 254–56

competitive electoral contests. *See* electoral competitiveness

Constitution, United States, 254n

consumers: capacities of citizens as, 10, 220, 244; citizens cast as, 85–86; of public goods, minimal standards for evaluating, 184, 186

Converse, P. E., 21, 28–30, 104

Corcoran, Paul E., 18, 76, 84

core political desires: cognitive representations of, 34–35; conceptualization of, 30–33; critical events and, 53–56, 71–72; electoral perturbations and, 181, 184–88, 202–12, 220–23; exogenous events and, 47–48; new information regarding, processing of, 35–36; normal voting patterns and, 120–21 (*see also* normal voting patterns); of political stewards (*see* stewards); role and importance of, 33–34. *See also* political belief systems

critical elections: inferences about popular efficacy and, generating, 152; normal voting patterns and realignments, 171–78; the patterned change thesis, 153–54; realigning (*see* realigning elections); realignment eras, 155–60; spatial order analysis of the patterned change thesis, 160–70; temporal order analyses of the patterned change thesis, 154–60. *See also* electoral change; enduring electoral change

critical events: catalysis of, 53–55, 61–62; characteristics of, impact on vote choice and, 55; competing stewards, actions and resources of in mediating, 59–64, 69, 73–74; duration of electoral change and, 64–70; electoral change and, 53;